Catholic Social Thought

This series focuses on Catholic social thought and its application to current social, political, economic, and cultural issues. The titles in this series are written and edited by members of the Society of Catholic Social Scientists. They survey and analyze Catholic approaches to politics, sociology, law, economics, history, and other disciplines. Within these broad themes, authors explore the Church's role and influence in contemporary society.

The Society of Catholic Social Scientists was formed in 1992 to rejuvenate a distinctively Catholic scholarship in the social sciences.

Toward the Common Good

A Catholic Critique of the Discipline of Political Science

Edited by
Robert F. Gorman

Catholic Social Thought, No. 5

THE SCARECROW PRESS, INC.
Lanham • Toronto • Plymouth, UK
2011

Published by Scarecrow Press, Inc.
A wholly owned subsidiary of The Rowman & Littlefield Publishing Group, Inc.
4501 Forbes Boulevard, Suite 200, Lanham, Maryland 20706
http://www.scarecrowpress.com

Estover Road, Plymouth PL6 7PY, United Kingdom

British Library Cataloguing in Publication Information Available

Library of Congress Cataloging-in-Publication Data
Toward the common good : a Catholic critique of the discipline of political science / edited by Robert F. Gorman.
    p. cm. — (Catholic social thought ; 5)
  Includes bibliographical references (p.   ) and index.
  ISBN 978-0-8108-7796-2 (cloth : alk. paper)
   1. Christianity and politics–Catholic Church.   2. Catholic Church–Doctrines.
I. Gorman, Robert F.
  BX1793.T69   2011
  261.7–dc22   2011008399

Contents

Chapter 1

TOWARD THE COMMON GOOD: INTRODUCTION

Robert F. Gorman
Professor of Political Science and International Studies
Texas State University

So Pilate said to him, "Then you are a king?" Jesus answered, "You say I am a king. For this I was born and for this I came into the world, to testify to the truth. Everyone who belongs to the truth listens to my voice." Pilate said to him, "What is truth?" . . . So Pilate said to him, "Do you not speak to me? Do you not know that I have the power to release you and I have power to crucify you?" Jesus answered, "You would have no power over me if it had not been given to you from above." (John 18:37-38; 19:10-11)[1]

Repay to Caesar what belongs to Caesar and to God, what belongs to God. (Matthew 22:22)[2]

Hence it is evident that the state is a creation of nature, and that man is by nature a political animal. (Aristotle, *Politics*, Book I, 1253a)[3]

Politics is the authoritative allocation of values. (David Easton, *The Political System*)[4]

From the earliest dawn of the systematic study of politics, philosophers understood that the common good was the end of the political life of man, who is designed for friendship in the family and wider society. As Aristotle understood and proclaimed it, man was by nature a political animal designed for common deliberation and action aiming at the preservation of concord, public order, justice, and the common good. Political science was a sister to moral philosophy, a study of virtue in formation and action. That was then. Now the very notion of the 'common good' is subverted, problematized, deconstructed, and trivialized. The intimate connection of political to moral philosophy and of politics to morals is too often minimized. Politics, increasingly devoid of its substance, becomes a mere matter of process and calculation. The soul of politics having been removed, a mechanical corpse remains in motion. The intimate intersections of the family, religious, economic, and political life of man fade into obscurity as government itself loses a grasp of its proper limits and knowledge of its vocation of pursuing the common good in the rich soil of subsidiary activity.

Writing in 1954 and already concerned about these very matters, Henry Schmandt and Paul Steinbicker observed in their introductory textbook *The Fundamentals of Government* that "[p]olitics without morality is like a human being without a conscience."[5] They explicated a politics of substance rather than a mere politics of process. They explored the fundamental principles of the natural law and systematically examined the moral dimensions of political life within the state, acknowledging the limits of government and the limits of individualism. In doing so, Schmandt and Steinbicker operated within an ancient stream of political analysis that refused to deny or ignore the supernatural origins and destiny of man, even when so many other political scientists operate in a strictly natural and material frame of reference. Not many political science textbooks today follow in the same spirit as that of Schmandt and Steinbicker. Indeed, one year before their book was published, David Easton had proposed a different way to understand the science of politics, asserting that politics is the "authoritative allocation of values."[6] From nature and the common good, Easton urged a turning of the political scientist's concern rather to the functions and processes of politics as a mechanism for resolving clashes of interests and value. Even Easton's use of the term "value"—although it can include clashes over ultimate goods, first principles, and foundational norms—implies a certain plasticity, removing modern political inquiry from its teleological moorings. For Aristotle, as he declared in the opening line of his *Ethics*: "Every art and every inquiry, and likewise every action and choice, seems to aim at some good, and hence it has been beautifully said that the good is that at which all things aim."[7] For Easton, and many other political scientists, changing attitudinal and behavioral matters occupy attention and study, rather than the question: "How ought we to live together?"

The two citations to the New Testament offered above and taken together, suggest that the Christian conception of politics involves both the ultimate ends of truth, and the finite and variable matters of power and process. The state, and the politics necessary to the state, has in the Christian conception, its proper place. However, the state is not the whole of the political question. There is a power and an end that lies beyond even the capacity of the state, and that the state is not at liberty to ignore. Above the natural world, in which politics is situated, there is a supernatural reality that demands attention and respect. When the state ignores the final ends of man, it runs the risk, as Schmandt and Steinbicker asserted, of becoming beastly and monstrous. Aristotle said as much, implying that the man who is by nature without a state, is either "a beast or a god."[8] In modern times, the state has evidenced a tendency to proclaim its own divinity, as once did tyrants in former ages. The result in ancient times and today is much the same: Where the state denies the God of truth, it becomes its own god, seeks its will through the contest of power, and too often this has led to the beastly treatment of man himself. Not a pretty picture. Christ offered a different theory of politics: The state should be given its due, but then so should God, who is the ultimate sovereign and the judge of the deeds of men.

Catholic Principles of Philosophical and Political Inquiry

As Stephen Krason has pointed out, modern social science disciplines tend first to approach human society through the lens of secularity that tends to distrust the existence of reality, or—if there is such a thing as reality—the human capacity to know it.[9] The Catholic approach to the understanding of society begins with the realist assumption of the intelligibility of the world.[10] Secular social science dispenses almost completely with the supernatural and spiritual nature of man. It has not disproved the existence of God or the spiritual nature of man; it simply believes in cosmological and anthropological systems that deny or ignore the supernatural and the spiritual nature of man. Catholic thought assumes the existence of both. One consequence of modern social science's banishment of the spiritual principle is that it is unequipped to deal with the problem of evil, and thus even to determine what the good is. Hence the modern distaste for a term such as "common good." A further consequence of this is that it is not uncommon for modern versions of Pelagianism and Manicheeism to lurk at the heart of much contemporary social science. The Catholic Church is well acquainted in its 2,000-year history with such optimistic and pessimistic cosmological and anthropological systems of thought. The Church's political teaching, embracing realism, rejects both the optimistic and pessimistic systems, insisting that the supernatural virtue of hope is at the heart of a textured appreciation of human prospects. The Church, accepting both the reality of material and final causes, leaves room for human moral responsibility and for the work of social and political institutions to grapple with the contentiousness of human interrelations. Human beings are not merely determined by the stars, as astrology proclaimed from ancient days, nor by their social environment, as contemporary behavioralists have often declared. Rather human beings, though influenced by their times, cultures, and backgrounds, still possess human freedom and consequently moral responsibility.

Secular social science, rooted deeply in relativist and subjectivist assumptions is empiricist and positivistic in its outlook, studying matters (often of questionable significance) that can be measured and quantified, and thus ignoring matters of a moral and spiritual nature. Having declared human persons and their governments the basis of sovereignty, modern social philosophy rejects or distrusts the power of reason and denies the existence of natural law, and so law becomes a matter of mere procedural decision-making—a plastic material in the hands of government manipulation. With traditional notions of natural justice no longer offering limits to the power and will of sovereign authorities, is it any wonder that totalitarianism arose and flourished in modern times? Moreover, the family and other subsidiary organizations such as churches and local partnerships no longer are regarded as being the natural basis of human activity, and instead states and markets everywhere claim to remake the foundations of human interrelationships, and the rise of big government and big business insists on their reformulation. The 'organization man,' a new kind of imperious pawn, emerges as the cellular basis of new Leviathans. The Catholic Church and its social teaching in contrast holds out for the dignity of human persons as precious beings made in the divine image and likeness, born into and molded by families who nurture and educate rising generations with the help of the church, which assists in spiritual and moral formation of flourishing, mature, moderate, prudent, and just persons and citizens.

Indeed a summary of the teachings of the Catholic Church (as expounded in its Catechism) and of its greatest doctors and teachers (Justin Martyr, Augustine, Bernard of Clairvaux, Bonaventure, Thomas Aquinas, Teresa of Avila, John of the Cross, Francis DeSales, and John Paul II, to name but a few) will indicate that Catholic thought embraces the full gamut of history and of human experience, always exploring the truths of particular human realities, without falling prey to developing a whole philosophical or religious system on just one aspect of reality. Rather, the Church in the fullness and richness of its thought and teaching holds the whole range of human experience in dynamic tension, starting with the complementary roles of reason and faith. The following offers a brief outline of the intellectual 'catholicity' of Catholic social and philosophical thought, which embraces:

- The complementarity of reason and faith as avenues to the acquisition of human knowledge, with faith completing reason where reason meets mystery.
- The subjective and objective orders of truth while avoiding subjectivism and objectivism.
- The deductive and inductive approaches as twin paths for the discovery of truth.
- The rational capacity and reality of the human mind and its ability to discover and know truth within the limits of human experience, while rejecting radical skepticism, solipsism, or rationalism.
- The reality and intelligibility of matter, not a monistic and deterministic materialism.
- The importance of behavior but not the obsession of behavioralism.
- The importance of facts to the attainment of wisdom, but not empiricism.
- The role of utility as a calculative faculty and civic goal, but not a reductionist utilitarianism.

- The unique importance of the human person, but not an atomistic or utterly autonomous individualism.
- The importance of human freedom for excellence, but not a libertine quest for unlimited and indifferent choice.
- The importance of community in the formation of human persons, but not communism or communitarianism.
- The quest of human beings for happiness, but not a myopic hedonism.
- The importance of history, but not a narrow historicism.
- The importance of culture and cultural diversity, of racial and ethnic identities, but not multiculturalism, racism, or ethnicism.
- The importance of human, voluntary, and positive law, but not positivism.
- The reality of nature and the natural law, but not naturalism.
- The importance of circumstances in weighing moral culpability, but not moral relativism.
- The importance of consequences in prudential moral judgment, but not consequentialism.
- The importance of proportionality in moral action, but not proportionalism.
- The value and importance of love of country, but not chauvinism, jingoism, or nationalism.
- The solidarity of people in the formation of the state aimed at the common good, but not to the usurpation of natural roles of subsidiary organizations such as the family and the church.
- The distinctiveness and equal dignity of men and women, and the natural complementarity of the masculine and feminine genders, but not radical "genderism" or feminism.
- The proper separation and complementarity of church and state, and the principle of religious liberty, but not secularism.
- The moral duties of human beings, but not a deontological rationalism.
- The dignity of human labor, but not economic determinism.
- The importance of play and leisure, but not sloth or indolence.
- The centrality of love and friendship to the fulfillment of human inclinations, but not romanticism or emotivism.

In the chapters that follow this introduction, the reader will notice repeated efforts by the contributors of this book to critique modern political science in light of this canon of Catholic principles. But before we address those contributions, we must first recall the historical development of the discipline of Political Science.

A Brief History of Modern Political Science

This book is written in view of an ancient and constant conception of human beings as naturally social and political beings. It may seem, therefore, and it is, countercultural, by virtue of its being a traditional critique of the modern discipline of political science. As a countercultural critique of the modern culture of political science, we begin first with a history of the discipline to recall how it has understood itself from its inception down to our own time. In its beginning, political science was well aware of itself as an interdisciplinary field of study with a special focus on the origins and operations of the state and interstate relations. Even before the American Political Science Association was formed in the early years of the twentieth century, many who thought of themselves as "political scientists" understood that the subject matter of politics was deeply imbedded in history, including the history of philosophy and in the domestic and constitutional law of countries and in international law. Furthermore, there was a deep appreciation that the study of law and politics was also built upon a foundation of moral principles and ethics. In the brief history of the discipline that follows, I cite the work of prominent political scientists, including presidents of the American Political Science Association, in an effort to chart the temperature of the discipline in regard to its most immediate concerns and preoccupations during its more than a century-long existence.[11]

For example, John R. Seeley—who was by profession first an historian and then a political scientist—recognized and discussed these deeply imbedded connections between history, politics, law, and ethical thought in his path-breaking book *Introduction to Political Science*, first published in 1896. Seeley is famous for his quip that "history without political science has no fruit; political science without history has no root."[12] His focus on the emergence of the state in history paid special attention to what we might call today 'political anthropology,' and given this optic, Seeley was impressed with how politics as an ancient reality of human society was at its beginnings "given by nature in the family relation."[13] He was impressed by the roots of the state in family and religion and its development in due course in distinction from them. He noted that "political theory forgets the influence of religion as it forgets that of the family because political theory commonly belongs to an advanced period of the state when it has become independent."[14] This might be true of much of political theory today, but it certainly wasn't true of Aristotle who saw even the basic regime types of monarchy, aristocracy, and democracy as having roots in the family relations of spouses, parents and children, and siblings.[15] Seeley traced the evolution of the organic state as increasingly larger communities of interest from ethnic, familial, tribal, and religious unions under the pressure of common suffering and external danger.[16] On the other hand, inorganic states, or empires, in turn emerged from conquest and force, rather than by natural inclination. And indeed the differences in politics between the organic city-state and the inorganic country-state or empire were dictated by size. A lively local and national politics flourished in the smaller and organic city-states, and Seeley thus saw a lively subsidiarity at work in the organic states that was too often lost in the empire states formed by force.

Seeley was not the only or the first scholar of his day to observe these and similar phenomena. French historian Numa Fustel de Coulanges in his *The Ancient City*, first published in 1864, offered another classical example of this kind of political anthropology of the early origins of the state in full awareness of the organic ties of society's four key institutions, the family, religious institutions, economic institutions, and government.[17] Fustel de Coulanges, like Seeley, was a classically and liberally trained person who was able to navigate with facility between history, law, ethics, political philosophy, religion, sociology, and anthropology. His importance is still attested to by inclusion of excerpts of *The Ancient City* in contemporary books on state and society.[18] Compared to Rousseau's rhetorical flights of fancy concerning the origins of the state, Fustel de Coulanges was a realist, fully steeped in a range of scholarly disciplines and empirically grounded. Because political scientists today rarely undertake this kind of integrated study, the interrelations of these basic societal institutions of family, religion, economics, and government often go unnoticed except for the ongoing preoccupation with the connection between politics and economics.

Albert Somit and Joseph Tanenhaus in their study on the development of political science note in an all too brief discussion of the early genesis of political science, that one of its first tasks was to legitimize itself as a discipline among many other disciplinary fields.[19] What was its proper object of study? How did it differ from other fields? In short, what was its proper scope and method? They report that most Americans desiring higher education before the Civil War traveled to Germany to study law and theology, but after the Civil War students of history and politics joined them. Undergraduate education in the United States was an interdisciplinary program in which the study of government, philosophy (metaphysical and natural), ethics, history, religion, constitutional law, mathematics, rhetoric, and logic were seen as of an integrated piece and often taught in conjunction with Greek and Latin as the classical languages of the educated person. Such a course of study was indeed common fare for well-educated persons, and in our own time often constitutes the basis of home school curriculum that now produces some of the very best students we have in this country. Somit and Tanenhaus, however, rebuked this traditional curriculum and its attendant pedagogy as sectarian, "incredibly stultifying" and "remorselessly didactic."[20] One wonders if that was the actual perception of the persons who were educated in such an interdisciplinary setting, and one detects more than a little whiff of secular prejudice in their claim that: "Even the advanced courses in ethics, philosophy, religion, economics, and politics. . .were manifestly designed to ensure that students developed into God-fearing, morally upright, sound-thinking citizens. . . . What then passed as political science would be called 'education for democratic citizenship' by a later and more sophisticated generation."[21] If modern sophistication is rooted in less knowledge of morals, piety, and sound thinking, one wonders what made later generations "more sophisticated." Still, what Somit and Tanenhaus admit even in their criticism is that politics was understood as having rich and multifarious ties to other arenas of thought and study. Catholic pedagogy and philosophy also would point out that the principle of the 'unity of knowledge' was still in evidence in those days. People educated in these wide-ranging and related fields of study were once known as 'Renaissance Men.' Today we are often surprised by what we call 'interdisciplinary discoveries.' But this should only be surprising to those who have lost the sense of the unity of knowledge in the first place. As John Cardinal Newman so pointedly asserted in his *The Idea of the University*, theology is the science that ultimately embraces every other science and the banishment of theology from university curriculum would necessarily lead to the balkanization of the disciplines, who might then only gradually rediscover the connections that exist between their departmentalized ghettoes of study.[22] His prophecy was uncannily accurate.

Still, even as theology was gradually banished from the increasingly secularized university curriculum, the architects of the discipline of political science appreciated in varying degrees the situation of political science in the wider sphere of human knowledge. When John Burgess founded the first School of Political Science at Columbia University in 1880, its curriculum was decidedly interdisciplinary with courses in politics and political theory, economics, history, and geography. Courses in sociology soon followed.[23] The method pursued was rooted in comparative analysis, including analysis of the nation-state and American states, public law, and philosophy imbedded in legal studies. Further elements of the philosophy of education at Columbia included a quest for collection of facts, interpretation of facts, and inductive theoretical approaches, all of which indicated a concern for a kind of prebehavioral empiricism or scientism. Indeed, from the time the American Political Science Association was founded in 1903, presidential addresses increasingly were preoccupied with how the discipline could become truly a science and in turn distinguish itself among other scientific disciplines. Frank Goodnow was struck by how much centralization of political activity was occurring even in his own day, thus contravening the principle of subsidiarity in favor of the activity of ever more comprehensive and intrusive governments.[24] In 1910 Lawrence Lowell observed that political science was at best an observational rather than an experimental science, but he also declared that the "ultimate object of political science is moral, that is the improvement of government among men."[25] A year later Woodrow Wilson mused that law is a product of the political process and the facts of a particular community. After avowing that "nothing that forms or affects human life seems to me to be properly foreign to the student of politics," including literature, art, history, and spiritual experience, Wilson then professed a dislike for the term 'political science' asserting that "human relationships whether in the family or in the state, in the counting house or in the factory, are not in any proper sense the subject matter of science. They are stuff of insight and sympathy and spiritual comprehension."[26] Wilson did not seem to recognize the contradiction or at least the tension implicit in these two statements. But it is striking that in both of the apparently contradictory assertions, he avowed the importance of the spiritual nature of man.

In 1926, in his famous call for political science to begin the long slog to a more behavioral and empirical approach in the discipline, Charles Merriam nonetheless bewailed the lack of a "central wisdom" given the overspecialization already apparent in his day.[27] John A. Fairlie in 1930, like Goodnow before him, observed the increasing centralization and scope of political power by regional and national governments and international organizations.[28] Absent in any formal way from these addresses was any mention of the family, but still observable was the constant recommendation that scholars in the discipline employ more empirical methodologies and approaches.

After World War II, the discipline entered into the behavioral revolution, a new and theoretically informed effort to improve on the barefoot empiricism that was too common prior to the War. David Truman's presidential address, "Disillusion and Regeneration: The Quest for a Discipline" is a representative species of this new expectation for a revitalized scientific approach.[29] But the battles that marked the 1960s and 1970s were actually quite fierce. During my graduate training in the 1970s, disputes raged between what we called then somewhat tongue in cheek, the behavioralist Prussians and the traditionalist Mushies. I thought the distinction at the time to be overdrawn and overheated, and my instincts on this score were thoroughly Catholic. In all of the disputes about method, the Church holds no particular position. Any method that can shed light on the human experience is welcome so long as it advances the truth. But there is also a caveat, in that empiricism itself can promote a diminished and trivialized understanding of the human person and the human person in society. Thus, the Church holds for the value of multiple lenses of analysis and varieties of methodology to explore the human condition. Where methodology only examines questions that can be answered by quantitative and statistical measures, it won't be touching on matters of politics and social life that defy such reductionism, including the interior life of man, his motives, his struggle with good and evil, the moral life, the contest between virtues and vices, and the timeless quests for justice, affection and love, and interior peace.

To the extent that modern political science has preoccupied itself with statistically measurable data and with attitudinal matters that are often the byproduct of passing fancy, it may be missing these larger and perennial concerns. That at least is the convincing position staked out by David Ricci in his *The Tragedy of Political Science*.[30] Ricci was convinced that the scientific preoccupation within the discipline largely sidelined and minimized the forms of inquiry that would lead to more complete and satisfying studies of political life and its intimate connection to ethics and moral thought. Moreover, he argued that it left the discipline, which increasingly discovered discouraging empirical results about the prospects for democracy, bereft of the intellectual resources to justify the commitment to democratic governance it desperately believed to be one of its primary professional imperatives. From the comedy of methodological wrangling was born the tragedy of a discipline of increasing irrelevance to democratic political life as such. Ricci's critique was penned before the dramatic changes in global politics that saw the collapse of global communism, the rise of globalist interaction, and the triumph of democracy over totalitarian and authoritarian forces throughout much of the world. Thus, while his critique of the discipline's behavioralist preoccupation still has force, his argument concerning the success of democracy and the discipline's inability to support democratic political life seems to have been somewhat vitiated.

In 1990, writing in the midst of the seemingly miraculous changes that had transpired in the contest between forces of freedom and those of totalitarian excess, Lucian Pye made observations similar to those of Ricci in his APSA presidential address, arguing that methodology and theory were often in tension with one another, especially when the humanistic aims of the discipline contend with its scientific aspirations. However by then the discipline had come to a truce, leaving room for those seeking empirical certitudes in the behavior of man in society to pursue their scientific quest, and for others to "search for meaning, for understanding and interpretation . . . for what is human in the blending of mind and spirit."[31] Matthew Holden, surveying the discipline 10 years later and nearly 75 years after Charles Merriam's call for greater scientific rigor, sought to take stock of its accomplishments. Like Pye, he admitted the value of a certain eclecticism, insofar as he recognized the importance of pursuing not only the behavioral methods of study, but also valuing what he called the "Old Literature and History." Still, Holden concluded that the main object of study and the special competence of political science is in the realm of "organization of power."[32] Naturally enough, bounding the discipline as such will lead to a preoccupation with the state/market grid, which his analysis reflects. Left out of mix is an appreciation of justice as a focus of politics. Also left out of the analysis in this view of political science are the agencies of mutual aid such as the church and the family. Pye had made a case for the discipline's attention to the identity-making institutions, whereas Holden 10 years later, made the case for centralized administration in the state/market grid, where power is organized, concentrated, and administered. There can be no doubt that a central concept of the discipline is that of power, but equally central is that of justice. The Church, paraphrasing its Master, reminds not only the state but also students of the state that "you would have not power, and no power to study, if it were not given from above."

Robert Putnam's observations about the discipline in 2002 were a manful attempt to remind it of its civic obligations, its need to "poach" across disciplinary lines, its need to tolerate a broad array of methodological and theoretical approaches, and its vocation to provide solid policy advice to practitioners and decision-makers.[33] Putnam addressed the very same set of issues and the problematique that Ricci had so trenchantly revealed, except with a more hopeful tone than Ricci's. Putnam's most important observation, increasingly sensed by many political scientists, if only in bits and pieces, like Milton's truth-seekers who find only the scattered shards of the originally beautiful and integrated vase of Truth, is that political science is not, after all and after more than a century of trying to prove the opposite, an autonomous field of study. Even an attempt to demonstrate what political science has to teach other disciplines—as Robert Axelrod did in his 2007 presidential address cagily suggesting that the discipline after decades of importing ideas, should recognize that it has good ideas to export to other disciplines—is at least a partial recognition of the interdisciplinary nature of all human inquiry.[34] Indeed, Catholic thought has always taught the unity of knowledge, maintaining that the knowledge and art of the common good and of political activity is connected by thousands of tendrils to the wider field of human existential awareness in which, as James V. Schall has put it:

> Granting the mystery of God, we can still make a pretty good case that science, politics, morality, and revelation belong coherently to the same world. The fact that this case is made increasingly rarely is, paradoxically itself, a problem of will and not of intellect. The effort of modernity to establish the complete autonomy of man on a planetary basis involves refusing precisely to consider any philosophical question that might suggest reason's own natural incompleteness.[35]

Margaret Levi, musing about the need for a theory and practice of effective government in her 2005 APSA presidential address, raised important questions about how to make government both more accountable and effective.[36] Questions that she didn't pose and frankly that many other political scientists don't pose include: Does government do too much? Does government violate not just individual but family rights and religious liberties? Does government's authority extend to questions that it has no right or competence to regulate? Does government respect subsidiary rights? Levi does mention briefly the role that traditional religious groups play in galvanizing their adherents, but her purpose is not to encourage governments to listen to the legitimate concerns of such constituencies, but rather to figure out ways to coax them into changing their beliefs, as though political leaders have a monopoly on the truth as policy experts. She writes:

> Attachment to traditional religions, even in extremist or fundamentalist forms, provide an accounting of the world that may fit with the reality adherents experience; changing the beliefs that support religious orthodoxies may require convincing adherents that they will get what they need from alternative sources. Leaders and government actors can change beliefs and help people to learn new ways of interacting in the society only to the extent that they can create confidence in the reliability and quality of government-provided information and services.[37]

The chutzpah and condescension of such an assertion may not be recognized by many political scientists. Three cheers to those who do. Indeed, true governmental accountability isn't just about processes, services, and information that an all-knowing and expert government or a nanny-state confers to its uncomprehending, helpless, and retrograde subjects. Rather, true accountability must ultimately respect the deepest held convictions of the members of the body politic (meaning not just individuals but also associations), including their deepest and most firm moral convictions. Communists made the mistake of intrusive "value re-creation" in the twentieth century. Hundreds of millions of human beings paid a high price for such governmental value engineering, and in the end communist governmental overreach into arenas they had no right to reach, was a major cause of their colossal failure and ultimate demise. Mikhail Gorbachev admitted as much on the occasion of his resignation from office: "An end has been put to the Cold War, the arms race, and the insane militarization of our country, which crippled our economy, distorted our thinking and undermined our morals."[38] One wonders if the kind of effective government entertained by our discipline today doesn't fulfill the prophecy of Alexis de Tocqueville, who warned Americans so long ago about the dangers of 'soft despotism' in overreliance on government for things that are just as well if not better done by an active citizen body in lively local interaction. Indeed, a key point in any assessment of modern political science is that it has to a very large extent lost sight of the moral principle of subsidiarity, a principle that lies at the heart of Catholic social and political thought, and one that is frequently raised in this book in criticism of contemporary political science inquiry.

For a very long time, political scientists have lived under the Hobbesian assumption that politics and power are the by-products of fear. Indeed, Hobbes tapped into an older stream of thought traceable to the nominalism of William of Ockham and the materialism of Epicurus, for whom no reality existed that the human mind could understand, so that only coercive exercises of power could compel behavior conducive to order.[39] Ira Katznelson, in his thoughtful 2007 APSA presidential address entitled "At the Court of Chaos: Political Science in an Age of Perpetual Fear," seemed to tap into this sense of modern angst without, however, discovering a satisfying answer to the problem of our fear.[40] For a very long time the philosophers of enlightenment regarded fear as the primary motive for religion itself, and blamed religion for the terrors of war that succeeded the Reformation and gave rise to the modern state system. Fear is indeed a passion of the human soul. The Catholic Church recognizes fear in its multifarious forms as part of its own anthropology, but unlike modern philosophers, it regards fear precisely and primarily as a deformation of the soul, which in fear loses its capacity for trust and love, the primary antidotes to fear in the first place. Physical fear rests in the sympathetic appetite and in our nervous systems. But moral fear is a work of fevered intellect posing to itself future obstacles to the preservation of a good that in the end warps prudence itself and leads to acts of evil. This kind of fear has a spiritual source and is not susceptible to medical or even to psychiatric intervention, because its source lies ultimately in the recesses of the soul. Indeed, the Church here expounds not just an anthropological theory, but also a cosmological answer, for the universe itself takes its origin from an act of Divine Love. Moreover, the natural desire of all men to know the origins of their existence, their purpose for living, and their final destiny is also a response to Love itself. The tedious and trivial quest for temporal goods becomes an opiate of the people, who can no longer recognize the greatest love and deepest yearning of their inmost spirit. Augustine summarized this universal human longing lapidarily: "Our hearts are restless Lord until they rest in you."[41] What modern thought, including political theory seems to have forgotten, is that love is the dominant goal in the "pursuit of happiness." Augustine pithily thus also asserted that "the happy life is joy based on the truth" and that well-ordered love was essential to tranquility.[42] Furthermore, we seem to have forgotten that love is more than a passion. St. Thomas Aquinas asserted that it is foremost a benevolent disposition of the will, a desire for the good of another, rather than a feeling or a constant pursuit of sensible pleasure.

Catholic Answers

Modern political scientists actually have much to learn from the Catholic tradition of social thought. They will not find there an obsession with methods of study, but rather a concern for matters of substance as they bear on the dignity of the human person in light of both her earthly aspirations and his supernatural destiny. On this score, several summary points may be offered from the Catholic perspective on the state and society. First, Catholic thinking is not limited to any one method of inquiry. It embraces both deductive and inductive reasoning, in the context of theoretical, descriptive, explanatory, and predictive approaches. It embraces both normative and empirical study. In the pages that follow, criticism of a narrow behavioralism will be frequently leveled as we examine the dominant methodological preoccupations of the literature in the subfields of political science. However, at the outset we emphasize that behavioral approaches are not in themselves objectionable. They can indeed advance our knowledge of political behavior. A fine example of the blending of behavioral method with value questions is provided in the path-breaking work done recently by Arthur Brooks, whose empirical studies of charitable giving and on the correlative factors to happiness have illustrated how behavioral and attitudinal studies can lead to a more profound understanding of what makes people happy. This work demonstrates quite conclusively that religious commitment and practice are the best predictors of both generosity and human happiness. Brooks finds conclusively that the least generous and least happy people on the planet are secularists, and that the most happy and generous persons are traditional churchgoers. Other factors that correlate to happiness include fruitful and meaningful work that leads to personal feelings of success, freedom tied to conservative values, generosity toward others, and, though its effect is lagged, the long-term benefit of sacrificial giving in the context of family life. Largely uncorrelated with happiness are variables such as equality of income and outcome, as well as wealth, liberal political values, and secular values.[43]

Second, and in a sense flowing from the findings just mentioned, but also from traditional Catholic teaching, is that the assumptions of the inevitable secularization of political life and the desirability of achieving secularization— assumptions and prejudices of the Enlightenment Age—must now be seriously reconsidered and questioned in light of modern global experience. Moreover, the history of the impact of religion on politics needs a thorough reworking as well. Such a reworking will discover that religion is not always and everywhere the culprit behind wars and rumors of wars, but rather in important ways and in particular settings, it is the actual force for the emergence of civilization and of the civilizing of political life. But this assumes that history itself is consulted seriously.

Third, the assumption that centralized and comprehensive political institutions are necessary for the advancement of human progress and inherently better than a lively local government and subsidiary activity by primary social groups, such as the family, local churches, partnerships, and mutual aid societies, must also be called into question. There is much favorable talk about the extension of national and international institutional powers and prerogatives as signs of human progress, but when such comprehensive bodies begin to violate the rights of local and more accountable and probably more efficient local bodies and initiatives, one must begin to question whether it is real scientific knowledge that demonstrates the superior efficiency, justice and accountability of agencies that are manifestly less personal, local, and accountable. When democracy itself comes to regard its vocation as merely a voting process that hands policies over to experts for enforcement, the substantive core of politics as a means of achieving the ends of respect for human dignity, autonomy of natural subsidiary institutions, including the family and marriage, and ultimately justice and the common good are threatened.

Fourth, when political science abandons this wider and substantive aspect of civic life and the study of such subsidiary bodies in light of the wisdom and scope of the liberal arts and social sciences, it risks becoming a ghetto incapable of engaging the broader quest for the advancement of knowledge and wisdom. Thus, political science is not an autonomous discipline any more than human persons are completely autonomous or atomistic existences. Epistemologically, political science cannot without damage to its own existence as a proper field of knowledge separate itself from the wider experience of knowing that embraces, as Plato himself understood, a continuum from phenomenological observations rooted in imagination (*eikasia*) and belief (*pistis*), to understanding (*dianoia*) to ultimate knowledge (*episteme*) of being and reality rooted in thought (*noesis*) in pursuit of wisdom (*sophia*). A line might be divided into segments but it is still a line, a whole, one might say, with parts that connect with one another forming a larger reality that is itself rooted in being.[44] Ontologically speaking, political science exists as a part of the whole of reality, just as the human person, mysteriously unique and unrepeatable, enjoys an integral subjective existence. The human person recognizes that she is neither the cause of herself nor that he is completely the author of himself, suggesting instead that there is a great chain or stream of being so much larger than oneself that must ultimately have its source in the Being who creates. Modernity has attempted to divide the order of knowledge from the order of being, and in doing so, has diminished both the order of love and of happiness. The casualties in ruined human lives and dysfunctional political communities have thus proliferated.

Fifth, the Church ultimately makes the case that politics is much more than a utilitarian quest for pleasure and avoidance of pain. Rather, the state and the common good must be regarded as being part of a love story that began with the creation of all things *ex nihilo*, including time and matter, as an act of Divine Love. Love is learned and fulfilled in relationships formed first in the family, the church, and local community where an awareness is cultivated that the most important love is the love of God followed by the love of neighbor as of self.

The political world is, from the Church's perspective, stitched into the warp and woof of Christ's articulation of the great commandment of love. Therefore, as John Paul II asserted, there can be "no genuine solution to social questions apart from the Gospel."[45] Statecraft, then, as even the ancients knew, is closely connected to soul-craft and to the formation of virtuous citizens. But the Church asserts that moral life of mankind is not merely the work of the regime, as Robert Hunt notes in his chapter to this book, but rather a work of subsidiary institutions where the arts of love are learned, and where civic institutions then continue to craft citizens capable of virtuous subordination of their own desires to the larger needs of the community, which is itself subject to limits and has as its highest goals the preservation of life and respect of human dignity.

Finally, though perhaps first in order of importance, is our need to recover the virtue of humility. Through the millennia, the Church has deeply appreciated and joyously affirmed the value of humility as the first step in the attainment of human spiritual maturity and as the doorway into a life of sanctity. Humility is a Hobbit who slays the Lord of Mordor. Humility learns to bow to mystery, even as pride ventures forth with confidence into realms beyond its comprehension. No one who has spent any time as a member of the professoriate or as an inhabitant of academia can fail to notice the bonfire of vanities that swirls within the ivy halls. Indeed, in sciences that call themselves social and humane are often found the most arrogant aloofness from and inhumane disregard for the common man. Yet, especially in the field of government, the discipline holds for the superiority of democratic political life and the human rights of the common man. That the common man is typically now, as they have been throughout human history, religious in practice and spiritual at heart, is a fact of human experience. Yet how often does our discipline show contempt for the little person, his life, her aspirations, his love of family, and her religiosity? Whose perspective is truly out of sync, that of masses, or that of the cognoscenti who claim to know better than hoi polloi? As individual students of political life, and as a discipline concerned with political knowledge, we need a large dose of humility to dispel the fog of pride. The homework we need most to do is to read the life of a saint. Connected with humility is recognition that Almighty God is ultimately the Sovereign Lord of all creation. This is not simply a theological assertion. Even the most recent findings in astrophysics imply a universe that in its physical constants and laws is fantastically improbable except on the hypothesis of a Designing Intelligence.[46] Are political scientists aware of this research? What difference might it make to their study of politics, if they were more completely aware of it?

The Catholic Church itself has developed, throughout its lengthy engagement with human thought, a coherent and expansive appreciation of the human experience in light of the deepest longings of the human heart. Thus it has cultivated a political and social method and a teaching of its own rooted in its long observation of the human soul, and articulated anew since the advent of modernity. From Leo XIII's encyclical *Rerum Novarum*, down to the issuance of Benedict XVI of *Caritas in Veritate* in 2009, the Church has served as a constant critic of modern innovations in thought. Numerous intervening popes also wrote beautifully on the predicament of modern man, including notably, John Paul II in a string of important political and social encyclicals. Political scientists rarely engage this wide body of political and social thinking, often to their impoverishment. Several of the contributors to this book offer examples of how the Church's social teaching continues to resonate with great relevance in modern times, and it is to a brief introduction of their work that we now turn.

Summary and Organization of the Book

Our book begins with two chapters on the Catholic appreciation of the central role of political theory and philosophy to the discipline. Steven Brust begins with an essay summarizing the key features and principles of a Catholic political theory, pointing out both the theological and philosophical dimensions of Catholic cosmology and anthropology as it has been revealed by God in nature, in Scripture and Tradition. He next takes up the explicit principles of Catholic social teaching growing out of these revelatory sources, and then articulates a spirited defense of political theory as a necessary basis of political inquiry. But political theory, he warns, needs to give due credit to both the evidences of reason and faith. Truth itself demands a full exploration of human behavior and human spiritual longing. The various schools of thought within the history of political thought are themselves admissible of a Catholic critique, with a view to the Church's expertise in the spiritual nature of human beings. Thus the Church offers a message concerning human rights and goods, the relationship of freedom to truth, the importance of solidarity in human relations, but also a right ordering of political activity under the principle of subsidiarity, and a long and rich tradition of protecting marriage and the family as the basic element of society along with other subsidiary associations, including the role of the Church and its own rights to freely exercise its spiritual functions in religious liberty. The Church, then, conveys an important treasury of knowledge about the appropriate activities and limits of the state.

Robert Hunt offers a reflection on a more particular but crucial question concerning the role of Christian political philosophy as an intermediary system of thought between the Ancients and Moderns. Hunt's argument is that the tendency of followers of Leo Struass, or Straussians, to regard the Medieval Christian thinkers as an appendage of the ancient classical world, and Modern political thought as a distinct break with the ancient system, disregards both significant ways in which Christian political theory built upon, revised, and mediated Ancient political thought, and how modernity was as much a reaction to this Christian synthesis as a break with an Ancient past. He proposes that a Catholic moral realism can serve today as a means of critiquing both the missing elements of Ancient philosophy, and the nihilist tendencies of modern thought.

Ryan Barilleaux offers an assessment of the subfield of American government, noting that it has too often ignored questions of substance and value owing to its preoccupation with the behavioral creed. Real knowledge and understanding have resulted nonetheless about political processes operating in the

American political system. But, he observes, too often the very ends and purposes of political action have been ignored, leading to the increasing irrelevance of much political science research to the actual art of politics itself. Restoring political science to a more respected position will require its recovery of the importance of virtue in political life, and thus of traditional political theory as a matter of serious engagement. He notes that the subdiscipline continues to offer distinctive insights into the political characteristics of American society. He suggests that an integralist approach as found in the work of Pitirim Sorokin offers a potentially fruitful synthesis of empirical method and cross-disciplinary value-orientation. Catholic thought naturally embraces such a unifying approach.

John Corso follows with an assessment of modern public administration, chiefly examining how this subdiscipline stands up under the scrutiny of the Catholic principle of subsidiarity. He takes up first a discussion of this important principle as it is defined in recent papal encyclicals, and then he notes that the concept is imbedded in the very federal system of government reflected in the Constitution of the United States. The whole discipline of public administration, he observes, is rooted in at least partial recognition of the principle, insofar as students of public administration regard themselves as being servants to politically elected legislators and leaders. But this older understanding of administrative science has given way to a preoccupation with efficiency and scientific management that can be oblivious to ultimate social values and the common good. Using the health care debate, Corso offers a textured analysis of how arguments over subsidiary rights have colored governmental action, and how the Church has attempted to engage legislators both to achieve solidarity and respect for subsidiary rights.

Anthony Brunello offers a critique of both the development and current preoccupations of the subfield of comparative politics. He first addresses the twin phenomena in very recent times of secularization and democratization. He cautions, however, that religion remains, despite secularization, a critical component of political culture, and thus also a tool for comparative analysis. Religion is a striving for human meaning and purpose. Comparative politics, Brunello asserts, thus has common cause with religion, since it too strives for meaning and understanding as it applies to the political life of peoples in different cultural settings. Students of comparative politics cannot thus fruitfully dispose of either the ends of its study or the forms of politics oriented toward the ends of political life, even if their orientation is limited to the pursuit of material goods. But clearly politics is a struggle not only for material goods but also norms and values. These tensions he traces from the beginning of comparative political analysis in Aristotle, through the High Middle Ages with Thomas Aquinas and into modern times, with its emphasis on behavioral study. But the limits of behavioralism lie precisely in its ignorance of *telos* and *eidos*, and so comparative politics has returned to a realization of the importance of ends and forms of politics. The Church, he asserts, continues to offer a lively and relevant teaching in the study of comparative government through its understanding of the human person and its long-held traditional of social teachings. The latter include the formal teachings of the modern papacy on the human person, the common good, the human striving for peace and justice, and the respect for both solidarity and subsidiarity. But Catholic social thought also includes nonmagisterial reflection, including liberation theology, which produced tensions with magisterial teaching. The massive changes that comparativists have witnessed in both global politics and in the individual politics of nations leave a good deal of room to examine the goods of political life through the long-standing treasury of the Church's teachings. Faith and experience in the spiritual life of man should not be divorced from reason's quest to discover not just how political behavior varies, but why it varies, and more importantly why the more things change, the essentials remain the same.

Subsequent chapters in the book focus on aspects of international relations. Andrew Essig begins with a critique of the dominant schools of international relations theory. His essay examines three dominant theoretical approaches, including Marxism, Idealism/Liberalism, and Realism, and less influential theoretical systems, such as constructivism and feminist and gender theory. Each of these schools of thought is assessed in regards to their 'key unit of analysis' (for Marxists, economic classes; for idealists, transnational organizations; for realists, the nation-state), their understandings of the chief motivations of primary actors, and their understandings of human nature. Finding each approach wanting in one respect or another, Essig, like Hunt, turns to Moral Realism as a distinctively Christian and Catholic lens through which to understand international relations more completely and accurately. Moral realism, he holds, embraces a fuller appreciation of human experience at the international level. Catholic thought comes to the rescue here as both a guardian of moral philosophy and a purveyor of realism, rooted in the assertion that the world and human existence and activity in the world is intelligible. Moral realism is capable of embracing elements of the other competing models for understanding international relations, precisely because it keeps in view the supernatural origins and destiny of mankind, not merely or only human temporal concerns. With man's eternal destiny in view, a fuller appreciation of human dignity becomes possible, even in the midst of political contention, social instability, and international war. Government of all kinds, local, national, and international, are at the service of human persons, and the subsidiary institutions that give life to, nurture, protect, and educate them toward an end of mutual flourishing. Thus government has both responsibilities and limits. Moral realism demands that human persons be respected in their dignity, that subsidiary bodies be given scope to perform their tasks of supporting human flourishing, and that governments attend to the maintenance of peace, justice, and order. Moral realism seeks peace and stability largely through cooperative mechanisms and 'soft power,' but recognizes that injustice and morally outrageous action are not to be tolerated but resisted, even to the point of using force for justice and the common good.

Finally, I offer an essay on global institutional studies. A survey of contemporary scholarship on international organizations, law, and humanitarian policy and human rights finds that scholars in this arena of political science appreciate the importance of interdisciplinary connections to other fields of study, although too often history is not fully appreciated and understood, and the dominant philosophical presuppositions are decidedly positivistic and relativist. In order to counter the ahistoricism that too often afflicts these areas of study, a brief history of the Catholic Church as a transnational organization is offered, along with a critique of the principles of organization that have marked this oldest and most continuous international institution. One of the secrets of its success turns upon its capacity to offer solidarity while respecting subsidiarity. These two principles, originating in Catholic thought and practice, are then applied to current approaches in studying collective security, international human rights and humanitarian policies, and matters concerning global economics and sustainable development, which are the major preoccupations of contemporary global studies. The dominant preoccupation in global studies is international solidarity. Although there are pockets of awareness in the literature and scholarship regarding the importance of subsidiarity, the overwhelming bias of international institutional studies today is in favor of statist and globalist rather than local solutions to local problems. In part, this prejudice proceeds from the very level of analysis at which scholars in this field operate, namely the international and state levels of analysis, largely ignorant of the actual activity, capacities, and aspirations of local peoples to resolve their own security, human rights, and economic situations. Scholars in this arena of study need to approach the study of Intergovernmental Organizations (IGOs) with a more realistic and practical eye, since IGO programs too often violate local rights and human dignity, even where they can claim some degree of material success as in the emergency and humanitarian assistance arena.

We offer this book to the profession of political science as Catholic scholars hoping that our discipline in its current preoccupations, approaches, and aspirations might benefit from a critical Catholic optic and ethos. We share with our fellow political scientists a common love of politics and society. In this book we hope as fellow workers in the field and as dressers of the vineyard to restore greater flavor to our labors, to illuminate aspects and corners of our discipline where shadows have obscured our vision, and to expand our awareness of political science beyond its self-imposed blinders. Our reflections, we hope, will offer Christian political scientists a window into the Catholic understanding of politics that might also be of value to them in their personal and professional endeavors. To our fellow Catholics in the discipline we hope this critique might spur them to shape their work in ways that could enlighten the fullness of the human experience as understood by their Church. From its beginnings the Catholic Church was the source of a rich reflection on the connections between moral and political philosophy, on the organization and relation of the church to the state, and on the human aspiration for justice and the common good. We hope then that this study will indeed prove to be salt of the earth, light to the world, and leaven to the dough, recognizing that our efforts are but a humble step in the right direction, not the final word, which is contained ultimately and fully only in the one who claimed: "I am the light of the world, the way, the truth and the life."

Notes

1. References to the Bible in this chapter are taken from the *New American Bible* Catholic Bible Personal Study Edition, ed. Jean Marie Hiesberger (Oxford: Oxford University Press, 1995). See Jn 18:37-38; 19:10-11.

2. *New American Bible,* Mt. 22:22.

3. Aristotle, *Politics,* Book I, 1253a.

4. David Easton, *The Political System* (New York: Knopf, 1953).

5. Henry F. Schmandt and Paul G. Steinbicker, *Fundamentals of Government* (Milwaukee, Wis.: The Bruce Publishing Company, 1954), 12.

6. Easton, *The Political System.*

7. Aristotle, *Nicomachean Ethics,* trans. Joe Sachs (Newburyport, Mass.: Focus Publishing, R. Pullins Company, 2002), 1. Consult also Aristotle's assertion in the *Politics* Book. I, 1252: 30: "the final cause and end of a thing is the best, and to be self-sufficing is the end and the best."

8. Aristotle, *Ethics.*

9. Stephen Krason, "The Importance of the Society of Catholic Social Science Apostolate," *Catholic Social Science Review* 11 (2006): 371-73.

10. See James V. Schall, *Roman Catholic Political Philosophy* (Lanham, Md.: Lexington Books, 2004), 116. For a full presentation of the Church's political and social teaching, see Pontifical Council for Justice and Peace, *Compendium of the Social Doctrine of the Church* (Citta del Vaticano: Libreria Editrice Vaticana, 2004).

11. APSA Presidential Addresses now can all be found on the internet at www.apsanet.org.

12. John R. Seeley, *Introduction to Political Science* (London: Macmillan and Company, 1896), 4.

13. Seeley, *Introduction to Political Science,* 55.

14. Seeley, *Introduction to Political Science,* 61-62.

15. Aristotle, *Ethics,* Book 9.

16. Seeley, *Introduction to Political Science,* 65.

17. Numa Fustel de Coulanges, *The Ancient City: A Study on the Religion, Laws, and Institutions of Greece and Rome* (Garden City, N.Y.: Doubleday & Company, 1956).

18. For example, see Reinhard Bendix, *State and Society* (Berkeley, Calif.: University of California Press, 1968), 87-106.

19. Albert Somit and Joseph Tanenhaus, *The Development of American Political Science: From Burgess to Behavioralism* (Boston, Mass.: Allyn & Bacon, 1967).

20. Somit and Tanenhaus, *American Political Science,* 12-13.

21. Somit and Tanenhaus, *American Political Science,* 13.

22. Cardinal John Henry Newman, *The Idea of the University* (London: Baronius Press Ltd., 2006). In the first paragraph of his now famous and controversial Regensburg Address, Pope Benedict XVI infers a position very similar to that of Newman, whom Benedict canonized as a Catholic saint in September 2010. In his address the pope wistfully recalled how in his days of teaching at the University of Bonn the theology faculties were in constant and lively interaction with the faculties of history, philosophy, and philology, in a common and coherent quest for reasonable discourse.

23. Somit and Tanenhaus, *American Political Science,* 18.

24. Frank Goodnow, "The Growth of Executive Discretion," *Proceedings of the American Political Science Association,* 40.

25. A. Lawrence Lowell, "The Physiology of Politics," *American Political Science Review* 4, no. 1 (February 1910): 14.

26. Woodrow Wilson, "The Law and the Facts," *American Political Science Review* 5, no. 1 (February 1911): 2-3; 10-11.

27. Charles Merriam, "Progress in Political Research," *American Political Science Review* 20, no. 1 (February 1926): 12.

28. John A. Fairlie, "Political Developments and Tendencies," *American Political Science Review* 24, no. 1 (February 1930): 12-14.

29. David Truman, "Disillusion and Regeneration: The Quest for a Discipline," *American Political Science Review* 59, no. 4 (December 1965): 865-73.

30. David M. Ricci, *The Tragedy of Political Science: Politics, Scholarship, and Democracy* (New Haven, Conn.: Yale University Press, 1984).

31. Lucian Pye, "Political Science and the Crisis of Authoritarianism" *American Political Science Review* 84, no. 1 (March 1990): 4.

32. Matthew Holden, "The Competence of Political Science," *American Political Science Review* 94, no. 1 (March 2000): 1-19.

33. Robert D. Putnam, "The Public Role of Political Science," *www.apsanet.org* 1, no. 2 (June 2003): 249-55.

34. Robert Axelrod, "Political Science and Beyond," *Perspectives on Politics* 6, no. 1 (March 2008): 3-4.

35. Schall, *Roman Catholic Political Philosophy,* 2.

36. Margaret Levi, "Why We Need a New Theory of Government," *Perspectives on Politics* 4, no. 1 (March 2006): 5-19.

37. Levi, "New Theory," 12.

38. John Lewis Gaddis, *The Cold War: A New History* (New York: Penguin, 2005), 257.

39. For a fine treatment on the ongoing influence of Epicurean materialism in modern thought, see Benjamin Wiker, *Moral Darwinism: How We Became Hedonists* (Downers Grove, Ill.: InterVarsity Press, 2002).

40. Ira Katznelson, "At the Court of Chaos: Political Science in an Age of Perpetual Fear," *Perspectives in Politics* 5, no. 1 (March 2007): 3-15.

41. Augustine, *Confessions* Book I: 1.

42. Augustine, *Confessions* Book X: 23.

43. See, for instance, Arthur C. Brooks, *Who Really Cares* (New York: Basic Books, 2007) and Arthur C. Brooks, *Gross National Happiness* (New York: Basic Books, 2008).

44. Plato's discussion of epistemology and his metaphor of the divided line may be found in *The Republic*, Book 6, following his famous Allegory of the Cave.

45. John Paul II, *Centesimus Annus,* para. 5.

46. See, for instance, Robert J. Spitzer, *New Proofs for the Existence of God: Contributions of Contemporary Physics and Philosophy* (Grand Rapids, Mich.: William B. Eerdmans Publishing Company, 2010).

Chapter 2

A CATHOLIC APPROACH TO POLITICAL THEORY

Steven J. Brust
Associate Director of the Tocqueville Forum
Georgetown University

"Do not conform your mind to this world, but conform your mind to Christ so that you may do what is pleasing and perfect in His sight." (Rom. 2:12)[1]

Introduction

When I first learned about this book on Catholic assessment of political science, I thought it long overdue. I was first introduced to the idea of a Catholic approach to political thought during my graduate studies in philosophy when I sat in on an undergraduate course titled Catholic Political Thought. Later on, when I returned to another graduate school to earn a Ph.D. in politics, I learned of the many different schools included in the subfield of political theory as well as all of the other subjects covered under the discipline of political science. Having read much of the Church's teaching on social and political matters, I had a benchmark from which to engage the vast subject matter. As I progressed in my studies and then in my teaching and research, I realized that a Catholic has much to offer the discipline of political science in general, and political theory in particular. In order to attempt to fulfill the perhaps immodest task of a providing a Catholic approach to political theory, I must begin with an understanding of what is meant by "Catholic" in order for there to even be a "Catholic approach" to political theory. Next, I will proceed to a defense and normative understanding of political theory itself, which will necessarily be undertaken from within this Catholic perspective. In addition, I will present the way in which a Catholic political theorist should approach his or her scholarly work and teaching, and briefly set forth an important contribution a Catholic can make in reference to contemporary political thinking and practice. This article, therefore, is addressed to Catholics and non-Catholics alike. In short, I attempt to explain both the "Catholic Approach," and the "Subfield of Political Theory," and assess the latter by means of the former.

A Catholic Approach

When one identifies himself as a Catholic, it means that one has been baptized into the Catholic Church. This membership in the Church includes an assent to the full substance that the term "Catholic" represents. There is an objective reality which one embraces and participates in, or claims to participate in.[2] This reality is the Person of Jesus Christ, God, Who is Truth itself. A Catholic accepts Christ as his savior and all truths that are necessary for his salvation. This includes all of Christ's teachings, which are found in the Church He established—the Catholic Church, which is the *pillar and bulwark of truth* (1 Tim. 3:2). Thus, when one self-identifies as a Catholic, it necessarily entails that one accept the whole content or substance of the Catholic faith. The whole content comes by means of Scripture and Tradition, which includes the Sacraments, liturgical celebrations, prayers, customs, and truths about God, His Church, the world, and man. And this content comes through the Church, including what the Church specifically teaches. The Church's teaching office is aptly named the *Magisterium.*[3] A claim to be Catholic includes the acceptance of what the Church teaches through the *Magisterium*. Exactly what the Church teaches is encapsulated under the term "faith and morals." Knowledge of these truths of faith and morals are for one's own salvation—eternal life with God, as well as for the salvation of all. Therefore, a Catholic is obligated to know these truths and to live them out, and to make them known to others, that both he and others may achieve salvation.[4]

However, salvation is not merely a life-beyond-death reality, for it begins in this world by living a good moral life, a life of holiness. This moral life is not one of isolation, but for most people, occurs while living in community. Thus, the Church's moral teachings include how one ought to live as a person living in relation to others. Man's social life includes every aspect of his life: nothing can be neglected or is irrelevant for salvation. Therefore, since man's social life also is a subject matter for the Church, then She teaches not only on matters of personal morality, but also of social morality (*CSD*, #10). The result of this is a body Catholic Social Teachings (CST).[5] The modern formulation of these teachings is symbolized in Pope Leo XIII's encyclical of 1891, *Rerum Novarum*, which addressed both the problems caused by the industrial revolution associated with liberal economic theory and practice, and the dangers of the ideas of communism and socialism.[6] However, I must add that CST did not commence in 1891, but originated with Christ and the first Christians, and developed on up through the centuries from the sources of Scripture and Tradition, theologians, philosophers, canonists, and the historical experience of the Church. It is only due to the great social disruption based on new ideas and practices of the modern world, rooted in socialism and liberalism, that the Church had to respond with more explicit, specific, and developed teachings regarding social matters.

Since these social teachings are part of the Church's evangelizing mission (*CSD*, #66-7), informing man of his need for salvation, they are intended to be normative and, as such, they consist of "principles of reflection, criteria for judgments, and directives for action" (*CSD*, #7). These principles, criteria, and directives are to help individuals create a new social and political order (*CSD*, #19) and to transform the world (*CSD*, #55) in accordance with them, thus facilitating the salvation of persons. This is not a straying from her supernatural mission, nor an immanentizing of it, but rather is essential to it: because the natural is raised to a higher plane by the supernatural, therefore nothing of the natural temporal order is excluded from the supernatural order of faith and grace (*CSD*, #64). Therefore, the Gospel of Christ (which includes the social teachings) should penetrate and reign throughout society (*CSD*, #62),[7] offering a path to follow in order to build up a society of justice and love which "anticipates in history, in a preparatory and pre-figurative manner, the 'new heavens and new earth in which righteousness dwells' (2 Pet. 3:13)" (*CSD*, #82). Since the social teachings ultimately have their source in moral theology, they have the same dignity and authority as the moral teachings, which obligate the faithful to assent to them (*CSD*, #9).[8]

Before summarizing the content of the Church's social teachings, it is helpful and instructive to underscore that although the social teachings are considered to be moral theology (*CSD*, #72), nevertheless, they are known either through reason and revelation or both and therefore are not exclusively theology. The Church considers truths for salvation to be divinely revealed through Scripture as well as through Tradition, both of which are not beyond reason or without rationale. What I mean by this is both that the truth of some of the teachings are not merely true due to the authority of the one claiming them—in this case God through his representative on earth, the Church—but also because many of the teachings can be known by reason, that is, by a rational reflection on the world and human nature, which is created by God. Furthermore, what is divinely revealed can be reasonable, or explained to some degree by reason. Furthermore, Revelation can provide more knowledge about the nature of man than can reason alone, and therefore affords a better and more complete understanding of man's nature. In turn, reason itself can help understand and explain revealed truth and integrate it into the truths of human nature known by reason, helping one to understanding more fully the very principles and concepts of the social teachings (*CSD*, #77). The Church's social doctrine is (natural) knowledge enlightened by faith, and therefore faith does not deprive it of rationality. As a result, it can have universal applicability, that is, be applied to and accepted by all (*CSD*, #75). It is not merely for those who have the gift of faith. As we shall see below, the very fact of revelation and its harmonious relationship with reason is important for political theory.

Besides deriving knowledge from theology and philosophy, the Church draws upon the contributions to knowledge discovered by the variety of natural, human, and social sciences. Whatever part of the truth about man and the world that can be gathered from a particular scientific discipline is integrated by the Church into its teaching either explicitly or implicitly. However, these different branches of science should themselves be open to the Church's teachings (*CSD*, #78).[9] Thus, the Catholic theorist can bring aspects of political theory into dialogue with the Church's teachings to deepen and increase the knowledge of political life. One might ask how it is that if a particular piece of knowledge within a social, natural, or human science is true and is taken up by the Church as true, then how could one examine that particular piece of knowledge in light of the Church's teaching to know if it is erroneous? The answer to this question, in one respect, touches on the point of this chapter: What is already known to be true according to the teachings of the Church cannot be contradicted, and any claim of knowledge in another science is measured by these teachings.

The 2,000 years of knowledge accumulated throughout history by means of divine revelation through Scripture and Tradition, philosophy, other sciences, and historical practice, bolsters the Church's claim to be an "expert in humanity" (*CSD*, #61). Those who are Catholic participate in this patrimony of expertise, so they should understand it, live out, and offer the teachings to everyone else in the world for their salvation, and the building up, organizing, and promoting of a society of justice and love. For as I mentioned above, although the world is not the kingdom of God, it can prefigure it to the extent that Catholics work for it in cooperation with the grace of God.

Principles of Catholic Social Teaching

I now turn to a summary of the specific content of the social teachings. Many think that the Church's social teachings touch exclusively or primarily on economic matters, and that the term "social justice" mainly captures this. However, this is mistaken. Since the Church claims to be an expert in humanity, Her teaching touches on every aspect of man's life—economic to be sure—but also political, legal, familial, cultural, and social, as well as the obvious spiritual. Since the subject matter is quite extensive, and the scope of this chapter is limited, I can do no more than provide a brief summary of the contents of the teachings, primarily its main principles.

The primary and foundational aspect of the Church's social teaching is the understanding of the nature and dignity of each and every human person as made in the image of God. Man is a unity of body and soul, with the faculties of intellect to know the truth and the will to choose the good, capable of self-knowledge, self possession, and self-giving as a social being, called to attain a life of virtue and holiness while living in communion with others. Yet man is afflicted by original sin, and therefore needs redemption by the grace of Christ, called to communion with God in this life, and in eternal life (*CSD*, #108-110). These realities are not merely slogans or nice sounding concepts, but contain very particular meanings. By beginning with the dignity of the human person, the Church points out that all of man's social life is to be for the good of the person, that man is "the beginning and end of all social life."[10]

With this foundation, the Church teaches other principles and values necessary for man's life: the principle of the common good, the universal destination of material goods, the principle of subsidiarity and participation, the principle of solidarity, and the values of truth, freedom, justice, and love. Each of these principles and values has its specific content, with clear descriptions of what they are, and how they are related to each other. Furthermore, the social teachings also include specific normative understandings of these values and principles as they pertain to different aspects of man's life and world: marriage and family life, human work and economic life, the political community and civil society, the international community, culture, and the environment. Each of these areas is not randomly or arbitrarily conceived or arranged, but represents an order based on God's divine plan of creation. They have a reality that one discovers and cooperates with, but does not create. Thus understood, one can discern the consistency in and coherence of the teachings. It is incumbent on a Catholic to take into account all of the teachings as a unified whole, especially according to the moral order in which the whole is presented by the Church (*CSD*, #9). Within this ordered whole is found the place of the more specifically political teachings. These include the nature of civil law and its relation to the natural law, natural and civil rights, the primacy and content of the common good, the proper understanding of freedom, the origin and nature of political authority, democratic governance, tyranny, punishment, civil friendship, Church and State relations, just war, just wage, and private property and its social use, and so forth.

I need to emphasize that a Catholic theorist doesn't merely think in light of principles, criteria, and directives, but in light of the totality of the faith and the living Tradition of which he is part—the liturgy, Sacraments, prayer life, parish life, and the like. In short, he should have a Catholic mind.[11] Having been transformed by the supernatural workings of grace, with a deep faith and abiding hope, one is called to go forth in love in order to bring Christ (from whom the teachings ultimately arise) to others. For the political theorist, this includes the domain of his research, scholarship, and teaching.

Political Theory: A Defense

Having given a presentation of the "Catholic" aspect—the reason for and general content of Catholic social teaching and its importance to a Catholic, I am now prepared to discuss the "political theory" component of this chapter. We start with an essential question: What is political theory? To answer this, perhaps one may need to presuppose the Catholic understanding of faith and reason that I am presenting here. Indeed it this understanding that is essential to the Catholic assessment of the political theory subfield and is one of the most important contributions a Catholic can make to it. However, before I present this understanding of faith and reason in relation to political theory and answer the question, it is first necessary to make the case for the subfield of political theory (even if one rejects revelation) in face of attempts to scale it back or eliminate its presence, or reject it as irrelevant to the study of political things.[12] This is most important: For regardless of the infighting within political theory itself about its exact nature—that is, the inclusion of theology and philosophy under the "theory" discipline—what is at stake is the legitimacy of this subfield as an actual source of knowledge or science as such.[13]

One notices that the contents of this book in which this chapter appears, include two chapters on political theory along with the other typical subfields of political science. From the perspective of a typical political science department, this would appear to be disproportionate. Indeed, in many departments, the theory field is usually the smallest, if it exists at all. The other subfields predominate, with a focus on methods of political processes, empirical analyses of political systems and events such as voting behaviors, how laws are made, or how political parties effect change, and other similar matters. They primarily are descriptive in nature, with perhaps some attempt to promote a normative "theory" based on this descriptive analysis. Included in this is the big emphasis on quantitative method and analysis—using mathematical formulas to tell us how and why the political system and behavior works, and providing formulas to predict future assessments.[14]

Departments typically offer a course or two on the history of Western political thought, ancient and modern, and depending on the college or university, these courses may or may not be required for a political science major. In a recent survey of political theorists revealing their perspective on the current state of the theory subfield, the most telling result is the fact that only 27.7 percent of Ph.D. programs require their students to take a political theory course.[15] If the day has arrived when the kind of thinking on political matters which existed for a couple of thousand years is not considered knowledge of political things, then that is all the more to lament the current state of the political science discipline which ignores its very origin and foundation.

In general, scholars in the dominant subfields do not take the time to address the theoretical/philosophical assumptions embedded in their scholarship or perhaps are not aware of these assumptions, and at worst, reject theory as irrelevant to their work and as useless because it is too subjective in its interpretation and not an objective scientific method based on empirically verifiable data. Since they are so focused on the descriptive case, they neglect to ask the principled questions such as: Why does this matter? Or what does this tell us about how the political community ought to be ordered?

Indeed, there is even the denial of the legitimacy of raising questions concerning these normative or "value" judgments—the separation of the supposed objective facts from subjective values. But while this neglect or denial occurs in speech or explicit inaction, professors don't hesitate implicitly or explicitly to adhere to particular views of the government process or events or behaviors as normative, that is, as good, however much they may be based on their undefended or unexamined personal ideological preferences. Basic theoretical and philosophical (and as I would include, theological) assumptions upon which many of the other disciplines are based are the very assumptions which need to be studied in a theoretical manner—that is, attempting to discover the fundamental principles of the political order, the nature of the good life, justice, freedom, etcetera. Yet it is precisely this theoretical study that is the smallest within many political science departments, and is at times neglected. I am not claiming that these other subfields are not valuable nor provide true knowledge, indeed they do. Rather, much more theory needs to be offered in the political science departments for its own sake, but also because it is essential to these other subfields—providing their ultimate context and purpose. Thus, from a Catholic perspective, political theory would be the most important subfield of a political science department, without excluding or neglecting the others. The number of chapters in this book devoted to theory is recognition of this.

"Political" and "Theory"

Having defended the need for political theory understood in a generic sense, I turn now to describe in a more precise way what the subject matter of the subfield of "political theory" ought to include. An answer to the question "what is political theory?" begins with understanding both the "political" and the "theory." By "political" I mean all things that pertain to man's life in political community, which is all encompassing, touching on every aspect, to lesser and greater degrees, of man's life—his economic, social, legal, cultural, moral, and yes even spiritual life.[16] This understanding of the "political" perhaps could be shared by most (except maybe the inclusion of spiritual); however, it is the understanding of "theory" which is more controversial.[17] What I mean by "theory" is the pursuit and attainment of knowledge of the whole of reality, of what is,[18] from two sources—reason and revelation (philosophy and theology). Therefore, political theory includes both political philosophy and political theology.[19] What I mean by this is as follows: Philosophy includes the knowledge obtained by the use of one's reason. Philosophy asks questions pertaining to life's meaning in all its aspects, and can find some answers to them by coming to the knowledge of man's origin, nature, and end. This is summed up in the inscription at the temple at Delphi: Know Thyself.[20] Knowing oneself better, means that one knows his own nature as well as the nature of things around him, both material and spiritual things, including God. By knowing oneself better, there is the possibility to live a more fully human life.[21] Thus, philosophy is not merely the questioning which originates in the wonder of things (*Fides et Ratio*, #4), but most importantly, it is the attainment of some true answers.

When one speaks of *political philosophy*, one means the knowledge of political things attained by man's human reason alone and not by any divine revelation. It should be noted that it is not only a descriptive exercise, but goes beyond that to making evaluative judgments about what ought to be with respect to political life and action, that is, it includes the nature of the good life, namely, how one ought to live in the political community, and hence, how the political community ought to be ordered. One can also think of this in terms of attaining knowledge of the best regime that is then used to judge all other existing regimes in their particularity. This is a normative claim and pertains to what ought to be done in the morally relevant sense.

I add that philosophy includes asking and answering questions pertaining to God and man's relation to God. This knowledge of God is attained by reason and not by any special revelation from a divine source, which one believes in based on one's trust or faith in that source. Therefore, one can classify this knowledge as *natural* theology, that is, knowledge of God attained naturally— through the use of one's reason alone—and not supernaturally, that is from a divine reality above nature. Questions such as whether God exists are important to an individual's life and the political community—as Plato demonstrates in *The Republic*. Since this knowledge is not based on any direct divine revelation, it would fall under political *philosophy*. The inclusion of natural theology under political theory is not necessarily controversial, or least it seems to me, it shouldn't be. Since reason is a faculty inhering in everyone, all can come to know truths about creation and a Creator, and about man with respect to his political and social life.

The more controversial claim is that divine revelation is also a source of political knowledge for the whole political community, even to nonbelievers, or at least is relevant to the whole political community, regardless of its composition of believers or nonbelievers. This is what I termed above as political *theology*: knowledge of God and man, and man's relation to God, which pertains to political matters either directly or indirectly. Some of this knowledge about God can also be known by reason, and in these cases, divine revelation would support or clarify this natural knowledge, and provide a deeper understanding of it. However, much of this theological knowledge can only be attained by specific revelation from a source beyond the power of human reason—a divine source, which comes as a gift from God and must be received as such. An example of this is the knowledge that God is one in three persons, and that the second person is Jesus Christ, who forgives sins and from whom man obtains salvation— an eternal life in communion with God.

However, what God reveals can be rationally understood. For instance, man can use reason to try to explain how there can be three persons in one God. Revelation also can enhance what can be known by reason: For instance, knowledge of man being made in the *imago Dei* provides a more profound understanding of what it means to say man has dignity as a rational and social creature. Or one can reasonably assess the consequences of revelation for political life. An example of this would be the revelatory claim found in St. Paul's book to the Romans 13:1-12, that all authority is from God, and one must obey all authorities; or the claim found in Acts 5:29, that a Christian must obey God rather than man when there is a conflict between God's law and human law. One can reasonably reflect on what these mean and what consequences they have for the political order. Lastly, revelation can provide reasonable answers to questions that reason itself proposes, but that it cannot answer on its own. For instance, questions such as: Why is there evil in the world and what is its remedy? Or can God be friends with man? Christian revelation provides reasonable answers to these questions.[22] In short, revelation can purify and clarify reason, can provide a deeper understanding of man's nature and moral life, and provide reasonable answers to questions reason itself asks, spurring reason on to accept what is revealed by God. But first, one must allow reason to be open to this revelatory source of knowledge.

Theology, then, is important for political matters, and there is a *political* theology that should be included within political *theory*. This is controversial primarily because it seems "unfair" and unacceptable to those who will not accept theological knowledge either because they do not believe in the God who has revealed this knowledge, or because they reject theology as having any relevance for how the political community should be ordered. They might object that the political must be free from revelation and theology, as it only leads to a fundamentalism leading to the imposition of theological truth claims by coercion through the use of political power as it was done at times in the history of the West and in other settings. Yet this should not preclude taking revelation into account when theorizing about political matters. One must work out an answer to this objection, which we don't have space to do. However, in brief, it would include an understanding of a distinction between Church and State, and political versus cultural/societal promotion of religion, religious freedom, the natural moral law, the origin of political power, and an inquiry into the historical reality of the relation between religion and cultures and in particular between the Christian faith and the very rise of Western civilization.[23]

Perhaps the most important way in which Christian revelation relates to political theory and politics is that it limits the political power: revelation reveals a spiritual life and kingdom that transcend the political and earthly realities. This prevents, or rather provides reasons to prevent, political theory and politics from expecting perfect justice and goodness in this world. A revealed God helps to prevent politics from becoming a substitute religion and metaphysics.[24]

Up to this point, I have primarily equated reason with philosophy, but it also includes truths known by reason found in other human, social, and natural sciences. Thus, knowledge of economics, psychology, culture, literature, medical science, technology, etcetera, all fall within the political theorist's scope as he takes into account the whole of one's life in the political community.

I conclude this section with a summation of what I believe to be the description of a political theorist: One who seeks out the truth of reality by using reason and revelation in order to obtain truth for its own sake, but also with the hope that man might live in accordance with the truth so that he may have a more complete and good human life in a political community. Looked at in another way, the theorist attempts to attain knowledge of the good life whereby he may judge the existing political life and call it on to live according to that standard as best as can be done in accordance with the virtue of prudence.[25]

Political Theory Courses and "Schools" of Thought

I now turn to a summary sketch of the political theory subfield and a Catholic approach to it.[26] In general, courses on the history of political thought are the most prevalent, ranging from ancient to contemporary. Other courses include a focus on particular thinkers such as Aristotle or Machiavelli. In the departments where political theory has a higher importance, there are a range of additional offerings including topical courses covering notions of justice, law and morality, freedom and authority, American political thought, democracy and liberalism, and the like.

There is a concern that political theory courses are treated as merely historical, that is, the texts are read for historical knowledge without asking whether the ideas argued for in the texts are true or not, or whether the principles can be applied to contemporary circumstances. This view, most prominently held by Quentin Skinner and other scholars at Cambridge,[27] contends that the political thinkers of the past only address "individual questions" with "individual responses" at particular points in time and do not have anything to tell us about our own problems nor are they addressing any "perennial problems" or providing any "universal truths." Suffice to say, the addressing of perennial problems and discovery of universal truths is precisely the point of political theory. No doubt, that in studying the texts of political thinkers, one must know the historical context in which they are written and the specific problems they are addressing. Thus, one can interpret the text and attempt to understand the author, and ask whether there is a correct interpretation. Yet one should not stop there; one should consider what the thinker appeals to in response to the specific problems he addresses. Usually the thinker appeals to a normative principle or idea that he does not claim to be historically relative to particular circumstances. This is where a theorist should ask whether or not the principles or ideas are true—i.e., do they reveal anything about the nature of reality? For example, many political thinkers have addressed the idea of tyranny, albeit in many different particular historical circumstances. Even though addressed particularly, the thinkers are attempting to understand what tyranny is, which in turn leads to understanding the origin, nature, and purpose of political power. Thus it is both a perennial problem that is addressed, and a universal understanding that is sought. John Locke surely argued for a universal understanding of the origin and purpose of political power in order to recognize when tyranny exists. Although a theorist should be concerned with what the thinkers intended to say, the most important task is to ask whether what they do claim is true or not. These questions are ultimately at the heart of political theory because they attempt to build up what Catholics know as a perennial body of truths about man, the world, and God.

The Canon and Catholic Political Thought

The typical canon of texts used in courses on political thought in most departments include ancient, modern, and contemporary texts, with those of the medieval era, or even the whole 1,500 years from Christ up to Machiavelli found missing. Even within topical courses—e.g., political authority and obligation—one might find the neglect of the Christian thinkers between the Greeks and Hobbes. This omission would seem odd considering the idea and reality of, and justification, for the origin and nature of political authority were debated and lived out from the coming of Christ on up to Hobbes and it is upon this history that the modern thinkers build (or destroy), theorizing about the origin of political authority in reaction or relation to the previous 1,500 years of thinking and practice. Any number of Christian political thinkers could be introduced in a course such as this. Indeed, since the West's development is linked with the history of Catholic theologians, philosophers, jurists, canon lawyers, and popes, it would seem appropriate to include more of them in the canon. St. Augustine and St. Thomas are the usual representatives, but one could include the Bible, the early Church Fathers, John of Salisbury, William of Ockham, and Francisco Suarez.

Related to the suggestion to include more Catholic thinkers in the canon, is the question of whether there exists a school of "Catholic political thought." This category of thought can be understood in two ways. It may be understood first as the existence of Catholic teachings that are social and political in nature, which I have summarized in the first section above. They are Catholic in the sense that they are teachings of the *Magisterium* intended for one's salvation as it relates to the social and political life and are included in the content of what one believes when one self-identifies as a Catholic. One could teach a course using the specific documents of the Church. Of course, these teachings are (partly) an expression of the accumulated wisdom of the Church's Tradition, which includes, but is not identical with, the wisdom contributed by Catholic theologians, philosophers, jurists, and canon lawyers throughout the centuries.

This latter admission leads to the second understanding of a category of Catholic political theory: There is a long tradition of Catholic thinkers throughout the history of the Church who have thought about political life in light of the Catholic faith and who have helped to inform the Catholic understanding of fundamental political and social principles. Now, understood in the broadest sense, this classification would include all thinkers who claim(ed) to be Catholic, and claim(ed) to be applying Catholic principles, whether Thomas Aquinas, Giles of Rome, or the heretical Marsilius of Padua. Thus, Catholic political thought could manifest itself in a few courses that might include a number of Catholic authors spanning the history of Christianity, or thinkers from a select time frame—e.g., contemporary American Catholic political thinkers. Examples of authors include the obvious—Augustine and Aquinas—but also the not so obvious—the Bible, early Church Fathers, Pope Gelasius I, William of Ockham, Francisco Vitoria, Francisco Suarez, Juan Donoso-Cortes, Joseph De Maistre, Orestes Brownson, Jacques Maritain, and Yves Simon.

In summary, a category of "Catholic political thought" makes sense in that the Church, existing for 2,000 years, has been instrumental in shaping the Western world in thought, deed, and institution. Catholic thinkers have had a tremendous influence on the course of history and on the very ideas debated throughout history—the origin and nature of political authority, freedom, rights, natural law, the common good, tyranny, Church/State relations, constitutionalism, democracy, law and legal procedures, the unjust law, and the like.[28] One can say that the Church and Her teachings have helped to shape most of Western political thought and action, which has been born out of either a harmonious relationship with, or hostility towards, or outright rejection of, Catholicism. This history of thought and action also has helped to necessitate the Church's articulation of Her teachings—indeed what is considered the modern social teaching is a reactive and proactive teaching brought on by the thought and action of the modern political world. From Gregory XVI, Pius IX, and Leo XIII, the Church found itself explicitly teaching principles for a just and good political order and society as political and social evils continued to spread across Europe and other parts of the world.

"Schools" of Thought

Whether or not one accepts the existence of a Catholic political thought, it is safe to say that different "schools" of political thought do exist within the subfield, each with a quite extensive variety of literature. A list of schools might include: Marxism, Conservatism, Classical and Contemporary Liberalism, Communitarianism, Libertarianism, Voegelinianism, Straussianism, Post-Modernism, and Feminisim. Of course, this list is not exhaustive, and each is not mutually exclusive, for some may overlap with others, and there may be some subsets of each school itself. I also add that these classifications might be somewhat contrived, as perhaps all attempts to group thinkers or ideas together in one sense are.[29] However, general classifications help us to look at particular thinkers and schools and ask questions such as: What are their fundamental substantive principles and/or starting premises? What do they consider to be normative? What are their hermeneutical methods?

After answering these questions, which pertain to understanding the substance and method of the thinkers and schools on their own terms, the Catholic political theorist should then ask the more fundamental and important questions such as: What in these schools is true? Is anything contrary to a Catholic perspective? Can anything in them complement what one knows to be true by faith and morals? Of course, one's responses to these questions depend on how well formed one is and what substantive principles, premises, and paradigms one has already accepted. In accordance with St. Paul's exhortation to the Romans (2:12), a Catholic should first conform his mind to the Church's teaching. Thus Catholics must use careful discernment in approaching these schools, and by doing so, they can help to break through their own ideological barriers or prejudices that prevent the discovery and development of truth for themselves and for other theorists and the broader political community. By ideology, I mean believing that one's reason has come to certitude about some principles that are not rooted in the whole of reality. Or put another way, a focus on one truth of reality while ignoring or neglecting or rejecting other truths results in a distortion of the interdependent complexity of the whole of reality.[30] As a result, one is less apt to examine ideas in light of the teachings, but to view and interpret Catholic teaching through the lens of one's school. Looking to the teachings to find support for the ideology can result in giving a meaning to the teaching that it doesn't have and perhaps is opposed to. It can also have the effect of diluting the teaching's effectiveness for transforming thoughts, actions, and institutions, and instead using it to support the reigning dominant ideology or some other set of ideas. A Catholic also might be inclined to claim that the teachings are historically situated and no longer relevant, or that they have changed and thus shouldn't be adhered to, or that they are merely prudential judgments so they can be rejected outright. Catholic theorists have a responsibility to resist succumbing to these temptations at the outset. Instead, one's priorities must be properly ordered, viewing the ideology or thinker through the lens of Catholic teaching first, which then allows one to open a dialogue with other schools with the hopes that it will be fruitful in the search for a deeper knowledge of the truth.[31] Indeed, a Catholic theorist ought to be the one to encourage members of these schools to move outside the confines of their ideational walls.

Suffice to say, the Catholic theorist has much to offer all of the schools of thought prevailing in political theory. Since the contemporary and historical literature is quite vast and varied, an extensive assessment of these schools would fill volumes, so therefore I will address what I believe to be the most important concern which implicates most if not all of the schools. However, first I would like to mention two influential schools: Voegelinism and Straussianism. These schools follow in the footsteps of and include the very influential twentieth century theorists Eric Voegelin and Leo Strauss. They both saw the importance and necessity of political theory while addressing the condition of modern liberal democracy. A Catholic ought to assess how they treated the relation between philosophy and theology (reason and revelation—especially Christian revelation), and whether their turn toward ancient political philosophy as an answer to shortcomings in modern political thought and practice is an adequate solution, and also whether their understanding of the natural law is compatible with the Catholic natural law tradition, especially as it relates to intrinsically evil actions—i.e., universal moral principles—as well as natural rights.[32]

The Fundamental Catholic Contribution to Political Theory

Although this assessment of each individual school of thought is necessary and important, I would like to suggest that the overall most urgent concern for the Catholic theorist is the present condition of modern liberal democracy, in theory and practice. What follows is an assessment of an assemblage of contemporary schools of thought and the general opinion of popular political culture and movements as well as courts. Although liberal democracy could include many things, what seems to be bound up with it is the profession and promotion of pluralism—the notion that the liberal democratic order is comprised of individuals who hold many, seemingly incompatible, understandings of morality, the good life, and overall comprehensive metaphysical and religious doctrines. This fact of profound pluralism is generally accepted as a good state of affairs, and appears as a guiding foundational principle and as a political and cultural goal. This pluralism is sometimes justified by an appeal to skepticism, namely, that one can't know the truth, or by an appeal to the claim that there is no one truth to be known and everything is relative to each person, or by an appeal to what is similar, that all the different comprehensive doctrines are equally true or of equal value. As a result, it is argued that the state should be neutral with respect to the good life as embedded in any comprehensive doctrine.

At the same time, there are claims concerning the existence of universal moral absolutes. These absolutes primarily come in the form of rights, especially rights to freedoms. Modern and contemporary political theory and practice have promoted an ever-expanding notion of freedom, beginning with a freedom from government interference in matters of religion—freedom of religion, to a freedom *from* tradition, custom, authority, government, and others, wherein the freedom of the autonomous sovereign individual is exalted. Finally, this freedom *from* has culminated in a freedom from the natural moral law and from virtue leading to true human flourishing and perfection. This freedom emphasizes the freedom of choice itself, without concern for what the content of that choice is.[33] This freedom *from* tends ultimately to encourage the fragmentation of community, resulting in relationships between persons more apt to be defined by mere voluntary contract at will or by power whereby the weaker person or one without power will most likely be harmed by the choice of the stronger.

This freedom to choose is also coupled with the fact that certain behaviors once considered to be morally evil are now considered to be morally good, and behaviors previously considered to be morally good are now considered to be morally evil. In the name of freedom to choose, these "new moral goods" are becoming something that adherents to the natural moral law must tolerate, respect, and at times personally support, and require the political community to provide. As a response, the Catholic political theorist should engage this notion of freedom and provide an alternative understanding of it that is linked to the truth of the human person, who has a nature and end in reference to which the freedom of choice is exercised. It is freedom *for* the good, true, and beautiful, not freedom *from* these, nor freedom of arbitrary choice based on subjective and plural notions of the human good. Furthermore, the freedom of the person is not to be understood in an individualistic manner, but rather as a freedom which is intrinsically social, whereby the person is already in relation to and for others, and finds his fulfillment with others. In this way, the person can participate in and promote the common good that he shares with others.[34] And this understanding of the common good should not be understood as a mere aggregate of individual interests, but rather one whereby persons share in common goods with others, and for others, whether they be material, cultural, moral, or spiritual. The more one has in common with others, the stronger the bond of community. Therefore the political community needs to have a certain "amount" of unity. The problem is that a unity centered around freedom—even a radical freedom—from others and as a choice indifferent to its content (or to be more specific, indifference to or rejection of the natural moral law and God) results in inevitable practical difficulties—an increased disunity on moral questions, and hence increased potential conflict and injustice among persons within the political community.

Therefore it is essential for Catholic theorists, who have an advantage in that they possess a body of truths about the moral and social nature of the human person—"expertise in humanity"—to promote the very unifying foundation of the political order itself. This pre-political foundation, based on the truth and good of the human person, is the *sine qua non* of the political community in contradistinction to the idea that there are plural forms of the human good.[35] What ultimately makes sense of the contradictory claims of a relativistic pluralism and of absolute rights and freedoms is the implied acknowledgment that there is no political, cultural, moral, and theological neutrality—that there is some view of the good, no matter what school of political thought or political practice one is associated with. In their dialogue with these schools of political thought and practices, Catholic theorists need to emphasize this fact, and then offer their understanding of the good of the human person. This offering includes a reaffirmation of the criteria one can use to judge the truth or falsity of political ideas and realities. First, we must advocate the use of a comprehensive understanding of reason, not limited to a mere scientific or utilitarian method, nor limited by an *a priori* definition of a political or public reason set up to fit specific political results. Second, we must look to revelation to complement reason in its search for truth. The schools within the subfield of political theory and the current political realities are in need of the truths of faith and reason, which provide the 'principles for reflection, criteria for judgment, and directives for action.'

Whatever the school, a Catholic theorist can provide a comprehensive understanding of the human person complete with a nature and end to those who deny it; a way to distinguish between true and false human rights; an understanding of freedom intrinsically related to truth; the importance of the principles of subsidiarity and solidarity; the correct understanding and importance of marriage and family as the first cell of society; the promotion of objective truth over the false and inconsistent claims of relativism, subjectivism, moral pluralism, consequentialism, selective absolutism, and state neutrality; and the importance of tradition, custom, authority, and community at all levels. Perhaps the most important is the recognition of divine revelation and its proper relationship with reason.

Conclusion

When a Catholic approaches the totality of the political theories and events, one's theorizing may very well be challenging with respect to the canon, schools of thought, and contemporary political and social life. However, this only means that a Catholic must engage them with all the more scholarly rigor and humility. The only way for a political theorist to harmonize his vocation as a theorist with his Catholicism is to first form himself. This means that if one self-identifies as a Catholic, he must know what this identification means and entails. This requires that he be properly catechized in all aspects of the Catholic faith, the sacraments and liturgy, and the teachings on faith and morals, especially the social teachings. As St. Paul exhorts, he must conform his mind to Christ (Rom. 2:12). He must take a posture of humility in seeking ever more to understand what the Church teaches and why, and give the appropriate response. One's mind is formed from many sources—a political ideology, a political party, etcetera—but the primary source for Catholics should be their faith and the teachings of the Church. Without this, there is simply no "Catholic" approach to political theory—one might as well be an atheist or believe in any other religion.

A Catholic should defend the very subfield of political theory itself and encourage the political science discipline to include more political theory in the curriculum. With respect to the subfield as a whole, a Catholic political theorist should also take a posture of humility in seeking to understand the political thinkers and schools on their own terms, and then should have the Church's body of truths and Catholic frame of mind influence his judgments on political thought and events, accepting any truth to be gained. At the same time he should also encourage and challenge others to take seriously these Catholic truths not only for the sake of knowledge itself, but also to help promote a good political order based on justice and love.

Notes

1. The *Holy Bible* Revised Standard Version, Catholic Edition.

2. I do not address here any degrees to which any specific individual is assenting to and or living out the faith—e.g., the baptized but "nonpracticing" Catholic. Rather, I am summarizing the normative understanding of what it means when one identifies oneself as "Catholic."

3. Pontifical Council for Justice and Peace, *Compendium of the Social Doctrine of the Church* (Citta del Vaticano: Libreria Editrice Vaticana, 2004), #79 (hereinafter *CSD*). For a general overview of the Church's *Magisterium*, see Avery Cardinal Dulles, *Magisterium: Guardian and Teacher of the Faith* (Naples, Fla.: Sapientia Press, 2007).

4. I do not here enter into any debate with those who wish to reject certain moral teachings of the Church whether they accept them as teachings but reject them anyway, or they outright deny that they are in fact teachings of the Church that are binding.

5. John Paul II, *Centesimus Annus* (1991), #4; *CSD*, #104.

6. By "modern," I do not mean an adoption of modern thought and practices, but rather I mean that the Church's responses to the modern practices which modern thought spawned have been written in modern times, not medieval or renaissance times.

7. This is what the *Catechism of the Catholic Church* (Citta del Vaticano: Libreria Editrice Vaticana, 1997), #2105 refers to as the social reign of Christ the King. If Christ doesn't reign, some ideology hostile to Him will.

8. The type of assent owed is an important aspect of the social teachings and how the theorist approaches it needs to be fleshed out more fully than what I can offer here. Briefly, the social teachings are comprised of teachings of different levels of authority, and so the type of assent required by Catholics differs according to the teaching (*CSD*, #8, #80). Basically there are three categories of teachings: 1) those divinely revealed, which are irreformable and are to be believed as such; 2) those definitively taught which necessarily follow upon divinely revealed truths, either historically or logically, and which are irreformable and must be firmly accepted and held; and 3) those not definitively taught, in matters of faith and morals, some of which might be reformable, but

nonetheless call for "religious submission of intellect and will." All of this means that a Catholic has certain obligations—to assent to teachings as authoritative, but also as reasonable. There are truths that are irreformable which Catholics must believe, and there are some teachings to which one must give a kind of assent, and this willingness to submit to possible, but not necessarily reformable matters, should be the rule. However this doesn't mean that the irreformable teachings can't be investigated and questioned, and explored with careful discernment, reflection, and prayer, in order to develop a deeper understanding of the teaching. Furthermore, on those teachings which might be reformable, one can investigate why it would not or would be reformable, and perhaps discover truths which would help to demonstrate why a certain teaching doesn't not conform to reality as the Church judges it to. If the theorist is in this latter area, the Church does caution about not providing an untimely public expression of his views that are contrary to the Church's (maybe reformable) teaching. See Congregation for the Doctrine of the Faith, *Donum Veritatis* 1990, #23-31; http://www.vatican.va. Also the *Code of Canon Law* 1983, Canon #747-755, esp. 752 and 754, with reference to having the faithful avoid erroneous doctrines which are contrary to the teachings of the Church which are not definitively taught: www.vatican.va/archive. Lastly, I caution that Catholic teaching is not merely acceptance of a set of certain propositions, but a way of life rooted in the life of the Church with Her sacraments, prayer, calendar, parishes, history, and saints: in sum, an overall approach to and understanding of reality.

9. This, one should recognize by now, is what I am arguing for in this chapter with respect to political theory.

10. *CSD*, #106-7. Obviously this doesn't mean an individualistic idea of man with no inherent relation and responsibility to others.

11. This term resembles that of the title to Father James V. Schall, S.J., *The Mind That Is Catholic*: *Philosophical and Political Essays* (Washington, D.C.: The Catholic University of America Press, 2008). The idea, which has been a part of the life of the Catholic Church, is that the whole of one's being and life should be shaped and formed by a Catholic understanding of reality.

12. Andrew Rehfeld, "Offensive Political Theory," *Perspectives on Political Science* 8 (2008): 465-86, points out that Penn State University wanted to remove political theory from its political science department completely. Although, strictly speaking, his article is about whether political theory should be included within political science as a social science, so perhaps the problem is the very restrictive meaning of science within the discipline and the university itself. Thus, if political science is defined in this narrow way, then perhaps it is right to exclude theory. Yet this is precisely the point—political science, as knowledge of political things, must include political theory.

13. Leo Strauss, *What Is Political Philosophy?* (Westport, Conn.: Greenwood Press, 1959), rightly defends political philosophy over against the claims of present day political science which claims to limit knowledge of political things to merely empirical and descriptive analysis.

14. For instance, the *American Political Science Review* (among other journals published by the American Political Science Association) is predominantly focused on articles centered on quantitative models. I also think it necessary to add that what I mean by theory is not what one might mean when referring to, say, a "theory of how voters behave politically," or a "theory of how the executive branch agencies, congress, and lobbyists work together to write laws and policies." They might be ways of explaining processes, and in fact, the explanation may be true, but they are not political theory in the sense I mean here. The political theorist would take this information and ask further questions such as: Is this process good for achieving the purposes of government? What does this say about the principle of separation of powers—is it a valid principle and why? Should

our government operate in this way? And, of course, these questions aren't looking for answers in terms of efficiency, or merely empirical goals, but normative metaphysical and ethical truths concerning the good life and a just and good government and political community.

15. Matthew J. Moore, "Political Theory Today: Results of a National Survey," *Political Science and Politics* 43, no. 2 (April 2010): 265-72.

16. I include the spiritual within the political in the sense that man's spiritual life is lived out within some political community, although it is not intrinsically dependent on it, and in fact transcends it.

17. There are some who want to limit political theory to pertain to power relations.

18. Fr. James Schall, S.J., uses these words throughout much of his writing. They emphasize that there exists a knowable reality that we discover but do not create. It is one's responsibility to live a life of discovering the truth of things, and this necessarily begins with *what is*.

19. This is in stark contrast to a thinker such as Leo Strauss who excludes, *a priori*, theology/revelation as a source of knowledge pertaining to the nature of political things. See "What Is Political Philosophy," in *Introduction to Political Philosophy*, 7. It is also in contrast to the contemporary liberal thinker John Rawls, who rejected theology as a source of political notions of justice unless they happened to coincide with the justice determined by his "public reason." See John Rawls, *A Theory of Justice* (Oxford: Cambridge Press, 1971). For another view of political theory from an influential theorist, see Eric Voegelin, "What Is Political Theory?" in *The Drama of Humanity and Other Miscellaneous Papers, 1939-1985 Collected Works* 33 vols., eds. William Petropulous and Gilbert Weiss (Columbia: University of Missouri Press, 2004). Thus, arguing that theology is relevant to political theory is one of the ways a Catholic can contribute to the subfield.

20. Pope John Paul II in his encyclical on the relation between faith and reason, *Fides et Ratio*, rightly references this inscription at the temple at Delphi, and it surely influenced Socrates who exhorted to his Athenian jury that the unexamined life was not worth living. Pope John Paul II's *Fides et Ratio* (Washington, D.C.: USCC, 1998), #1. Plato, "Apology," in *The Trial and Death of Socrates*, trans. G. M. A. Grube (Indianapolis: Hackett Publishing Company, 2000), #38.

21. *Fides et Ratio*, #1,3,4.

22. This is an example emphasized by Fr. James V. Schall, S.J., who has written extensively concerning the proper relation between philosophy and revelation from the Catholic perspective. See *Roman Catholic Political Philosophy* (Lanham, Md.: Lexington Books, 2004). See also Josef Cardinal Ratzinger, who has helped to shed light on the dialogical relation between reason and revelation, in *The Church, Ecumenism, and Politics* (San Francisco: Ignatius Press, 2008), and in *Values in the Time of Upheaval* (San Francisco: Ignatius Press, 2005), 69. See Pope John Paul II, *Fides et Ratio*, #76.

23. For this last point, see Christopher Dawson, *Religion and the Rise of Western Culture* (New York: Doubleday, 1957).

24. Again, I follow Fr. Schall who has done great work in this area. See his *At the Limits of Political Philosophy: From 'Brilliant Errors' to Things of Uncommon Importance* (Washington, D.C.: Catholic University of America Press, 1996), 49-56. See also Schall, *Roman Catholic*, and Ratzinger, *Values in the Time of Upheaval*, 70-72, one of his many works where he writes of this danger.

25. I add this condition "as best as can be done in accordance with the virtue of prudence" to underscore that one should not be looking for a utopia or perfection on earth.

26. Here I include in political science departments any and all of them.

27. See Quentin Skinner, "Meaning and Understanding," in *Meaning and Context: Quentin Skinner and His Critics,* ed. James Tully (Princeton, N.J.: Princeton University Press, 1988), 29-67. See also his other articles as well as the responses by critics.

28. Indeed, Martin Luther King, Jr., in his explanation for his disobedience to the civil law found in his Letter from a Birmingham Jail, references St. Augustine and Thomas Aquinas with respect to their understanding that the civil law must not contradict the natural moral law, and if it does, it is considered an unjust law.

29. For instance, classical liberalism may overlap with libertarianism. And a Catholic can ask whether these classifications are even helpful or destructive to arriving at truth—they could act as barriers to attaining truth, by building up an ideology which pits itself against another "school," and prevents one from accurately assessing the school of thought. I expound on this below.

30. An analogous example is that of heresy, which contains a partial truth but to the diminishment or rejection of another truth—e.g., the Monophysite heresy, which holds that Christ is truly God but rejects that He also is truly man.

31. I must remind the reader that this temptation must be understood in light of my earlier reference to teachings and the assent owed to them.

32. See "Symposium: The Ancients/Moderns Distinction—Catholic Perspectives," *The Catholic Social Science Review* 14 (2009): 9-84 for differing views among Catholics regarding these topics with respect to Leo Strauss. Dr. David Walsh is a notable among those Catholics who have engaged the thought of Eric Voegelin; Fr. James V. Schall, S.J., is a notable one among those Catholics who have engaged the thought of Leo Strauss.

33. The most strident example of this present day understanding of liberty is found in the Supreme Court Case, *Planned Parenthood v. Casey,* 505 U.S. 833 (1992), Justice Anthony Kennedy writing for the majority: "At the heart of liberty is the right to define one's own concept of existence, of meaning, of the universe, and of the mystery of human life."

34. Cardinal Joseph Ratzinger, "Truth and Freedom," *Communio: International Catholic Review* 23 (Spring 1996). *CSD*, #135-143.

35. Congregation for the Doctrine of the Faith, *Doctrinal Note on Some Questions Regarding the Participation of Catholics in Political Life,* 2002, #3.

Chapter 3

THE ANCIENT/MODERN DISTINCTION AND THE CATHOLIC INTELLECTUAL TRADITION

Robert P. Hunt
Professor of Political Science
Kean University

Moral Realism and Contemporary Catholic Social Thought

Almost sixty years ago, Professor John H. Hallowell of Duke University delivered a series of lectures at the University of Chicago that was to become a book entitled *The Moral Foundation of Democracy*.[1] The lectures were delivered at a particularly propitious time, when prominent political theorists were attempting to provide philosophical grounds upon which to defend their preferences for limited, constitutional government over more totalistic political systems. Hallowell, an Episcopalian, rejected one of the fashionable credos adopted by many of the more prominent political "scientists" of his day, namely, that constitutional democracy was preferable to totalitarianism precisely because it took no view of the goods that make for human flourishing. These scientific proponents of a "value-free" political science believed that one could understand the workings of political institutions and the ideologies that supplied "rationalizations" for those institutions without reference to some transcendent source of human meaning and purpose. In fact, the very effort to objectify transcendent truths made it more likely, in the eyes of these value noncognitivists, that we would fall victim to these potentially totalistic claims.

By contrast, Hallowell maintained that the American experiment in self-government could be sustained only if it were grounded in a moral realist view of human nature, a view that depended at least in part upon the insights of ancient political theorists such as Plato and Aristotle. In opposition to those political philosophers who argued for governmental neutrality on the question of the good life, Hallowell argued that every society defined itself by how it answered certain basic questions about human nature and the goods appropriate to it. The decision not to answer these questions was, paradoxically, just as much an answer as any other, and the consequences for our constitutional way of life would be profound:

> Underlying every system of government there is some predominant conception of the nature of man and the meaning of human existence. More often that not, this idea of man is implicit rather than explicit. But if not explicit, it is always fundamental. For what we think government can and ought to do will depend in large part upon what we think about the capacities of men and the purpose of human existence. If our conception of man's essential nature is false, i.e., unreal, we may be led to seek and apply political solutions to human and social problems that at best are useless and at worst harmful.[2]

Hallowell's moral approach to the subject of democracy—and, more generally, to the study of politics—was viewed at the time by many political scientists as naïve. It has become even more controversial over the past half century as the behaviorist confidence in scientific, neutral reason has given way to a more radical brand of philosophical skepticism under which postmodernist and post-structuralist critics question the very capacity of the human mind to know anything about the nature of reality.

At both the theoretical and practical levels, the consequences of this deracination and de-moralization of politics have been profound. Contemporary anti-perfectionist liberals such as John Rawls and Ronald Dworkin have argued that, while there might or might not be any moral furniture in the universe, political morality requires that those who wish to participate fully in a liberal, democratic constitutional order must leave their truth claims at the door of the public square. To do otherwise, they claim, is to violate the canons of "public reason." Other postmodernist liberals, who are more honest in their unwillingness to place a brake on their philosophical nihilism, go even further. They argue, with Richard Rorty, that even the preference for the modern liberal model of man and society is merely that: a preference to be indulged because we will for it to be so indulged.

Given this seeming movement of liberal modernist philosophy toward the deracination of politics, one of the central questions confronting contemporary Roman Catholic social and political theorists is the relationship between Catholicism and liberalism, especially in the wake of the Second Vatican Council and its reflections on the politico-juridical order and the proper foundations for constitutional government and religious freedom in the modern world. In raising such questions, the Catholic theorist is often placed at a seeming rhetorical disadvantage. As just noted, Rawlsian and Dworkinian liberals, in the name of "public reason," ask that teleological moral truth claims be left at the door of the public square. To the extent that Catholics fail to conform to this deontological conception of "public reason," they are deemed to violate the terms of the liberal social compact by attempting to impose their own conception of the good upon the whole of society, especially those who do not share their thicker conception of the moral and political good.

Some Catholic integrationists such as David Hollenbach, J. Leon Hooper, and R. Bruce Douglass seek to effect a rapprochement between Catholicism and modern liberalism by emphasizing the Second Vatican Council's support of "liberal" political institutions, or by de-emphasizing those intractable moral issues upon which Catholics and liberals disagree. They hope thereby to establish a quasi-Hegelian philosophical synthesis of Catholicism and liberalism.

For example, Hooper, arguing for a historicized and relativized version of John Courtney Murray, transforms Murray's attempt to reconstruct an American public philosophy on discernibly Roman Catholic grounds into a recipe for ethical proceduralism:

> [I]t is in the public commitment to human attentiveness, intelligence, and judgment that finally, for Murray, the core and timeless moral reality of human society resides. Without personal and collective commitments to the processes of human social reasoning, the discussion of any moral, justice, or religious issue quickly resolves into a factionalistic play of blind force.[3]

Hooper defines Catholicism down to a point where it is forced to adopt a watered down view of the political common good, commits itself to public discourse of a purely procedural variety, and establishes a modus vivendi with the liberal model of man and society as a precondition for Catholic involvement in the public square.

R. Bruce Douglass, in his introductory essay to *Catholicism and Liberalism: Contributions to American Public Philosophy*, argues that "on any number of matters that are of real consequence [Catholics and liberals] now deserve to be thought of much more as allies rather than as adversaries." They could become even greater allies if they would get over the "myopia born of the heat generated by the 'culture wars,'" and relieve themselves of being "obsessed with certain particularly divisive issues on which they continue to have deep, abiding differences." These divisive issues include abortion, gay rights, and "the status of women" where the Church "still has, needless to say, a long way to go."[4] One suspects that under the modus vivendi advocated by these Catholic integrationists, Roman Catholics are expected to go a much longer way in accommodating themselves to the politics of liberal modernity than are their liberal counterparts in accepting certain key elements of the Catholic view of man and society.

To counter the liberal secularist defense of ethical neutrality or Rawlsian public reason, many of those operating from within the Catholic intellectual tradition argue for an approach to liberalism different from that of the integrationist. They contend that anything other than a merely prudential accommodation to some aspects of liberal modernism constitutes a threat to the integrity and distinctiveness of the Catholic intellectual tradition. They insist that liberal secularism itself is based on a nonrational faith that attempts to set norms for a whole society. As Francis Canavan has noted (following Hallowell), for liberal secularists "normlessness . . . turns out to be itself a norm. It is a steady choice of individual freedom over any other human or social good that conflicts with it, an unrelenting subordination of all allegedly objective goods to the subjective good of individual preference."[5] The modernist liberal secularist articles of faith elevate choice to the highest of social goods and charge the state with the responsibility of enforcing this voluntaristic, individualistic orthodoxy.

Nonintegrationist Catholic social and political theorists argue for the integrity and substantive distinctiveness of the Catholic intellectual tradition and the philosophical and practical inadequacy of the liberal model of man and society. They reject the liberal assumption that some variant of "moral autonomy" (as in David A. J. Richards) or "equal concern and respect" (as in Rawls) can serve as foundation for contemporary "rights talk," and, more broadly, question whether the liberal intellectual tradition contains within itself the resources needed to sustain its purported commitment to democratic self-government. On this reading of intellectual history, secular rationalist liberalism tends to create a culture of disbelief and leads toward statism rather than truly limited, constitutional government.

Canavan was one of the first Roman Catholic theorists to point out how the liberal, individualist model of man and society inclined toward statism, especially, for example, in its influence on the recent development of American constitutional law:

> Recent constitutional law in the United States has limited government by insisting more and more upon individual rights. Still more recently, so has civil rights legislation enacted by Congress or by the several state legislatures. This undoubtedly limits what government may do to individuals, but by the same token, and necessarily, it increases what government may do for individuals and institutions.
>
> Consequently, government is obligated to be, at one and the same time, individualistic and statist. It is individualistic when it serves an expanding array of rights. But insofar as it uses the power of the state to impose those rights upon institutions, government is statist, and the fingers of the bureaucracy reach more and more into all of the institutions of society.[6]

Or, as contemporary Catholic political philosopher Robert Kraynak has noted, "Unless the rights of persons are clearly specified from the outset as serving the true hierarchy of ends, those rights will be seen in contemporary secular terms and will weaken subsidiarity by increasing demands to expand the centralized bureaucratic state."[7]

In sum, liberal political philosophy, and the model of man and society that flows from it, threatens to dissolve the matrix of institutions, virtues, and convictions on which a free society depends for its vitality. It does not supply an adequate moral foundation for limited constitutional government. Any establishment of a principled *modus vivendi* with modernist liberalism threatens, therefore, to undermine the integrity of the Roman Catholic intellectual tradition.

Strauss, the Ancient/Modern Distinction and Catholic Political Thought

In light of the inherent theoretical and practical weaknesses of liberal political philosophy (i.e., its epistemological slide into value noncognitivism and failure, therefore, to provide what Murray called a theory of *ordo iuris*), the call for a return to what Leo Strauss described as principles of natural right and classical political philosophy presents what seems to be an attractive alternative to the modern liberal project, particularly to many of those Catholic nonintegrationists who wish to restore the notion that politics can be, at its best, a great and civilizing activity.[8] In short, Roman Catholic social and political theorists who reject the philosophical and political foundations of liberal modernity must confront the question of the relation of the Catholic intellectual tradition to ancient political philosophy.

Leo Strauss's effort to rekindle an appreciation of classical political philosophy in the face of the challenges posed to it, and to any serious effort to recover the truth about political things, is to be commended. Like Hallowell, Strauss's seeming moral realist approach to the study of political life was viewed by many of his contemporaries, influenced as they were by the tenets of value noncognitivism, positivism, and historicism, as hopelessly naïve. As Strauss ably pointed out, however, these "value-free" efforts were doomed to trivialize the study of political things, replacing political philosophy ("a doctrine which claims to be true") with the history of political philosophy ("a survey of more or less brilliant errors").[9] For Strauss, liberal modernity was incapable of providing sustenance for an experiment in self-government, most especially that experiment explicitly grounded in an acknowledgment of the "truthfulness" of natural rights claims.[10]

For Roman Catholics in particular, Strauss's work—and the work of the scholars who express an intellectual indebtedness to him—is of special importance. It has forced them to reconsider the relationship between the Roman Catholic intellectual tradition and classical political philosophy. It has also forced them, as already noted, to reconsider the wisdom of any full-throated embrace of liberal modernity, particularly in light of the development of Catholic social and political thought as embodied in the teachings of the Second Vatican Council. Moreover, as Father James V. Schall has noted, Strauss (along with Hannah Arendt and Eric Voegelin) has "forcefully raised the question about the relation of reason and revelation, of modern and classical political philosophy to each other," thus challenging "the very philosophy upon which the modern state has rested."[11]

Central to the Roman Catholic tradition's quest for a fuller understanding of its own intellectual premises, however, is a need to understand the relationship of the tradition to Strauss in particular and to the reading of intellectual history upon which the Straussian distinction between "ancients" and "moderns" rests. The use of the word *distinction* here is important, for most Roman Catholics would agree that there is indeed a distinction between a type of philosophical and moral realism that acknowledges the existence of a hierarchy of ends within nature itself—usually associated with the tenets of "classical" or "ancient" philosophy—and a philosophical and moral voluntarism and nominalism that acknowledges no natural teleology and reifies human choice as the highest human good—usually associated with "modern" philosophy.

To the extent that the Straussian distinction between "ancients" and "moderns" points Catholics back to this fundamental philosophical "turn," thereby assisting Roman Catholics to appreciate the consequences of liberal modernity's rejection of the aforementioned transcendent norms and standards that are not a product of human will, it is helpful. To the extent to which it is hardened into something more than a useful distinction—that is, into a principled dichotomy where the person who employs it seems to be pushed into embracing either classical or modern philosophy, especially as Strauss characterizes the distinction—it might fail to do full justice to the richness and integrity of the Catholic intellectual tradition and that tradition's reflections upon the nature, purpose, and limits of political life. I will argue that Strauss's distinction between "ancients" and "moderns" in general and between "classical" and "modern" political philosophy in particular does tend toward a dichotomizing of intellectual history where under even an ostensibly Catholic view of political life is, upon even a favorable reading of Strauss's distinction, more classical than Catholic in its philosophic orientation and political ramifications.[12]

Ted McAllister has pointed out that "Strauss devoted little space [in his works] to an examination of Christianity," but that "he often employed a more expansive language" in his analysis of natural right and natural law "designed to suggest to the uninitiated reader a broad Judeo-Christian tradition when he meant the Jewish heritage simply." [13] McAllister's reference to "the uninitiated reader" and the inference he draws from it are based at least in part on Strauss's famous hermeneutic distinction between exoteric and esoteric writing and the need for the philosopher, in the interest of the commonweal, to cloak or disguise his true philosophic intentions. On this reading, "the great quarrel" and tension between Jerusalem (representing revelationally based societal adherence to divine law) and Athens (representing the corrosive character of reason and of true philosophic inquiry) is "the root of Western civilization," not the transition from Greek particularism to Roman universalism.[14]

The recovery of the root of western civilization, therefore, requires not merely a return to classical political philosophy as Strauss understands it, but to an awareness of the tension between the conflicting demands of reason and revelation. The effort to dissolve the tension in the interest of revelational norms or philosophic truth is one of the hallmarks of modern philosophy and its proclivity toward political utopianism. Even as sympathetic a Roman Catholic reader of

Strauss as Gary Glenn acknowledges that Strauss "lived that tension: he understood that the claims of reason when fully developed as philosophy were incompatible with those of revelation. But he regarded their mutually exclusive claims as not resolvable on any basis that both could accept."[15]

Under Glenn's favorable interpretation of Strauss's contribution to the recovery of political philosophy, Strauss's view that the claims of reason and revelation are "mutually exclusive" need not be accepted by Roman Catholics. Rather, the Roman Catholic political philosopher can appropriate Strauss's teaching in support of moral realism in the battle against subjectivism and relativism. In other words, Strauss shares with Roman Catholics an aversion to liberal modernity and provides a powerful philosophical argument for rejecting it, particularly in its positivist and radical historicist dimensions. The "ancient"/"modern" distinction is a powerful hermeneutic tool through which one can embrace the moral realism of the "ancients" and reject the increasing nihilism of the "moderns."[16]

And yet a closer reading of even the exoteric Strauss should give Roman Catholics pause before they embrace Strauss's distinction. First, Strauss's brand of moral realism is one that seems to be at best ambivalent to Christianity's contribution to the history of political philosophy, particularly in its political ramifications. Second, Strauss's distinction between ancients and moderns seems to be based primarily on the relationship between the philosopher and the city, not on whether the human mind has the capacity to grasp truths grounded in the nature of things. The first point is addressed obliquely in *Natural Right and History*, the second more directly in *What Is Political Philosophy?*

In his introduction to *Natural Right and History*, Strauss seems to indicate that "Roman Catholic social science" is preferable to most of "present-day American social science" in that it is not necessarily committed to "the proposition that all men are endowed by the evolutionary process or by a mysterious fate with many kinds of urges and aspirations, but certainly with no natural right."[17] In short, Strauss implies that Roman Catholic social science is at least open to the possibility of some view of natural right, implying for political philosophy the argument for a hierarchy of natural ends. The problem, however, is that "the modern followers of Thomas Aquinas" (i.e., neo-Thomists) have been forced to accept "a fundamental, typically modern, dualism of a nonteleological natural science and a teleological science of man" that seems to break with the views of Aristotle and Thomas Aquinas himself, thus pushing, one infers, much of contemporary Catholic social thought in a nonteleological, imperativist direction.[18] A possible implication: for Roman Catholics to salvage their own tradition from the shoals of the liberal politics of modernity, they must embrace a more fully (as envisaged by Strauss) Aristotelian Christianity and its hierarchical, prudentialist view of politics rather than a form of Kantian Christianity with its egalitarian and imperativist implications.[19]

And yet, at the very end of Strauss's chapter on "Classical Natural Right"—at the virtual center of the work itself—Strauss indicates that the problem with even St. Thomas Aquinas himself, a Thomas not read through the prism of neo-Thomists such as Jacques Maritain and Heinrich Rommen, is that "the Thomistic doctrine of natural right, or more generally expressed, of natural law is free from the hesitations and ambiguities of the teachings, not only of Plato and Cicero, but of Aristotle as well."[20] Thus, for St. Thomas there are certain immutable first principles of natural law that "suffer no exception, unless possibly by divine intervention." Under a Thomistic dispensation, reason and revelation are reconciled in such a manner as to imply (1) that all men are conscience-bound to obey the natural law, even in its immutable first principles, and (2) that this places an undue burden on the latitude exercised by statesmen in their pursuit of the common weal.

Thus, Montesquieu (a "modern" under any reasonable interpretation of Strauss's "ancients"/"moderns" distinction) "tried to recover for statesmanship a latitude which had been considerably restricted by the Thomistic teaching." The seeming gap between the "ancient" teleological view of political life and at least the early "modern" view (embodied in the writings of Machiavelli and Montesquieu) is bridged by a common rejection of immutable first principles that would limit the statesman's capacity to do what might be necessary to serve the regime.[21] It would seem, therefore, that the only way for political philosophers to salvage political wheat from the chaff of St. Thomas's effort to reconcile reason and revelation is to return to a more overtly "classical" view of politics, or perhaps to argue for a Christian view which minimizes the difficulties caused by the "Christianizing" of "classical" political philosophy by portraying the Christian view of politics as an interesting footnote to Greek classicism.[22]

Kraynak's Reconsideration of Catholic Thought

One of the best recent examples of a Christianized Straussian reading of intellectual history is supplied by Robert P. Kraynak in *Christian Faith and Modern Democracy*. Kraynak argues that there are "three great periods of Christian theology, each associated with a dominant philosopher": (1) the Platonic or Neo-Platonic Christianity of the early Church fathers; (2) the Aristotelian Christianity of medieval Scholastic theology; and (3) the Kantian Christianity of modernity (154ff). He implies that premodern (i.e., Platonic or Aristotelian) Christianity was teleological, hierocratic, prudentialist, and, in its more immediately political implications, not favorably disposed to natural rights talk or democracy. By contrast, modern Kantian Christianity is deontological (i.e., it adopts a morality of categorical imperatives), egalitarian, rights-oriented, and pro-democratic.

At a number of points in his book, Kraynak seems to assume that all rights talk is liberal/modernist. For example, he argues that "today, the term 'person' refers to a human being with a duty to forge his or her own identity or moral personality by an assertion of the will" (154), that "the deep premise of rights is the natural freedom and natural equality of the autonomous self" (172). Even though modern Christian theologians believe that rights can be detached from these voluntaristic premises, the subversive nature of "the deep premises" gradually take over because "rights are essentially ungrateful claims against authority, either for protections and immunities against authority or for entitlements against authority" (172).

At other points, particularly in his analysis of contemporary Catholic social thought, he retreats slightly from the assumptions that all rights talk is liberal/modernist and that liberal democracy and constitutional democracy are synonymous. For example, he acknowledges that the Second Vatican Council's embrace of religious freedom and constitutional democracy was "qualified" by the Church's historic commitment to a teleological view of human flourishing that subordinated human will to truths made accessible to man through revelation, reason, and the teaching authority of the Church itself. Moreover, "the modern synthesis of Christianity and Kant's philosophy of freedom is not inherently wrong. Like all syntheses, its validity depends on the precise formula for putting the different elements together" (163). Something resembling a proper synthesis is put together by Pope John Paul II, who subordinates rights to Christian natural law.

However, despite minor concessions to contemporary Christian personalism, the major theme of Kraynak's analysis remains the same: even legitimate efforts to control the Kantian component of a Christian synthesis are doomed to fail. The Kantian preoccupation with moral autonomy will ultimately devour the more teleological (and traditional) components of the synthesis. The fundamental choice for Kraynak is between Platonic/Aristotelian (and its hierarchical, prudentialist view of politics) and Kantian Christianity (and its egalitarian, imperativist view of politics). Assuming this fundamental dichotomy, which seems to be a Christian variation on the Straussian distinction between "ancients" and "moderns," Kraynak hopes that the traditionalist (i.e., nonintegrationist) Christian will opt for the former and reject the latter.

Kraynak's argument seems for the most part to be an extension to the whole of contemporary Christianity of themes addressed by the late Ernest Fortin—also influenced by Strauss's reading of intellectual history—who focused on what he perceived to be the weaknesses of contemporary Roman Catholic social thought. Fortin wondered whether any Catholic defense of human rights and religious freedom as anything other than a prudential concession to contemporary political realities might not place contemporary Catholic social thought in conflict with its historic commitments to "virtue, character formation, and the common good." For Fortin, this might produce within the Catholic tradition "a latent bifocalism that puts it at odds with itself and thereby weakens it to a considerable extent."[23] Those who would wish to preserve these historic commitments to a hierarchically ordered view of nature should ground their arguments in a philosophical anthropology that takes most of its political bearings from the insights of classical antiquity. For Fortin and Kraynak, to endorse human rights and constitutional democracy as a matter of principle is to endorse liberal modernity.

Kraynak's Christian variation on Strauss's major thematic distinction invokes the Augustinian doctrine of "the two cities" to explicate what he believes to be a Christian view of the proper relationship between spiritual and temporal realms. Given the dichotomy he has established between "ancient" Christianity and "modern" Christianity, and his clearly enunciated preference for the former over the latter, Kraynak's political theory collapses back, however, into a baptized variation on classical political philosophy.

Nowhere is Kraynak's effort to baptize classical political philosophy more evident than in his treatment of Plato's and Cicero's defense of a "mixed regime." The ancients understood "the advantages of a mixed regime in promoting a stable and balanced order that combines freedom and virtue in the citizen body with feelings of filial affection and piety for the foremost ruler." "The only point [at which a worldview inspired by the New Testament supplied an "important amendment"] that is missing in the classical philosophers is a proper distinction between the spiritual and temporal realms that the Greeks and Romans (and non-Christian cultures in general) were unable to grasp in all its implications" (236-237).

The Greeks and Romans were unable to grasp the implications of a proper distinction between spiritual and temporal realms *because they made no such distinction in the first place.* If they had made the distinction, they might have foresworn the need for the "regime" to instill in "the citizen body" feelings of "piety for the foremost ruler," and deemed any such effort to be itself an act of cosmic impiety.

Kraynak's Christian commitments seem at times to be subordinated to a view of human nature and of the role and purpose of the state that is more overtly Platonic. For example, Kraynak decries "the replacement of a culture that aspires to spiritual, philosophical, artistic, and heroic greatness with one dedicated to mundane pursuits and the tastes of ordinary people" (26-27). This aristocratic distinction between a "high" culture of aspirational greatness and a "low" culture of "ordinary" tastes leads Kraynak to argue that Jesus Christ himself distinguished between "higher" and "lower" human beings. "Jesus' very words require us to distinguish between higher and lower human beings and imply that fundamental human rights can be negated in order to satisfy the demands of divine justice" (174). The hierarchy of ends that distinguishes human nature from other natures seems to have been replaced at certain points in Kraynak's analysis by a terminology that implies a hierarchy of natures among human beings themselves.

A Catholic Response to Strauss and Kraynak

However, one of the most significant contributions that Christianity has made to our understanding of the goods that make for human flourishing, and for a proper appreciation of the relationship among those goods, is what Charles Taylor has called "the affirmation of ordinary life." According to Taylor, "ordinary life" designates "those aspects of human life concerned with production and reproduction, that is, labour, the making of the things needed for life, and our life as sexual beings, including marriage and the family." Ancient philosophy, whether Platonic or Aristotelian, saw these activities as necessary to attaining the good life, but playing an "infrastructural role in relation to it." Under this moral and social ontology, the natural institutions of civil society (e.g., family, village, trade associations, etc.) are subordinated to the series of intellectual and moral activities that make for the truly human life of contemplation and participation in the life of the polity. For the ancients, according to Taylor, truly good men "deliberate about moral excellence, they contemplate the order of things; of supreme importance for politics, they deliberate together about the common good, and decide how to shape and apply the laws."[24] By virtue of this ancient notion of the hierarchical subordination of the "ordinary" goods of production and familial life to the truly human goods of contemplation and deliberation, it was easy for the ancients to value the life of the philosopher over the carpenter, *zoon politikon* over the family man. The political consequence: ancient political philosophy exalts the polis, and the good of these other institutions of "ordinary" life must be subordinated to the well-being of the polis. The most important questions in the ontology of social life, therefore, are regime questions.

On the other hand, "the Jewish-Christian-Islamic tradition" effected what Taylor describes as a "radical revaluation of ordinary life"—"that God as creator himself affirms life and being, expressed in the very first chapter of Genesis in the repeated phrase: 'and God saw that it was good.' Life in a calling could be seen as participating in this affirmation of God's."[25] No longer are the natural institutions of civil society "infrastructural," as they were for ancient political philosophers. Rather, these institutions assume an increased dignity and importance in the economy of social life.

The notion of the *intrinsic* superiority of the contemplative and deliberative life is replaced by the more egalitarian idea that the lowly artisan can be just as much a member of God's Kingdom as the philosopher or the prince—if he participates in the sacramental life of the Church as a mediating force (as in Catholicism) or follows God's word more directly (as in Protestantism). And if the human person and the associational institutions of ordinary life are to be given a new and more important place in the social economy, it stands to reason that the polis can no longer assume the preeminent place in that economy that it had under the aegis of classical philosophy. The most important questions in the ontology of social life are not necessarily political ones.

Under the auspices of this tradition, one could argue that whether one assumes either that politics is primarily a consequence of human sinfulness (e.g., Augustine and Martin Luther) or that it is natural to man (e.g., Aquinas), it cannot lead man to his true transtemporal good. Nor is it univocally responsible for promoting the entirety of the temporal common good. Politics is thereby de-divinized, its functions and purposes limited by more than merely the Aristotelian canons of political prudence. The natural institutions of society (e.g., family, village, etc.) are elevated in importance, and it is no accident that even Aquinas, influenced as he was by Aristotle, could modify Aristotle's ideal of *zoon politikon* by stating that man was by nature a *social* and political animal. Kenneth L. Grasso summarizes the significance of that distinction and its social and political implications:

At the heart of Catholic tradition we find a rejection of the classical insistence on the primacy of the political in favor of what might be called the primacy of the social. For the Catholic tradition, society is not only sharply distinguished from the state, but enjoys primacy over it. Government is not merely one order in society, but is obligated to pursue its limited purposes under the latter's direction and correction. Rather than being seen as the unchallengeable ruler of the social world, the center of social gravity, the state is now understood to be limited in its jurisdiction, subject in its operations to the rule of law, responsible to those it governs, and required to share the stage of social life with a wide variety of other institutions whose integrity, autonomy, and distinctive responsibilities it must respect.[26]

However much Catholics and Protestants might disagree about the nature of the institutional Church, they can agree that the very idea of a hierarchy of natures among human beings and the assumption of the preeminent position of the polis in acknowledging that hierarchy is inconsistent with an Incarnation-inspired humanism and the integrity and dignity of the human person and the natural "ordinary" institutions of social life.

Strauss's concern about the practical political dangers caused by (the Christian) adherence to immutable first principles of natural law arises precisely because Strauss—and, one could argue, many of those who adopt a Straussian reading of intellectual history—believes that "the guiding theme of political philosophy is the regime rather than the laws." The fundamental questions of political life become "regime questions." In his analysis of Plato's *Laws* in *What Is Political Philosophy?*, Strauss provides the following definition of "regime":

Regime is the order, the form, which gives society its character. Regime is therefore a specific manner of life. Regime is the form of life as living together, the manner of living of society and in society, since this manner depends decisively on the predominance of human beings of a certain type, on the manifest domination of society by human beings of a certain type. Regime means that whole, which we today are in the habit of viewing primarily in a fragmentized form: regime means simultaneously the form of life of a society, its style of life its moral taste, form of society, form of state, form of government, spirit of laws. We may try to articulate the simple and unitary thought, that expresses itself in the term *politeia,* as follows: life is an activity which is directed towards such a goal as can be pursued only by society; but in order to pursue a specific goal, as its comprehensive goal, society must be organized, ordered, constructed, constituted in a manner which is in accordance with that goal; this, however, means that the authoritative human beings must be akin to that goal.[27]

In short, "classical political philosophy"—that form of political philosophy which Strauss most admires—"is guided by the question of the best regime." And the best regime itself is, in principle, concerned with the comprehensive ordering of society consistent with its collective telos.[28]

To argue that Strauss wants merely to return to the classical model of *politeia* as the self-sufficient and comprehensive form of human association is to miss the point here. For example, Strauss would undoubtedly find the modern liberal regime's commitment to religious liberty to be an improvement upon the classical view of society. Yet in his very adoption of the classical idea of "regime," he seems to endorse at the political level what John Courtney Murray described as "a single, homogenous structure, within which the political power stood forth as the representative of society in its religious and in its political aspects."[29] Strauss's very embrace of the question of what constitutes "the best regime" and his philosophical assumption of a conflict between reason and revelation cannot permit him—or anyone, for that matter, who commits himself to classical regime questions in the same manner as Strauss—to appreciate the extent to which a revelation-inspired worldview renders and transforms such classical regime questions and, perhaps, renders them largely irrelevant.

A number of prominent twentieth-century Catholic political philosophers (e.g., John Courtney Murray, Jacques Maritain, and Heinrich Rommen) have argued that a permanent goal of the Church in its relation to the state is to resist all forms of juridical and social monism. For the monist, there is one sovereign entity—usually the state—that is univocally responsible for advancing the common good and to which all persons and institutions must be subordinated. Whether this sovereign defines its purposes in individualistic or communitarian terms is not as significant as that it emphasizes the primacy of the political and sees itself as the ultimate bearer of human destiny. By arguing that *politeia* is concerned with the most comprehensive questions of human destiny and purpose, Strauss (and those of his adherents who subscribe to "regime questions" in the same manner as does Strauss) seems to embrace a form of political monism that ultimately expects too much of politics in the pursuit of our temporal common good.

As noted earlier, Robert Kraynak supports a Christianized amending of ancient political philosophy, but his discussion of the proper role of the state displays a similar fondness for the raising of classical regime questions, however much that view is "amended" by his ostensible indebtedness to Christian theorists such as Augustine and Aquinas. For example, in his discussion of contemporary formative influences on his own political views, Kraynak expresses his indebtedness to Dutch neo-Calvinist statesman Abraham Kuyper's defense of "sphere sovereignty" and the Catholic doctrine of "subsidiarity," each of which recognizes "certain corporate spheres of spiritual authority" that limit the pretensions of the state (206-7). Yet Kraynak pays little attention to the question of whether a principled attention to these spheres of authority might not require Christians to reconsider the sense in which the state is, as Kraynak argues at several points, "a provider of civil peace and moral order" and the maintainer of civic piety (xv, 88, 189).[30]

Kenneth L. Grasso has ably pointed out that the Platonic-Aristotelian tradition has modified rather than broken from the social ontology of pre-Socratic collectivist and elitist Greek culture:

> One thinks . . . of Platonic-Aristotelian philosophy's fusion of Church and state, and of state and society; its absorption of the individual, the family, and all of human social life in the all-embracing, undifferentiated, unity of the polity; its advocacy of infanticide; and its relegation of large segments of the populace to

the status not of "parts" of the city (partners in the polis, as it were), but mere "conditions" of its existence.[31]

Robert Kraynak is not calling for a return to the polis of classical antiquity, and he is most certainly not endorsing infanticide, but his criticism of persons of "ordinary tastes," his implicit acknowledgment of persons of fundamentally different natures, and his admiration of the mixed regime's ability to instill a spirit of proper "piety" in the foremost ruler are more ancient than Christian in tone and substance. His implicit adoption of the Straussian dichotomy between "ancient" and "modern" political philosophy forces him, when push comes to shove, to embrace a modified version of the former in light of the weaknesses of the latter. If Kraynak's philosophical elitism is consistent with the tenets of the Christian intellectual tradition, then he is most certainly correct in arguing that a New Testament-inspired worldview "amended" classical political philosophy.

John Courtney Murray has cogently argued, however, that Christianity has done much more than this. It has "freed man from nature by teaching him that he has an immortal soul, which is related to matter but not immersed in or enslaved to its laws. . . . It has taught him his uniqueness, his own individual worth, the dignity of his own person, the equality of all men, the unity of the human race."[32] For the committed Christian, this conception of man's personal spiritual dignity does not sit atop the classical conception of man as a rational animal. Rather, it transforms that conception with the light of its radiance into something other than "Platonic," "Aristotelian," or "Kantian" Christianity. In freeing man from nature, it has rendered the most fundamental of classical regime questions largely irrelevant since no "regime" short of the Kingdom of God in its fullness can satisfy man's thirst for heaven. In fact, the very effort to answer such a question (i.e., "What is the best regime?") in anything resembling political terms (either "ancient" or "modern") might be indicative of the fact that one has applied categories of political analysis more characteristic of a resident of the earthly city. Father James Schall has argued,

> [Aquinas's] reposing of the question of the best form of government could . . . be placed in an atmosphere in which it had never before found itself. That is, the problem of the ultimate destiny of man, his personal happiness, related to his individual life no matter what its context, could be considered a different question from that of the life of the polis.[33]

We must ask whether a truly Christian understanding of the ultimate destiny of man, and the extent to which that understanding suffuses and illuminates our appreciation of the inherent limits of politics, requires that we reconsider whether the concept of "regime," as Strauss defines it, is adequate for the consideration of the purpose and limits of politics within a Christian dispensation. Or, as Kenneth L. Grasso has pointedly asked,

> To what degree . . . is the Aristotelian conception of the polity as a self-sufficient community (i.e., as a community which supplies members with all that is necessary for human fulfillment), and with it the whole distinction be-

tween perfect and imperfect societies, compatible with the Christian conception
of man as a being possessing a transcendent destiny, a being who can find fulfillment only in the beatific vision?[34]

    The Catholic tradition of social and political thought is not simply a form of
baptized Platonism or Aristotelianism. Ancient political philosophers saw man
as a polis animal who realizes his social nature only insofar as he participates in
the organized activity of politics, that activity which distinguishes man from
God and beast. The Christian conception of man as *imago Dei* does not sit atop
the Aristotelian conception of man as political animal and supply an interesting
footnote to the history of political reflection. For the committed Christian, a lov-
ing God has created each person and has ordered each and every person to a life
that transcends nature. The political order must recognize the superior intrinsic
dignity of the human person and the natural goods and institutions (e.g., families, churches, neighborhoods, voluntary associations) that make for human
flourishing. As Murray argued in 1948, the state's political duty to the human
person is to create, or assist in creating, those political, social, economic, and
cultural conditions that "favor the ends of human personality, the peaceful en-
joyment of all its rights, the unobstructed performance of all its duties, the full
development of all its powers."[35]

    On this view, the state exists to serve the human person, not vice versa. This
task, while limited in nature, is both material and moral. In fact, the moral law
itself limits the authority of the state in its offices to the person and society. By
demanding that the state recognize and protect man's personal and social rights,
we do not make ungrateful claims against the authority of the state. Rather, we
demand that the state subordinate itself to the claims of a higher authority.
Grasso notes that "in keeping with its pluralist ontology of a society, [Catholic
social thought] has made clear that the state does not bear 'the primary responsibility' for the protection and promotion of the whole order of human rights, and
thus that the state's responsibilities toward this order are limited in nature."[36] In
fact, the whole notion of the equation of the state and society, or, in a more contemporary Straussian context, of the "subordination" of the plural structures of
society to the regime or to classical "regime questions," needs to be reconsidered.

    The Catholic intellectual tradition emphasizes the primacy of the spiritual,
the freedom of the Church to define itself and to discharge its divinely appointed
mission, and the inherently plural (rather than monistic) structure of the temporal common good. While the state has a degree of autonomy commensurate with
its fundamental purpose—securing public order as *an aspect* of the temporal
common good—it must respect the primacy of man's spiritual end and of the
natural social institutions that contribute to human flourishing. It must not impose on society an alien ideology that would subordinate the truths of religion
(i.e., the *res sacra*) to the perceived requirements of statecraft (i.e., the *res poli-
tica*). By respecting its inherent limits, the state honors the dignity and fundamental integrity of the human person as a child of God who seeks both spiritual
and temporal fulfillment.

Rethinking the Faith versus Reason Dichotomy

Leo Strauss's discomfort with any premature reconciliation of the possible truths made known through reason itself and the truths known through promulgation of the Divine Law forces him to "distinguish" political philosophy from political theology. "By political theology we understand political teachings which are based on divine revelation. Political philosophy is limited to what is accessible to the unassisted human mind." Moreover, "political philosophy rests on the premise that the political association—one's country or one's nation—is the most comprehensive or the most authoritative association." [37]

Why one should base one's political philosophy on any such premise Strauss does not answer fully, but it does provide insight into his distinction between "ancients" and "moderns." Ancient political philosophers defined "the best regime" as one in which moral virtue was promoted and the hierarchy of natures within human nature itself was given its due; modern political philosophers lowered man's sights and grounded "the best regime" in man's passions, self-interest, and some conception of human equality. In other words, the fundamental shift in political philosophy for Strauss is a shift in what characterizes the best regime. For Strauss, to begin from the revelation-inspired premise that any effort to define the most comprehensive or authoritative association in political terms is itself impious is to be untrue to the goals of political philosophy, whether ancient or modern. (This might explain why many political theorists who adopt Strauss's hermeneutic become concerned with "regime questions" and seem determined either to rescue the Catholic intellectual tradition in general and Aquinas in particular from modernity—as do many Christian Straussians—or to place it and him at the heart of modernity—as do many non-Christian Straussians: because the intellectual categories they have adopted prevent them from appreciating fully the distinctiveness of Christianity and its revelation-inspired understanding of political life.)

Christian political philosophers need not accept Strauss's charge precisely because, unlike Strauss, they do not assume that reason and revelation are in conflict with each other. Nor do they assume that the most comprehensive and authoritative association must be defined in political terms. Rather, they begin from a contrary premise, laid out eloquently by Etienne Gilson:

> If we admit, as we really should, that the miracles, the prophecies, the marvelous effects of the Christian religion sufficiently prove the truth of revealed religion, then we must admit that there can be no contradiction between faith and reason. . . . When a master instructs his disciple, his own knowledge must include whatever he would introduce into the soul of his disciple. Now our natural knowledge of principles comes from God, since He is author of our nature. These principles themselves are also contained in the wisdom of God. Whence it follows that whatever is contrary to these principles is contrary to the divine wisdom and, consequently, cannot come from God. There must necessarily be agreement between a reason coming from God and a revelation coming from God. Let us say, then, that faith teaches truths which seem contrary to reason; let us not say that it teaches propositions contrary to reason. . . . Let us rest as-

sured that apparent incompatibility between faith and reason is similarly reconciled in the infinite wisdom of God.[38]

Robert P. George has argued that religious faith and religiously informed
moral judgment can be based upon and defended by appeal to publicly accessible reasons provided by principles of natural law and natural justice.[39] The
Catholic social and political philosopher maintains that there is no inherent conflict between faith and reason, between the truths made known to man through
the Christian revelational dispensation and the truths that are naturally accessible
to man's intellect. In fact, Catholic social and political thought fulfills the promise of the philosophical realism of Plato and Aristotle by encouraging the human
mind to remain truly open to whatever it is capable of knowing, even if the fullness and implications of the truth attained surpass the mind's own unaided efforts.

This metaphysical openness to a richer understanding of reality than that
understanding contemplated from within the confines of ancient political philosophy in no way derationalizes philosophy or politics. Nor does it turn political philosophy into political theology, as Strauss would have it. James V. Schall
has noted that Christianity's influence on philosophy is philosophic to the extent
that it is itself subject to philosophic examination and can be seen to be related
to genuine philosophic questions about the nature of the human good.[40] The
questions asked by ancient philosophers about the nature of the human good
have received their most adequate response from within that tradition of thought
stimulated by Christian revelation.

Gilson's account of the reasonable basis for assuming a fundamental com-
patibility between faith and reason reflects the view of St. Thomas Aquinas,
whose main point, as Gilson notes, was "not to safeguard the autonomy of philosophy as a purely rational knowledge; rather, it was to explain how natural
philosophy can enter into theology without destroying its unity."[41] By seeing the
Divine as "infinite wisdom," St. Thomas—and those Christian philosophers who
follow in his footsteps—renders such an explanation less problematic. By con-
struing the Divine primarily as supreme lawgiver, Strauss actually seems to
adopt a more voluntaristic view of revelation-inspired norms, thus making his
desire to protect the autonomy of philosophy against the incursions of political
theology more understandable. At the same time, however, it leads the careful
reader to wonder precisely what a purely autonomous natural (as opposed to
political) philosophy—as Strauss understands that term—can tell us about the
nature of things.

The Case for Moral Realism

The Christian philosopher begins with an assumption that the universe is intelligible, Strauss with the assumption that "philosophy is essentially not possession
of the truth, but quest for the truth. The distinctive trait of the philosopher is that
'he knows that he knows nothing,' and that his insight into our ignorance con-

cerning the most important things induces him to strive with all his power for knowledge."[42] Whether a purely autonomous natural philosophy can take us anywhere beyond the acknowledgment that there are important questions to be asked is a question that Strauss leaves unanswered.

One who reads intellectual history under the Straussian hermeneutic dichotomy sees the course of intellectual history as an ongoing conversation about important philosophical questions, a conversation within which "ancients" and "moderns" provide two distinctively different sets of answers to the question of the role (and dangers) of true philosophy and its place within a political regime grounded either in the promotion of moral virtue (for the ancients) or the satisfaction of the appetites (for the moderns). If there is a dramatic moment in the course of that history, it is the moment at which "Machiavelli radically changed, not only the substance of [classical] political teaching, but its mode as well."[43]

The Christian philosopher can certainly appreciate the extent to which modern political philosophers such as Machiavelli, Hobbes, and Rousseau elevated what Servais Pinckaers describes as a nominalistic freedom of indifference over both a classical and/or medieval freedom for excellence.[44] The movement away from the philosophical and moral realism of St. Thomas Aquinas toward the nominalism and voluntarism of William of Ockham and his disciples was an important intellectual moment that has had profound historical consequences. And yet the most profound of historical moments, for the Christian, is not a philosophical moment at all, though the latter moment's impact on a revelation-inspired philosophy is profound. The true moment of significance for the Christian is that of the Incarnation. Christopher Dawson describes that moment, and the doctrine that it inspired, in the following way:

> For the Christian doctrine of the Incarnation is not simply a theophany—a revelation of God to Man; it is a new creation—the introduction of a new spiritual principle which gradually leavens and transforms human nature into something new. The history of the human race hinges on this unique divine event which gives spiritual unity to the whole historic process.[45]

"Viewed from this center the history of humanity became an organic unity. Eternity had entered into time and henceforward the singular and the temporal had acquired an eternal significance," says Dawson.[46] The whole of human history "finds its center in the life of an historic personality who is not merely a moral teacher or even an inspired hierophant of divine truth, but God made man, the Savior and restorer of the human race, from whom and in whom humanity acquires a new life and a new principle of unity."[47]

True Christian freedom, as Walter Kasper notes, is "the freedom of the sons and daughters of God, a freedom we have only in Jesus Christ and in the Spirit of Jesus Christ."[48] George Weigel has captured this understanding of freedom in his embrace of Pinckaers's freedom for excellence: "the capacity to choose wisely and to act well as a matter of habit . . . Freedom is the means by which, exercising our reason and our will, we act on the natural longing for truth, for goodness and for happiness that it built into us as human beings."[49] True Christian freedom reaches beyond the confines of the earthly polis and cannot be satisfied with questions asked and answers supplied from within the confines of either ancient or modern philosophies of man. *Gratia naturam non tollit, sed perficit.*

Under this dispensation, and the light it sheds upon the whole of human creation, a truly free choice for man is not limited to the choice between Athens—representing a truly autonomous view of human reason and the political consequences that flow therefrom—and Jerusalem—representing societal adherence to Divine Law. Nor does it require a political choice between "ancient" political philosophy—and its ultimate practical commitment to some variant of (baptized or unbaptized) Aristotelian regime—and "modern" political philosophy—and its ultimate commitment to an individualist regime of radical personal autonomy. Any effort to embrace one or the other pole represented by these dichotomies—or to portray Christian political philosophy simply as some variant of either—runs the danger of losing sight of the distinctiveness of a truly Christian understanding of political things and to harden Christian social and political philosophy into an old and discredited political and legal monism.

Notes

1. John H. Hallowell, *The Moral Foundation of Democracy* (Chicago: University of Chicago Press, 1954). Much of the first part of this essay is taken from Robert Hunt, "Political Philosophy," a contribution to *Encyclopedia of Social Thought, Social Science, and Social Policy* (Lanham, Md.: Scarecrow Press, 2007): 827-29.

2. Hunt, "Political Philosophy," 80.

3. J. Leon Hooper, *The Ethics of Discourse: The Social Philosophy of John Courtney Murray* (Washington, D.C.: Georgetown University Press, 1986), 203.

4. R. Bruce Douglass, "Introduction," in *Catholicism and Liberalism: Contributions to American Public Philosophy*, ed. R. Bruce Douglass and David Hollenbach (New York: Cambridge University Press, 1994): 9-10, 12.

5. Francis Canavan, S.J., *The Pluralist Game: Pluralism, Liberalism, and the Moral Conscience* (Lanham Md.: Rowman & Littlefield, 1995), 76.

6. Canavan, *The Pluralist Game*, 139.

7. Robert P. Kraynak, *Christian Faith and Modern Democracy: God and Politics in the Fallen World* (Notre Dame, Ind.: University of Notre Dame Press, 2001), 223. All further references to Kraynak's work in this chapter are to this edition.

8. Much of the rest of this essay restates and develops themes I raised originally in "Christianity, Leo Strauss, and the Ancient/Modern Distinction," *Catholic Social Science Review* 14 (2009): 53-63 and "Kraynak: Christianity v. Modernity?" *Catholic Social Science Review* 9 (2004): 47-52.

9. Leo Strauss, *The City and Man* (Chicago: University of Chicago Press, 1964), 8.

10. Leo Strauss, *Natural Right and History* (Chicago: University of Chicago Press, 1953).

11. James V. Schall, *Reason, Revelation, and the Foundations of Political Philosophy* (Baton Rouge, La.: Louisiana State University Press, 1987), 12.

12. One need not go so far as to embrace the claims of Shadia Drury, *The Political Ideas of Leo Strauss* (New York: St. Martin's Press, 1988) that Strauss was an esoteric Nietzschean in order to question whether one's adoption of the Straussian distinction between "ancients" and "moderns," conjoined with a hermeneutic that encourages the

reader to believe that most great philosophers engage in the art of secret writing to won-der whether Strauss's brand of moral realism fits altogether comfortably with a Christian worldview.

13. Ted V. McAllister, *Revolt Against Modernity: Leo Strauss, Eric Voegelin, & the Search for a Postliberal Order* (Lawrence, Kans.: University Press of Kansas, 1995), 198-99.

14. McAllister, *Revolt Against Modernity*.

15. Gary Glenn, "Defending Strauss Against the Criticism That His An-cients/Moderns Reading of the History of Political Philosophy Unjustly Depreciates Christianity's Contribution to That History," paper presented at the annual meeting of the Society of Catholic Social Scientists at St. John's University School of Law, Queens, N.Y. (October 2007), 1.

16. Glenn, "Defending Strauss," 6-8.

17. Strauss, *Natural Right and History*, 2.

18. Strauss, *Natural Right and History*, 8.

19. See Robert P. Kraynak, *Christian Faith and Modern Democracy* as an excellent example of this approach.

20. Strauss, *Natural Right and History*, 163-64.

21. Strauss, *Natural Right and History*, 164.

22. For another interesting effort to minimize the differences between Aristotelian natural right and Thomistic natural law, see Edward A. Goerner, "On Thomistic Natural Law: The Bad Man's View of Thomistic Natural Right," *Political Theory* 7, no. 1 (1979): 101-122. Goerner applies the Straussian hermeneutic of secret writing to Aquinas, argu-ing that St. Thomas didn't really believe in exceptionless moral norms. Ironically, Goerner's effort to refute Strauss's claims about the inflexibility of Thomistic natural law in matters of statecraft is resolved not by arguing in favor of what appears to be Aqui-nas's natural law position, but by pushing Aquinas in the direction of Strauss's position. Again, here it seems that the only way to salvage Aquinas and the tradition he represents is to transform him into something other—a baptized Aristotelian—than what he seems, at first glance, to be.

23. Ernest L. Fortin, "The Trouble with Catholic Social Thought," *Boston College Magazine* (Summer 1988): 37-42. For a more extended treatment of Fortin's reading of intellectual history, and of Christianity's place within that history, see J. Brian Benestad, ed., *Ernest L. Fortin: Collected Essays* (Lanham, Md.: Rowman & Littlefield, 1996).

24. Charles Taylor, *Sources of the Self: The Making of the Modern Identity* (Cam-bridge Mass.: Harvard University Press, 1989), 211-12.

25. Taylor, *Sources of the Self,* 218.

26. Kenneth L. Grasso, "Neither Ancient nor Modern: The Distinctiveness of Catho-lic Social Thought," *Catholic Social Science Review* 14 (2009): 49.

27. Leo Strauss, *What Is Political Philosophy?* (Westport, Conn.: Greenwood Press, 1959), 34.

28. Strauss, *What Is Political Philosophy?*

29. John Courtney Murray, *We Hold These Truths: Catholic Reflections on the American Proposition* (New York: Sheed and Ward, 1960), 202.

30. For an important Catholic defense of subsidiarity and its political implications, see Kenneth L. Grasso, "The Subsidiary State: Society, the State and the Principle of Subsidiarity in Catholic Social Thought," in *Christianity and Civil Society: Catholic and Neo-Calvinist Perspectives,* ed. Jeanne Hefferan Schindler (Lanham, Md.: Lexington Books, 2008), 31-65. American Neo-Calvinist defenses of the Kuyperian principle of "sphere sovereignty" can be found in David T. Koyzis, *Political Visions & Illusions: A Survey and Christian Critique of Contemporary Ideologies* (Downers Grove, Ill.: Inter-

Varsity Press, 2003), and James V. Skillen, *Recharging the American Experiment: Principled Pluralism for Genuine Civic Community* (Grand Rapids, Mich.: Baker Books, 1994).

31. Grasso, "Neither Ancient nor Modern," 45.

32. Murray, *We Hold These Truths,* 192.

33. James V. Schall, *The Politics of Heaven & Hell: Christian Themes from Classical, Medieval and Modern Political Philosophy* (Lanham, Md.: University Press of America, 1984), 173.

34. Grasso, "The Subsidiary State," 54.

35. John Courtney Murray, "Governmental Repression of Heresy," *Proceedings of the Third Annual Meeting of the Catholic Theological Society of America* (Chicago, 1948), 72-73.

36. Grasso, "The Subsidiary State," 56-57.

37. Strauss, *What Is Political Philosophy?,* 13.

38. Etienne Gilson, *The Christian Philosophy of St. Thomas Aquinas* (Notre Dame, Ind.: University of Notre Dame Press, 1956), 18.

39. Robert P. George, *The Clash of Orthodoxies: Law, Religion, and Morality in Crisis* (Wilmington, Del.: Intercollegiate Studies Institute Books, 2001).

40. Schall, *Reason, Revelation, and the Foundations of Political Philosophy,* 1-38.

41. Gilson, *Christian Philosophy,* 14.

42. Strauss, *What Is Political Philosophy?,* 10.

43. Strauss, *What Is Political Philosophy?,* 44.

44. Servais Pinckaers, *The Sources of Christian Ethics*, trans. Sr. Mary Thomas Noble, O.P. (Washington, D.C.: Catholic University of America Press, 1995).

45. Christopher Dawson, *Dynamics of World History,* ed. John J. Mulloy (Wilmington, Del.: Intercollegiate Studies Institute Books, 2002), 248.

46. Dawson, *Dynamics of World History,* 268.

47. Dawson, *Dynamics of World History,* 288.

48. Walter Kasper, *The Christian Understanding of Freedom and the History of Freedom in the Modern Era: The Meeting and Confrontation between Christianity and the Modern Era in a Postmodern Situation* (Milwaukee, Wis.: Marquette University Press, 1988), 8.

49. George Weigel, "A Better Concept of Freedom," *First Things* 121 (March 2002): 15.

Chapter 4

POLITICAL SCIENCE AND THE STUDY OF AMERICAN POLITICS

Ryan J. Barilleaux
Professor of Political Science
Miami University, Ohio

At the climax of *The Wizard of Oz*, Dorothy's dog Toto pulls away the curtain behind which an ordinary man manipulates switches and levers to project a fiery image that everyone thinks is the wizard. In truth, there is no wizard, only a middle-aged man with special powers. He offers Dorothy and her companions some practical advice on how to find the things they want (a brain, a heart, to go home), but he cannot solve their problems for them. *The Wizard of Oz* is often presented as a political allegory that maps late nineteenth-century American populism (try an Internet search on "Oz" and "politics")—although there is considerable controversy about this interpretation—but it more readily serves as an allegory of much of contemporary academic scholarship. It certainly applies to the state of the discipline of political science, especially in the field of American politics. The academic study of American politics is not exactly smoke and mirrors, but there is less there than meets the eye.

Consider these incidents:

The Humphrey Brush-off: Early in 1969, outgoing Vice-President Hubert Humphrey, having lost his bid for the presidency but determined to recover a future in politics, returned to his native state of Minnesota. He was intent on returning to Washington as a senator, but in the meantime he would have to wait for the ebb-and-flow of electoral cycles to make that possible. So he inquired at the University of Minnesota's Department of Political Science about whether that institution might be interested in having him teach a course or two on politics. The answer came back that the faculty of the Department did not think that Mr. Humphrey had much to say about contemporary political science. After all, he had not published his work in a refereed journal and the M.A. in political science he had received at Louisiana State University was by now hopelessly out of date.[1]

The Wilson Indictment: Several years ago, the American Political Science Association bestowed on James Q. Wilson its prestigious James Madison Award. This honor recognizes one scholar's exemplary work in applying knowledge obtained through political science to real-world problems. In the public address he gave on accepting the award, Wilson tweaked his colleagues by pointing out that the estimable Madison would never have received the award himself. After all, Madison had never published in a refereed academic journal. Wilson then went on to make several points about what is wrong with much of contemporary political science. He observed that the discipline is caught up in a quest for mathematical precision in its analysis of politics, focusing much scholarly attention and consuming many pages of journal space with models based on a kind of pseudo-calculus. Wilson admonished his colleagues to return to the kinds of questions that stimulated the thinking of Madison, Tocqueville, and other practitioners of political analysis.[2] These thinkers were not interested in mathematical models of politics, but in answering important questions about how to establish, maintain, and defend a good political system.

The "Truth in Advertising" Failure: Not long ago, this author participated in a workshop at which university faculty offered advice to a national organization on content standards for a college-level course on the introduction to American government and politics. Several of the participants dismissed the standards presented to these faculty as little more than low-level "civics lessons," because they failed to reflect the discipline as it was taught in their own department's courses. Asked to identify what should be in the standards, these critics could point only to "collective action problems" as an example of what was missing. One particularly vocal critic, from a major state university with a reputation for "cutting-edge" research, proclaimed that the introductory American politics course in his department was a course in the "science of politics." After hearing this claim, the person sitting next to me leaned close and whispered, "My daughter took that course in his department. It was *nothing* like the way he describes it. It was a standard American government course."

The Coburn Amendment: In the fall of 2009, Senator Tom Coburn (R-OK) introduced an amendment to the bill funding the National Science Foundation that sought to abolish National Science Foundation funding for research in political science. In an statement released by his office and posted on his Senate website, the senator explained his thinking:[3]

> During this time of economic challenges, few taxpayers, in fact, would believe that the NSF's political science program is contributing to our nation's ability to meet future challenges in science, engineering, or innovation. . . . If taxpayers are going to get their money's worth from the significant funding increases being entrusted to the National Science Foundation, the agency should be held

accountable for how those funds are being spent. . . . Theories on political behavior are best left to CNN, pollsters, pundits, historians, candidates, political parties, and the voters, rather than being funded out of taxpayers' wallets, especially when our nation has much more urgent needs and priorities.

The amendment was defeated, but not before igniting considerable discussion about whether Senator Coburn was a No-Nothing or maybe he was onto something. In an article asking the question "Just how relevant is political science?," at least one scholar admitted that "we political scientists can and should do a better job of making the public relevance of our work clearer and of doing more relevant work."[4]

While a few anecdotes will not prove anything, they suggest the sort of problems that plague contemporary political science. Like so many of their colleagues in the humanities and social sciences, the political science scholars of American politics seem determined to relegate themselves to irrelevance. Their work is often ignored or dismissed by those who actually practice politics or analyze current events, because it suffers from materialism, scientism, and obscurantism. It suffers by comparison with the older mode of political inquiry that James Q. Wilson admonished his colleagues to embrace.

What Happened to Political Science?

The older mode of political analysis represented by Madison, Tocqueville, and others is what is known as *traditional political science*. As James Ceaser described in a compelling plea for its revival, "For the authors of *The Federalist* and for Tocqueville, the *science of politics* or *political science* was, in its practical sense, knowledge directed at ascertaining the factors that maintain or destroy different forms of government."[5] This mode of analysis examines important and fundamental issues about politics in order to search for, build, and maintain a good regime in which human beings can live their lives in a manner consistent with their nature.

Wilson's remarks reveal much about the state of the discipline of political science, which has made itself nearly irrelevant to the art and practice of politics. Where once Philip of Macedon hired Aristotle to teach the young Alexander the Great, budding Humphreys, Kennedys, or Obamas largely ignore academic political scientists when they want to prepare for public life or seek counsel about politics. Indeed, political scientists have been eclipsed by a professional class of "political operatives" whose advice is considered far more valuable to practicing politicians than the mathematical models that prevail in the leading journals of the discipline.

Of course, it has not always been this way. In *Nicomachean Ethics* (I.2), Aristotle teaches that politics is the most authoritative science, and statesmen often looked to political philosophy for lessons about statecraft. In the twentieth century, however, political science abandoned its heritage in favor of more "modern" modes of thought, and in consequence it has strayed far from its roots in philosophy, ethics, and the practical issues of statecraft. It is not surprising, then, that when filmmaker Ken Burns produced his documentary *Congress: The History and Promise of Representative Government* (1987) to mark the bicentennial of the national legislature, he interviewed several journalists, politicians, and historians, but no political scientists. (In truth, he did interview James Macgregor Burns, who is a political scientist, but billed by Ken Burns as an "historian.") None of the "big names" in the academic study of congressional politics seemed relevant to a film that was intended as a meditation on the role of the legislature in democratic government.

Of course, not all political scientists have succumbed to the "physics envy" that marks much of the discipline, and even within the American Political Science Association there has been a movement to break away from the tyranny of the quantitative methodologists (known, with tongue planted firmly in cheek, as the *perestroika* movement). There are also many political scientists, mostly disciples of Eric Voegelin and Leo Strauss, who take political theory seriously. But the establishment of the discipline remains dominated by behaviorists seeking ever more precise—and ever more irrelevant—mathematical models of political phenomena.

Traditional political science has not been completely lost, but it needs to be restored to its central place in the discipline. While the intellectual study of politics has much to offer citizens and leaders, it can do so only if it is political science properly understood. For those who want to see political science maintain a place among the human sciences that can contribute to the good of humanity, and especially for those interested in building a Catholic social science, restoration of the discipline is the order of the day.

Materialism, Scientism, and Obscurantism

As anyone who has taken a course in psychology, sociology, or political science can attest, contemporary social science is dominated by behavioralism. This is an approach that took form most clearly after World War II and which overturned more traditional means of analyzing human beings and their societies. In political science, the tenets of behavioralism came to be crystallized in a set of principles known quite self-consciously as the "Behavioral Creed."

As defined by Albert Somit and Joseph Tanenhaus in their authoritative history of American political science,[6] the Behavioral Creed contained eight key "articles of faith" (the use of a religious metaphor is appropriate):[7]

1. Political science can ultimately become a science capable of prediction and explanation.
2. Political science should concern itself primarily, if not exclusively, with phenomena which can actually be observed—i.e., with what is done or said.
3. Data should be quantified and "findings" based upon quantifiable data.

4. Research should be theory oriented and theory directed (usually accomplished through the development of hypotheses that can be tested against empirical data).

5. Political science should abjure, in favor of "pure" research, both applied research aimed at providing solutions to specific, immediate social problems and melioratory programmatic ventures.

6. The truth or falsity of values (democracy, equality, freedom, etc.) cannot be established scientifically and are beyond the scope of legitimate inquiry.

7. Political scientists should be more interdisciplinary.

8. Political science should become more self-conscious and critical about its methodology.

These articles gained dominance in the discipline in the 1950s and 1960s. In some academic political science departments, faculty and graduate students were required to subscribe to (indeed, sign) some version of the Creed. In other departments, battles between the behavioralists and their adversaries lasted until well into the 1960s. Traditionalists objected to behavioralism precisely because they thought it dangerous to try to create a "value-free" social science, and because they rejected the behavioralists' assumption that the only political phenomena that matter are those that can be counted. By the 1970s, however, the behavioralists became the ruling party in the discipline, opposed only by pockets of resistance in a few places.

As a consequence, research on American politics tended to focus increasingly on those questions and subjects that lent themselves to quantitative analysis: voting studies, public opinion, the "attitudinal model" of judicial decision-making (which sees judges as driven by ideology rather than any sense of jurisprudence), and socioeconomic analyses. The study of political institutions, such as the American constitutional system or its components, was also dominated by behavioralists. Despite their claims of a "value-free" social science, they brought to their work a skeptical agenda.

Materialism

Political science had been a secular enterprise since its creation as a separate discipline in the late nineteenth century. With the rise of behavioralism, the largely passively secular discipline had become (like nearly all other academic disciplines) aggressively and self-consciously materialist in orientation. In short, it had little room for those who did not share the materialist assumptions of positivism. Those who wanted to discuss ideals or virtue—which are dismissed as "values" to be avoided in a value-free science—often took recourse in the study of political philosophy, whether under the influence of scholars such as Leo Strauss (who taught his students that the Greek classics were the primary source of wisdom) or Eric Voegelin (who subscribed to what he called "pre-Reformation Christianity," but who also openly criticized the Church for what he considered its excessive dogmatism). At the other end of the political spectrum, a number of scholars adopted Marxist analytical concepts—whether implicitly or explicitly—and were allowed to work within the "mainstream" of social science because of Marxism's self-described "scientific" analysis of human society. Either way, ideals and virtue were relegated to the dustbin of research.

This materialist foundation continued to dominate the discipline even as a new approach came to prominence. Beginning mostly in the 1970s and 1980s, an analytical method called rational choice theory (sometimes called public choice) became influential in political science. This approach, borne among economists, views human beings as rationally directed decision-makers interested (mostly *self*-interested) in maximizing utility—i.e., doing what will most likely achieve their preferences. It, too, is a behavioral approach to humanity. While "rat choice" methods are not necessarily inconsistent with a Catholic view of the world—indeed, Kenneth Arrow, one of the leading economists in this area, was named to the Pontifical Academy of the Social Sciences—many practitioners of this analytical method proceed from decidedly materialist assumptions. Their world is almost Hobbesian in its makeup: It is composed of self-interested sovereign individuals who engage in a kind of calculation to maximize their personal preferences; one person's preferences are as good as another's, and the individual's preferences and social actions "are entirely concerned with their own welfare."[8]

For some aspects of American political institutions, this secular or materialist orientation does not create problems. Studies of the organization, powers, and operations of the three branches of American government often examine technical political and organizational problems rather than questions of ultimate ends. But for other aspects of political institutions, such as the kinds of issues raised in assessments of presidential performance or the policy outcomes of government, questions of ends and means cannot be brushed aside. In consequence, contemporary political science finds itself called upon to deal with issues that it claims are beyond its scope.

Scientism and Obscurantism

Beyond this materialist orientation, much of contemporary political science is dominated by a pseudo-scientific precision that leads to sometimes laughable results. In one episode in which the author was directly involved, a promising young scholar (one of the hottest candidates on the job market that year) interviewed for a position in international relations and gave the standard academic "job talk" presenting his research. Employing a rational choice approach, complete with several calculus-based formulae designed to model the behavior of countries in alliances, he concluded that the greatest threat to one country in international politics comes from its allies. Asked whether the United States should fear an attack from Israel, he replied, "That's what the model shows." When pressed that his findings were not very helpful for understanding the workings of international politics, he proclaimed, "I am interested in precision." Out of the audience, one scholar (a Straussian) responded, "I thought we were interested in truth." The meeting dissolved in disarray.

The obsession with precision has led to a lot of scholarship that is increasingly narrow and removed from political reality. This is the kind of work that helped to provoke the *perestroika* movement earlier in the decade—one of its central charges was that political science (especially, but not exclusively, the rational choice variety) was irrelevant to any understanding of the real world of politics. Additionally, some practitioners of the more advanced and esoteric quantitative research methods delight in the inaccessibility of their work: only the elite can understand and appreciate the elegance and precision of it, and to ask what it means or why it matters is to invite scorn. Indeed, another charge made by the *perestroika* movement was that rational choice practitioners display a particular kind of arrogance that leads them to dismiss any non-calculus-based political science as mere journalism.

Whether it is the sort of behavioralism practiced since the 1950s or the rational-choice variety developed more recently, contemporary political science can do only so much. It has given us important insights into those areas of politics and political institutions that it can reach—albeit, usually freighted with hidden assumptions that the reader must uncover and consider—but it cannot address the most important questions of political life.

Assessing Contemporary Political Science

Contemporary political science is like so many other of man's intellectual enterprises: impressive for its cleverness and sophistication, disappointing for its limitations. Academic research as it is conducted by the vast majority of scholars can teach us important lessons, but it cannot teach us the most important ones.

Contributions

There are major contributions that contemporary political science makes to our understanding of political institutions. It makes contributions to our understanding other aspects of politics as well. These include:

1) Insights into the structure and operations of political institutions—These insights are not trivial, because they can help us to understand why government does what it does and how to make it work better.

2) Insights into the costs and tradeoffs involved in the various forms of political institutions—Political science research has shown us how different electoral systems affect political outcomes, how the separation-of-powers system has influenced government policies in the United States, how different representational schemes affect which groups have influence in a political community, and how the form of government can affect the long-term stability and prosperity of a political community.

3) Insights into public opinion and political behavior—Again, in a democratic political system, such insights are important. Nevertheless, knowing a lot about how people think and how they behave politically does little for explaining why they think and act as they do, or how to distinguish between opinion and behavior in free societies and authoritarian societies.

Limitations

Despite these contributions, contemporary political science faces three sharp limitations in advancing our understanding of the political world.

1) The divorce of "facts" and "values" renders political science ineffective for answering some of the most important questions about politics—As noted above, the contemporary discipline cannot sort out the legitimacy of different ends and means adopted by governments. As far as secular social science is concerned, there is no difference between the Nazi Final Solution and the Obama health-care reform plan, except in the scope of the undertaking. To be fair, we should acknowledge that it is this limitation that most troubles the practitioners of contemporary political science: They are troubled by an approach to the study of politics that does not make room for distinguishing between charity and genocide. Yet they have no effective way to remedy their problem.

2) Behavioralist political science is not value-free—This is a problem that occurs more in the practice of political science than in its conception. Because the behavioralist approach does not distinguish between one government policy and another, researchers often place their own biases at the center of their work.

Consider a volume assessing Bill Clinton's presidency, *The Clinton Presidency: First Appraisals*, edited by Colin Campbell and Bert Rockman.[9] According to its publisher, the book became a best seller (by textbook standards) on the date of its release, indicating that it is well in the mainstream of contemporary political science.[10] One of the central chapters is an ostensibly objective assessment of President Clinton's management of the White House by Colin Campbell, a political scientist at Georgetown University. Professor Campbell's essay is riddled with a variety of assumptions, value judgments, and other statements that belie the scientific neutrality of secular social science. For example, Campbell writes disapprovingly of the 1980s as "a period in which neoliberals began to look longingly across the Atlantic at Margaret Thatcher."[11] Then he passes judgment on the Reagan and Bush administrations in terms that can be described as ideological: Reagan "did great damage" to American government that resulted in "an exacerbation of malaise and distrust."[12] These conditions set the stage for the election of George Bush, who incurs Campbell's wrath for misdirecting the attention of European leaders away from the crisis in the Balkans to deal with Saddam Hussein's invasion of Kuwait.[13] Any of these statements may or may not be true, but none of them is value-free science.

Other examples compound the problem. Consider articles published in *The American Political Science Review* (*APSR*), the flagship journal of political science. According to the official values of the discipline, the feminist and environmentalist agendas are accepted as given. In June 1994, *APSR* featured an article by Courtney Brown of Emory University on "Politics and the

Environment," which opened with the statement that "The relationship between presidential elections in the United States and the degradation of the environment is not thoroughly understood."[14] In the next issue, Lyn Kathlene of Purdue University analyzed "Power and Influence in State Legislative Policymaking."[15] She begins by effectively defining the influence of women in state legislators as the success of the feminist women; later, she attributes the limited influence of female state legislators to "our culture and the social construction of male power."[16] The science practiced in this leading journal of the discipline is shaped by ideology.

When the ideological positions of scholars are passed off as science, the result is a kind of radical individualism in morals (which is certainly consistent with—and perhaps at the base of—contemporary American culture) in which each researcher creates his own definition of good and bad policy, right and wrong action. The practice of secular social science thus becomes a kind of editorializing through hidden—or not-so-hidden—assumptions.

3) Contemporary political science is ultimately blind to questions of ethics and behavior among political actors—This problem became very real for secular social scientists in their discussions of events such as the Watergate and Iran-Contra scandals or the war in Iraq. Limited to issues of success/failure, legality, or constitutionality, secularists have little to say about right conduct by political actors. After all, if we are ultimately the only judges of our own "private morality" (as one popular expression puts it), then so long as we do not commit a criminal act, we are free to do what we please.

The upshot of these strengths and limitations is that secular social science makes a very real contribution to our understanding of the political world, but alone it is insufficient for leading us to the truth. That is why there is a palpable need to restore political science to its roots in philosophy, ethics, and statecraft.

Facing Ultimate Questions

Contemporary political science has made great strides in advancing our understanding of the workings of political institutions. Scholars learned much about the way in which Congress is organized and Members conduct their business, about how presidents make and carry out decisions, about how the Supreme Court decides cases, and about how the bureaucracy shapes and implements the policies of elected officials. The increasingly sophisticated methods employed to undertake all this research could be truly impressive (and at times ludicrous), offering researchers tools to move beyond the impressionistic kinds of studies that often characterized traditional political science.

Yet the behavioralist approach runs headlong into a number of problems inherent in its very assumptions. For example, scholars found that their research often raised questions that their sophisticated methods could not even begin to answer: questions about the ends to which political power is employed, about what kinds of political action are justified and under what conditions, and about how to evaluate individual political actors, groups, and political systems. With an explicit separation of "facts" from "values," such questions were technically off-limits. Many scholars thus end their studies by pointing out that the most important questions are beyond the scope of their research; others editorialize about the answers to these ultimate questions on the basis of their own preferences.

In my own work, I found myself crashing into the limits of contemporary political science. My early work examined the issue of how to evaluate presidential performance in the conduct of foreign policy.[17] Without boring the reader with a recitation of my work, I will get to the point at which the standard contemporary approach failed: I found that the approaches and methods of the political science I had been taught in graduate school could not answer the questions that it pointed to as most important.

Proceeding from a study that sought to assess presidential success or failure in a series of case studies of foreign-policy conduct, my research indicated that the kind of evaluation I was attempting to develop—and that others told me it would be useful and important to conduct—required answers to questions about what are the appropriate ends and means of presidential actions.[18] In other words, in order to evaluate what a president had done in foreign affairs, a utilitarian idea of leadership (as success or failure in achieving express goals) was insufficient. Rather, it became apparent that judgments about "where presidents wish to lead us, by what means, and at what cost"[19] were needed: These are exactly the kinds of "values" that behavioralist social science declares both off-limits and unnecessary.

Behavioral political science is not equipped to make these judgments, nor does it officially recognize that such judgments ought to be made. Since it condemns a discussion of "values," it assumes that values are irrelevant to the enterprise of social science—yet its own methods lead to the conclusion that it is values that really count in politics. Consequently, behavioral political science cannot go where it points its practitioners. Furthermore, to discuss "values" is to raise questions about ultimate ends in politics and life, which inevitably lead us to questions about God.

Certainly, questions about appropriate ends and means of government policy can and must be conducted within the everyday world of politics. But the problem that faces the political community—and the scholars who work in it— is that the behavioralist view of the world is incomplete and therefore incapable of leading to the truth. A behavioralist analysis of the presidency can tell us much about the organization of the White House and the instruments of executive power, but it ultimately fails on the question of the uses to which political power is put.

Consider what would happen if President Obama really were to propose setting up "death panels" with the power to order elderly patients to "do us all a favor and die." Of course, most political scientists would agree that such a scheme would be inhuman—but it is not political science that teaches that lesson. After all, the Behavioral Creed told us that "values" are beyond the scope of legitimate inquiry. What, then, are political scientists to do? They can allow their methods to score a presidential success for an inhuman action and maintain their pristine analytical neutrality, or they editorialize by introducing their own values into their work while pretending not to do so.

Each of these responses can be found in the array of presidential rating studies mentioned above. Some analysts maintain strict neutrality that leads them into strange conclusions about what is political leadership, while others engage in editorializing under the guise of positivism. Either way, these scholars end up in the same borderlands in which secular political science points to ultimate questions but cannot of themselves offer ultimate answers. That is why traditional political science is needed.

Traditional Political Science

Until the rise of behavioralism, the central concerns of political science were framed by three issues raised by Aristotle in his *Politics*. Not all thinkers in this tradition arrived at the same conclusions, but their focus on the same concerns formed the great tradition of political science as an intellectual discipline. As James Ceaser has outlined it, traditional political science consists of three main elements: a knowledge of place; a general political science of regimes; and the political science of a particular place.[20]

Traditional political science is not an art of reasoning in a vacuum. Rather, it seeks knowledge within a context: historical circumstances, geography, and the character of a nation or people. A consideration of the American regime, for example, would be grounded in the history, geography, and "genius" of the American people. This context is intended to prevent the sort of abstracted reasoning that pervades exercises in women's studies, multicultural studies, and other efforts to fit all human institutions on a Procrustean bed of "race, gender, and sexual orientation."

A knowledge of place does not mean that traditional political science keeps its gaze to the ground and never looks toward the sun. It is also concerned with more general issues: regime types, the factors that support or undermine different regimes, and the general human nature that characterizes people in all regimes. In contrast to plastic notions of human nature found in most Enlightenment and post-Enlightenment thinking, practitioners of traditionalism accept human nature as it is.

The general part of traditional political science looks to different types of regimes and seeks to discern the factors that help them to work or fail. It examines how human nature interacts with each regime type and what benefits and hazards exist for people living in different types of political systems.

The final part of traditionalism is the search for knowledge about the working of a particular regime at a particular time. It involves applying the knowledge from the first two elements to a specific place. For example, an analysis of the state of the contemporary American regime could provide cautionary insights for the citizens and policy makers of the United States.

If Ceaser is right about the basic outlines of traditional political science—and I believe that he is, because he is pointing to the influence of Aristotle in Western thought—then it is a mode of analysis consistent with Catholic thought. Traditional political science is an application of human reasoning, but does not exalt reason, abstraction, or ideology. It can be used to apply principles of Catholic social teaching, which are employed with a sense of the context of time and place. It can be used to restore political science to its rightful place as an authoritative science, and it requires a sense of the importance of virtue.

The Politics of Virtue

The idea of virtue is one of the oldest in Western thought, and came to be thought unnecessary or dangerous only in the ideological revolution of the twentieth century. As long ago as Plato, the four cardinal—or political—virtues were seen as prudence, justice, temperance, and fortitude. Traditional political science—what Aristotle, Augustine, Aquinas, Shakespeare, Thomas More, James Madison, and Abraham Lincoln all knew—was built in part on these virtues. Contemporary political science wants to remember James Madison as a kind of proto-Ayn Rand: one who celebrated self-interest and rejected the idea of virtue. But Madison saw virtue as essential to the success of free government, and counseled only that designers of political institutions take into account the reality of political self-interest (in the form of factions). But where does the teaching about the threat of factions come from? It permeates Aristotle's *Politics*, and it is the case that James Madison was looking for a new solution to a very old problem. Despite the efforts of some contemporary interpreters of Madison to have it otherwise, the Founder recognized the importance of virtue.

Reviving the Study of Virtue

Political scientists need to return to a study of virtue. Traditional political science understood the role of virtue, and even contemporary secular philosophers grasp its importance as well. Take, for example, Andre Compte-Sponville's book *A Small Treatise on the Great Virtues*, which was a best seller in France and received much attention in the United States. This book argues that we must study, admire, and practice virtue in order to have civilization, and Compte-Sponville examines a list of virtues that affect everyday life. His treatise is a reminder that virtue has long been part of the Western tradition, that it is compatible with a free society, and that it does not imply a thought police or an inquisition. Among sociologists, the followers of Pitirim Sorokin likewise point to virtue and altruism as the foundations of society.

Contemporary political scientists are out of touch with reality, both political and philosophical reality. The return to virtue is not a step backward, but a step forward. To be fair, many political scientists today understand the importance of virtue—the disciples of Strauss and Voegelin, along with others such as J. Budziszewski (whose book *The Nearest Coast of Darkness* is subtitled

"Vindicating a Politics of Virtue")—but these scholars have been "marginalized" (to use a trendy term) by dismissing them as *merely* political theorists. Other scholars have also attempted to integrate the wisdom of traditional political science into modern research. One, Ethan Fishman, has gone so far as to apply an "Aristotelian approach to presidential leadership." His book on *The Prudential Presidency*[21] is a rare and welcome exception to the behavioralist mainstream. All of these developments are hopeful ones, but they are movements against a larger tide of behavioralism.

Political theory or philosophy is at the heart of political science, and the preceding discussion of the limits of the mainstream of contemporary scholarship reminds us that behavioralism points to ultimate questions while denying that there are ultimate questions. So political science is left with a dilemma: continue down the track of behavioralism and point to questions for which behavioralism has no answers, or admit the limits of behavioralism and restore political science to its authoritative place by recovering the study of virtue and ultimate questions.

What would a political science that acknowledges virtue look like? It would look more like traditional political science, even if it were now equipped with quantitative techniques for measuring those political phenomena that are truly measurable. It would look less like pseudo-calculus and more like the best policy analysis that has been undertaken in recent years by various "think tanks" around Washington. These institutions employ explicit values in their analyses of public policy, and use evidence and reason to arrive at judicious judgments about public affairs. The work of "policy analysts" may often be blighted by the tendency of many to employ a materialistic cost-benefit analysis to public questions, but at least these analysts are clear about the standards they use to evaluate policy and their studies are interesting exercises in prudent judgment. Their work is reminiscent of the P. G. Wodehouse line about why Bertie Wooster admired the House of Commons for prohibiting peers from membership—at least, Wooster observed, the Commons drew the line somewhere.

There are those among us political scientists who have not forgotten the importance of virtue, and who still read Aristotle and other scholars in the great tradition of political science. Political science as an academic discipline has much to learn from these scholars, and it can be restored when behavioralists see that the parameters of the Behavioral Creed describe a narrow and unrealistic world.

The Catholic Contribution

Peter Kreeft once observed that the atheist makes the mistake of believing that his universe is larger than the theist's, because his is a universe that does not need God in order to operate. Kreeft's response is that the theist's universe— especially in the cosmology of the Judeo-Christian tradition—is actually the larger one, because it includes everything in the atheist's universe plus the spiritual realm. The same is true for Catholic social scientists: Our world includes everything in the secularists' universe, plus the spiritual realm beyond the borderlands of conventional scholarship.

The Catholic contribution to social science generally and political science specifically is to help scholars make the final ascent—as the mountaineers call it—toward the truth. Catholic theology and social thought provide a moral compass to search through the borderlands of social science, as well as serious and sophisticated understanding of universal standards of justice—that is, the natural law. By bringing in the spiritual realm—that is, by talking about God—Catholic social scientists can make sense of what secular social science finds imponderable, such as questions about the propriety of different ends and means of political action.

There are many issues for which the Catholic study of political institutions can provide answers unavailable to secular social science. One example relevant to American politics might be in the assessment of presidents. How can we evaluate Barack Obama's performance in office, or that of George W. Bush? We can weigh the costs and benefits of different initiatives and actions of his administration, and different observers can rationally disagree on the final record of accomplishments and failings of the Obama or Bush administrations. But a complete assessment of the Obama presidency must include his administration's pro-abortion policies, from funding international clinics that provide abortions to seeking increased domestic abortion funding through community health centers, as well as his active support for a "culture of death." Likewise, evaluating the George W. Bush presidency must include weighing the costs and benefits of the invasion of Iraq. An assessment of the Clinton presidency requires attention to the amount of time, energy, political capital, and public money that his administration put into supporting abortion: not only did he lift the "gag order" on abortion counseling in federally funded clinics, but actively promoted abortions and contraception both at home and abroad. In the end, Bill Clinton's tenure in office did serious damage to the cause of life in the United States. Did George W. Bush's administration promote the cause of life? What about the Obama administration? Final results are not in, but the record so far is not good.

Even in areas where Catholics legitimately disagree, such as on other aspects of the Obama health-reform plan or Bush policy measures on taxes or overtime pay, Catholic teaching and social thought provides a foundation on which to build analyses of government operations, policies, and ideologies. Catholic leaders have made it clear that some proposed policies—such as cutting off funding for welfare mothers having children out of wedlock—are morally unacceptable. In other cases, statements on public questions by the Public Policy and Church Affairs Committee of the Society of Catholic Social Scientists (e.g., on health care reform and other issues)[22] have helped to provide clear thinking on important policy questions. On a larger front, work such as Stephen Krason's Catholic analysis of liberalism and conservatism can help provide fresh insights into the political debate in the United States.[23]

The Catholic contribution to the study of political institutions specifically and politics and society more generally is an important one. It is not mere sectarianism: it is a more complete search for the truth. Catholics can play an important role in the restoration of political science.

Restoring Political Science

Restoring political science is not some sentimental exercise in turning back to old books and ignoring the twentieth and twenty-first centuries. Rather, it requires an intellectual enterprise devoted to recovering the insights and contributions of traditional political science. Catholic political scientists can play an important role in this recovery because their intellectual tradition is so deeply connected to traditional political science, and because Catholic social thinkers have been so busy in our time studying what Pope John Paul II called the "whole truth about man." Catholic scholars have much to offer to a restored political science, and what follows is an agenda for the recovery of our ancient discipline.

Rediscovery of Virtue

It is not a foregone conclusion that modern social scientists cannot learn. Take, for example, the recent "discovery" of the importance of civil society. For decades, political scientists focused almost exclusively on the state, and those scholars who studied groups in society (e.g., interest groups, parties, social movements) tended to treat them as appendages of the state or in terms of their influence on the state. In recent years, however, there has been an almost Tocquevillian interest in the importance of civil society. Robert Putnam, author of *Bowling Alone*—one of the most talked-about books on civil society in the United States—was president of the American Political Science Association. Civil society is now a hot topic in political theory and political sociology. The intermediary institutions of society—the family, civic associations (including bowling leagues), churches, neighborhoods, youth organizations, and other non-state gatherings of people—are once again recognized as important. But what is it that creates and sustains these associations? A certain amount of self-interest, yes, but it is virtue that is the real glue of civil society.

The rediscovery of the importance of civil society points to the importance of virtue. Hard-nosed political scientists need not fear that virtue is some sort of airy abstraction or idealistic dream; virtue is a fact and a social necessity. Secular social scientists such as Putnam and his colleagues can go far in identifying the problems that develop when virtue declines (hence the decline of citizen associations that he summarizes with the term "bowling alone"), but where Catholic scholars can be helpful is directing their secular colleagues to the great tradition—from Plato and Aristotle to Aquinas and Shakespeare and George Washington and Tocqueville and Maritain and John Paul II and Benedict XVI—that has meditated on the importance of virtue in society and how to cultivate it.

Rediscovery of Natural Law

It is hard to understand why the idea of natural law, once at the core of Western thought, is not embraced today. After all, our contemporary public discourse is filled with implicit invocations of natural standards of justice. The discussion of the abuse scandal among the American Catholic clergy is one example: There is no one who disagrees with the notion that there is something inherently disordered about the sexual importuning of minors by adults. Why not? Because it is "just plain wrong," to use the conventional explanation. Likewise, former President Bill Clinton liked to use a similar rationale when he found something morally repugnant—it was "just plain wrong."

How can anything be "just plain wrong" unless there are natural standards of right and wrong? Many commentators have made this observation, although contemporary American society resists the logical consequence of this type of thinking. The idea of natural law is ridiculed by most of our cultural elites, even as they denounce what they disapprove of—whether it is the oppression of Tibet, female genital mutilation in certain societies, the restrictions imposed on Muslim women, segregation, slavery, damage to the environment, SUVs, and so on—as "just plain wrong."

Why are invocations of natural law so common, while the idea of natural law so suspect? The answer is simple: Natural law thinking requires rigor, and it means that one cannot simply pick and choose what to find right and what to find wrong. To think about natural law is to move from denouncing the Taliban for keeping girls out of school to serious thinking about why activities such as abortion are wrong. Natural law thinking runs contrary to the selective moral indignation that is a hallmark of our time.

Nevertheless, natural law thinking is important and necessary to the restoration of political science. Catholic scholars know this to be true, but so do others as well. Pope John Paul II gave us powerful encyclicals and other teachings on natural law. J. Budziszewski, before his conversion to Catholicism, wrote eloquently and accessibly on natural law in books such as *Written on the Heart*, *What We Can't Not Know*, and *The Line through the Heart*. Catholics and their allies in the cause of natural law must continue pointing to the importance of this tradition and logic to help restore political science.

A New Paradigm for Social Science

Since the Behavioral Creed became the Decalogue for modern political science, its principles have shaped the thought and work of political scientists. If political science is to be restored to its place as a discipline that has much to say about humanity and politics, then a new paradigm is needed to replace the reigning behavioral one.

There are several contenders for this honor. The intellectual disciples of Leo Strauss offer his approach to politics as an alternative paradigm, and there is much that is appealing about Straussianism. Straussianism takes the lessons of classical political philosophy seriously, it takes the words and works of thinkers and statesmen seriously, and it understands the importance of virtue. But one problem that Straussianism presents for Catholics (and others) is that many of its practitioners seem to think that only in a *polis* can humanity meet true happiness. That implies more than just a thick political community; in the case of some it implies a civil religion that is not consistent with Catholicism (Catholics never quite fit into the old generically Protestant civil religion that once dominated American political culture). But there is much to admire in Straussian political science, if it can be developed in such a way that it does not exclude orthodox Catholicism.

Another alternative paradigm can be found in the work of Eric Voegelin, who identified himself as a "pre-Reformation Christian" and whose worldview was far more consistent with Catholicism. Voegelin's *The New Science of Politics* offers an interpretation of history and politics that is explicitly Judeo-Christian, and his method focuses on political ideas and writings. But Voegelin's work is not very accessible, even for many scholars, and will require much interpretation. Moreover, there are many elements of politics that Voegelin himself did not explore and which would need to be addressed for his work to offer an alternative paradigm to behavioralism.

A third and promising possibility lies in integralism, i.e., an integral approach to social science such as is found in the work of Pitirim Sorokin. Sorokin is almost unknown to political scientists, but he and his work have many characteristics that could make him appealing to contemporary political scientists—his work is interdisciplinary in nature (which is what behavioralism also claims to be), it is as much empirical as philosophical, and it is the product of an intellectual who was once chair of the Sociology Department at Harvard and president of the American Sociological Association (so the godfather of the paradigm has the right credentials to appeal to snobbish American academicians). But there are elements in Sorokin's work that seem to be more wishful thinking than social science (especially in his later work on peace in the international system), and these need to be addressed by his disciples and interpreted for a new audience. Integralism is an empirical paradigm for social science that takes virtue seriously, takes the wisdom of what Voegelin called "the Mediterranean tradition" seriously, and offers a coherent account of humanity that is consistent with the Catholic worldview. Political scientists need to become better acquainted with integralism, and students of Sorokin need to explain his work to political scientists.[24]

Conclusion

Catholics are not the only ones who are interested in the restoration of political science. Many within the discipline have found fault with its course since the triumph of the Behavioral Creed. But Catholics can play an important role in the restoration of the discipline if they contribute to developing an alternative to behavioral political science. Given the agenda described above, it is clear that Catholic political scientists have much to offer: They have a theology and a tradition of social thought that appreciates virtue and respects natural law, and they can aid in building a new paradigm for the social sciences (such as integralism) that will give a coherent account of the "whole truth about man" in terms that social scientists can understand. There is much work to be done.

Notes

1. Humphrey was vindicated after his death. The University of Minnesota is now proud home to the Hubert H. Humphrey Institute of Public Affairs.

2. James Q. Wilson, "Interests and Deliberations in the American Republic," *PS: Political Science & Politics* 23 (December 1990): 558-62.

3. "Coburn Amendment 2631—Prohibits the National Science Foundation from wasting federal research funding on political science projects," http://coburn.senate.gov /public/index.cfm? (22 February 2010).

4. Patricia Cohen, "Field Study: Just How Relevant Is Political Science?" http://www.nytimes.com/2009/10/20/books/20poli.html (22 February 2010).

5. James W. Ceaser, *Liberal Democracy and Political Science* (Baltimore, Md.: Johns Hopkins University Press, 1990), 24. Emphasis is in the original.

6. Albert Somit and Joseph Tanenhaus, *The Development of American Political Science* (Boston, Mass.: Allyn & Bacon, 1967).

7. The following points are drawn from Somit and Tanenhaus, *Development of American Political Science,* 177-79.

8. Peter Abell, "Sociological Theory and Rational Choice Theory," in *The Blackwell Companion to Social Theory*, ed. Bryan Turner (Malden, MA: Blackwell, 2000), 223-44, especially at 231.

9. Colin Campbell and Bert Rockman, eds., *The Clinton Presidency: First Appraisals* (Chatham, N.J.: Chatham House, 1995).

10. The publisher, Edward Artinian of Chatham House Publishers, made that claim to the author at the annual meeting of the American Political Science Association, Chicago, Illinois, September 1995. The statement was part of a sales pitch, but clearly intended to boast about the academic reputation of the book and its contributors.

11. Colin Campbell, "Management in a Sandbox," in Campbell and Rockman, *The Clinton Presidency,* 55.

12. Campbell, "Sandbox," 55.

13. Campbell, "Sandbox," 55.

14. Courtney Brown, "Politics and the Environment: Nonlinear Instabilities Predomi-nate," *American Political Science Review* 88 (June 1994): 292.

15. Lyn Kathlene, "Power and Influence in State Legislative Policymaking: The Inter-action of Gender and Position in Committee Hearing Debates," *American Political Science Review* 88 (September 1994): 560-76.

16. Kathlene, "Power and Influence," 573.

17. Ryan J. Barilleaux, *The President and Foreign Affairs: Evaluation, Performance, and Power* (New York: Praeger, 1985); and Ryan J. Barilleaux, "Evaluating Presidential Performance in Foreign Affairs," in *The Presidency and Public Policy Making,* eds. George Edwards, Steven Shull, and Norman Thomas (Pittsburgh: University of Pittsburgh Press, 1985), 114-29.

18. Ryan J. Barilleaux, "Presidential Conduct of Foreign Policy," *Congress and the Presidency* 15 (Spring 1988): 1-23.

19. Barilleaux, "Presidential Conduct of Foreign Policy," 19.

20. Ceaser, *Liberal Democracy,* chapter 3.

21. Ethan Fishman, *The Prudential Presidency* (Westport, Conn.: Praeger, 2001).

22. *Public Statements of the Public Policy and Church Affairs Committee of the Society of Catholic Social Scientists, 1993-95* (Steubenville, Ohio: Society of Catholic Social Scientists), mimeograph.

23. Stephen Krason, *Liberalism, Conservatism and Catholicism: An Evaluation of Contemporary American Political Ideologies in Light of Catholic Social Teaching* (Catholics United for the Faith, 1991).

24. Two valuable recent editions of his work include Pitirim Sorokin, *The Crisis of Our Age* (Oxford: Oneworld Publications, 1992) and, Pitirim Sorokin, *The Ways and Power of Love* (West Conshohocken, Pa.: Templeton Foundation Press, 2002).

Chapter 5

TOWARD A SUBSIDIARY PUBLIC ADMINISTRATION: A CATHOLIC PERSPECTIVE

John A. Corso
Georgetown University
Center for Continuing Professional Education

Brief Overview of the Field of Public Administration

Man has shown a preoccupation with the affairs of governance since ancient times.[1] The science of public administration, however, defined as the application of the sciences, primarily social sciences, to the solution of public problems,[2] is generally reckoned has having distinguished itself as a separate field of study from political science in the late nineteenth century, around the time of the writing of Woodrow Wilson's watershed essay "The Study of Administration" in the *Political Science Quarterly*.[3] Published in 1887, Wilson, then a scholar at Princeton, argues in this essay that an objective or detached "science of administration" has emerged from the study of politics in his century.[4] This "science of administration" is to be distinguished from political studies in that it focuses on the execution or operation of government as opposed to its constitution or the public policies it promotes. For Wilson, Public Administration is not uninterested in these latter two topics, but sees them as ancillary to the study of matters pertaining to the equitable and efficient administration of policies derived from competent legal and political authority. This distinction is a bright line, a clean break from political questions and issues. Frank Goodnow stated it this way: "[while] the function of politics…consists in the expression of the will of the state…the function of executing the will of the state has been called administration."[5] Herbert Kaufman uses the term "politically neutral competence" to reflect one of three basic values that inform Public Administration, the other two being representativeness (of the electorate) and executive leadership.[6]

Wilson's views largely reflect the zeitgeist of the post-Pendleton Act era of American government with its emphasis on proper and fair conduct of public officials and the "scientific management" movement exemplified by industrial management progressives such as Frederick Taylor. This managerial theme, which evolved into the line of inquiry and practice known as Public Management, was eventually tempered by a more pragmatic view that suggested that politics cannot be reasonably disentangled from the execution of policy. The 1968 Minnowbrook Conference, led by Dwight Waldo, produced H. George Frederickson's paper "Toward a New Public Administration," which promoted social equity as the underlying principle of the discipline.[7] I will examine the implications of Frederickson later in this chapter.

The Fundamental Concept of Subsidiarity in Catholic Social Teaching

As an initial definition in the context of Catholic social teaching (CST), the *Catechism of the Catholic Church* (CCC) states the following:

> Excessive intervention by the state can threaten personal freedom and initiative. The teaching of the Church has elaborated the principle of subsidiarity, according to which a community of a higher order should not interfere in the internal life of a community of lower order, depriving the latter of its functions, but rather should support it in case of need and help to coordinate its activity with the activities of the rest of society, always with a view to the common good.[8]

Understandably, the *Compendium of the Social Doctrine of the Church*[9] goes into a much deeper treatment of the subject. Specifically focusing on subsidiarity and the state, the *Compendium* cites Pius XI's encyclical *Quadragesimo Anno*[10] in sharply admonishing a higher order association (e.g., a governmental entity) that oversteps its bounds in such a manner as to undermine the rights of individuals and lower-order associations (e.g., families, community associations) to accomplish what they are able for themselves:

> *The necessity of defending and promoting the original expressions of social life is emphasized by the Church in the Encyclical Quadragesimo Anno, in which the principle of subsidiarity is indicated as a most important principle of "social philosophy."* Just as it is gravely wrong to take from individuals what they can accomplish by their own initiative and industry and give it to the community, so also it is an injustice and at the same time a *grave evil* [my emphasis]

and disturbance of right order to assign to a greater and higher association what lesser and subordinate organizations can do. For every social activity ought of its very nature to furnish help to the members of the body social, and never destroy and absorb them. *On the basis of this principle, all societies of a superior order must adopt attitudes of help ("subsidium")—therefore of support, promotion, development—with respect to lower order societies.* In this way, intermediate social entities can properly perform the functions that fall to them without being required to hand them over unjustly to other social entities of a higher level, by which they would end up being absorbed and substituted, in the end seeing themselves denied their dignity and essential place. Subsidiarity, understood *in the positive sense* as economic, institutional or juridical assistance offered to lesser social entities, entails a corresponding series of *negative* implications that require the State to refrain from anything that would de facto restrict the existential space of the smaller essential cells of society. Their initiative, freedom and responsibility must not be supplanted.[11]

The *Compendium* further adds with respect to the family, or what it calls the "cell of society":

Society, and in particular State institutions, respecting the priority and "antecedence" of the family, is called to *guarantee and foster the genuine identity of family life* and to avoid and fight all that alters or wounds it. This requires political and legislative action to *safeguard family values* [my emphasis], from the promotion of intimacy and harmony within families to the respect for unborn life and to the effective freedom of choice in educating children. Therefore, neither society nor the State may absorb, substitute, or reduce the social dimension of the family; rather, they must honor it, recognize it, respect it and promote it according to *the principle of subsidiarity.*[12]

The profound implications of this concern for a right-ordered public policy will be examined later in this chapter.

The Roots of Subsidiarity in Public Administration

We can see that subsidiarity is certainly a concept that forms part of the foundation of CST. However, the concept can also be found in works such as the *Federalist Papers*, which promote a robust yet subsidiary republic; that is, one that is both responsive and deferential to the rights of lower levels of government (such as states) and individuals. Tocqueville observed that Americans have a distinct tendency to favor local self-government and civil associations as practical mechanisms for solving public problems.[13] J. J. Kirlin offers that one of the seven great questions of public administration in a democracy is "how shall tensions between national and local political arenas be resolved?"[14] He notes that the administration of all domestic policies and programs is suffused with this tension.

Subsidiarity in the Public Management Paradigm

Wilson's essay describes objective, detached career public officials who execute policy derived from the political process without imposing their own personal biases. This very detachment forms a sort of subsidiarity, which presumes that elected officials represent the people who elected them, and should therefore be unquestioningly and loyally served by the faithful execution of the policies developed by the elected officials. In *The Tides of Reform*, Paul Light writes of four philosophies or "tides" of governmental reform, one of which is "Scientific Management." This "tide" has yet to fully recede from the sphere of public administration, despite the shift represented by the Minnowbrook Conference.[15] Generally speaking, the term "scientific management," as mentioned in Section I of this paper, refers to an industrial reform movement focused on improving productive efficiency. For Light, scientific management is the product of a plethora of scholars and commissions influenced by the precepts of this movement, advocating greater administrative efficiency as its goal using prescribed principles of administration, structure, and rules informed by objective expertise embodied in career civil servants. Efficiency is the focus, and that efficiency is agnostic, or at least indifferent, to the ultimate outcomes of the process, which is the regime of policymaking and politics. As I will discuss later, there is a clear moral danger such indifference presents, but it nonetheless can be argued that this approach constitutes a form of subsidiarity to elected officials and, ultimately, to their electorate.

Subsidiarity in the New Public Administration Paradigm

The New Public Administration has a completely different view of subsidiarity. In this view, in promoting social equity, the needs of the people are well served. In contrast to scientific management, Light describes the tide of "Watchful Eye," which advocates openness and transparency. Frederickson writes of "client involvement" as a modality for enhancing change toward greater social equity.[16] In *The Spirit of Public Administration*, Frederickson describes a vision of an "administrative discretion"[17] in which public preferences are reflected and the common good pursued:

> Within the framework of the Constitution and American regime values, public administrators have a responsibility to structure relations between organizations and the public so as to foster development of an evolving concept—on the part of both organizations and the public—of the common good. Elections, legislative decisions, executive policy implementations, court decisions, and the continual pattern of interaction between public officials and the public are all expressions of public preferences. We must nurture and protect these forms of interaction to come as close as possible to an evolving creation of the public, an evolving definition of the public will, and an evolving spirit of public administration.[18]

In light of Frederickson's vision for administrative discretion, we must ask if the public's preferences are being represented in the performance of public administration. Is administrative discretion, in the sense of respecting subsidiarity, moving toward these preferences as expressed by Tocqueville's observations of American democracy or Kirlin's "core values,"[19] or is something else, such as special interests and agendas, being pursued? An intriguing parallel exists between Light's concept of openness in government as a "tide of reform" and the Second Vatican Council's "aggiornamento," the idea of opening the Church to a greater awareness and interaction with contemporary culture. I have already mentioned that there is a moral danger to the managerial focus in administration, in that it may promote action that is oblivious to societal values. Are there also dangers intrinsic to the New Public Administration similar to the dangers that were presented by the openness of the Second Vatican Council's "aggiornamento"? It may be more correct to use the term "pseudo-aggiornamento," a term coined by Cardinal Rode, Prefect of the Congregation for Institutes of Consecrated Life, to describe a distortion of the intended meaning of aggiornamento on the part of some in which a naturalistic view of man discounts or even discards supernatural humanism as a valid concept.[20] In the following sections, I will discuss the state of administrative affairs we find ourselves in, with a specific focus on health care reform as a timely, relevant case, in order to probe the notion that a naturalistic view of man that does not respect subsidiarity is currently dominant in public administration.

Subsidiarity in Today's Public Administration

Where do we find ourselves today? Administrative government in the U.S. has expanded to a considerable degree over time.[21] The Executive branch of the government began small, with the departments of War, State, Navy, and Treasury, along with Office of the Attorney General, being the constituent agencies. The size of the executive government has more or less expanded steadily since that time, through the establishment of additional departments and agencies under the theory that the managerialism promoted by new bureaucracies would bring about greater effectiveness and efficiency. This also represented a shift of power from elected political officials to executive agencies and the career officials operating within them. Meanwhile, transparency is emphasized by the current administration, suggesting that we are in Light's "Watchful Eye" tide of the reform cycle.[22] But is subsidiarity as a principle—a "core value" of the American people in de Tocqueville's sense—well served by either of these trends of expansion and transparency? Expansion has been debated since the late twentieth century, whereas transparency on its face seems beyond debate. Let us try to answer this question by examining what may be an ideal public administration case in point: health care reform in the United States. Let us also try to keep in mind the analogy of "pseudo-aggiornamento" as a cautionary concept—the idea that openness to all forms of so-called progress is always beneficial.

Prior to the passage of the Patient Protection and Affordable Care Act of 2010 (Public Law 111-148), leading legislative proposals in Congress (such as HR 3200)[23] envisioned an expanded bureaucracy to administer a so-called "public option." In turn, American bishops were reluctant to endorse "universal health care" despite universal access being an important teaching of the magisterium. R. Walter Nickless, Bishop of Sioux City, Iowa, points out that, while rationing or denial of access to needed health care as a principle violates Catholic social teaching, the means of providing universal health care is a prudential matter which, when administered by the government, arguably at best violates subsidiarity in creating a monopoly that potentially allows arbitrary denial of care, or worse, has a government bureaucracy unduly intrude upon life and death decisions.[24] Bishop Robert Finn and Archbishop Joseph Naumann jointly and directly address the equitable interests of society when they caution that "societal principles of justice" must be safeguarded via the provision of care in a context of love and reason at the lowest reasonable level.[25] Most pointedly, Bishop Samuel Aquila, Bishop of Fargo, North Dakota, admonishes that progress in the administration and technology of medical care must not trample upon human dignity: "Any provisions for actions which deny the dignity of human life, especially abortion, euthanasia, whether passive or active, and embryonic stem-cell research must be excluded [in principle] from all health care plans."[26]

Catholic Prescriptions for
Public Administration

What does Church teaching have to say on the topic of subsidiarity in public administration? As touched upon earlier, Pope Pius XI's encyclical *Quadragesimo Anno* is the first to fully articulate the notion of the *subsidium* as a means of the state supplying help to members of society without "destroying or absorbing them."[27] Most recently, Benedict XVI's encyclical *Caritas in Veritate* makes clear that subsidarity is "the most effective antidote against any form of all-encompassing welfare state."[28] The Holy Father further warns that, with respect to subsidiarity and solidarity, its balancing principle of concern for the welfare of fellow human beings, "the former without the latter gives way to social privatism, while the latter without the former gives way to paternalist social assistance that is demeaning to those in need."[29] Of these two dangers, in the case of U.S. health care reform, the more pressing may seem to be the demeaning (or worse) paternalism. Bishops Finn and Naumann defend the principle of subsidiarity in this case by pointing out:

> This notion that health care ought to be determined at the lowest level rather than at the higher strata of society, has been promoted by the Church as "subsidiarity." Subsidiarity is that principle by which we respect the inherent dignity and freedom of the individual by never doing for others what they can do for themselves and thus enabling individuals to have the most possible discretion in the affairs of their lives. . . . The writings of recent Popes have warned

that the neglect of subsidiarity can lead to an excessive centralization of human services, which in turn leads to excessive costs, and loss of personal responsibility and quality of care.[30]

However, the neglect produced by the privatistic instinct must also be guarded against:

There are many people—typically cited as 47 million—without medical insurance. . . . The cost of health insurance continues to rise. . . . The Medicare Trust Fund is predicted to be insolvent by 2019. . . . Mandated health insurance benefits for full-time workers have created an incentive for companies to hire part-time rather than full-time employees. . . . Similarly, the much higher costs to employers for family health coverage, as compared to individual coverage, places job candidates with many dependents at a disadvantage in a competitive market. . . . Individuals with pre-existing conditions who most need medical care are often denied the means to acquire it.[31]

The greater challenge at this juncture, however, seems to take the form of threats to respect for subsidiarity. Frank Morriss summarizes this challenge well.

The attempt to divert American Catholics from concern about pro-abortion politics is badly abusing Catholic social doctrine. The line goes: "Never mind the single abortion issue, but consider the many issues of human need held by candidates who might incidentally include the right of a mother to abort her child among them." This, of course, implies that every proposal for welfare programs fits Catholic understanding in the area of human need. This often amounts to a deception and even falsehood for the reason that Catholic social doctrine begins with the principle of subsidiarity—namely, that fulfillment of human needs begins at the lowest level possible, starting with the individual. Only when necessary should social welfare turn to higher levels of society, and that means that government is the very last resort for the working of social justice.

Pope Leo XIII in *Rerum Novarum* . . . condemned such taxation that amounts to public interference with "the productive activity of the multitude [which] can be stimulated by the hope of acquiring some property in land." . . . Nowhere in papal teaching or other magisterial statements do you find endorsement or recommendation of the welfare state, or for forced distribution of income, or for ever-widening entitlements. . . . It is a major mistake to equate welfarism with compassion, and a worse one to consider it called for by one's Catholic duty to love one's neighbor.[32]

In the end, a prudential way forward in any administrative undertaking will properly take both subsidiarity and solidarity into account. It is for this reason that the Catholic perspective must be one that presumes no particular method of solving public problems (which the reader will recall is the definition of the public administration field), whether public, private, a combination of the two, or executed at higher or lower levels, is inherently "good" by virtue of these characteristics, but is judged rather by how well it respects foundational principles of Catholic social teaching.

A "Subsidiarity Problem" within the Church?

Despite the obvious foundational status of the subsidiarity concept in CST, it appears that in some Catholic circles, subsidiarity may suffer under a sort of benign neglect in actual practice. Samuel Gregg, for instance, examines the USCCB's media statement in the wake of the passage of the health care reform legislation and finds it distressingly silent with respect to how well this legislation shows appropriate deference to the subsidiarity principle.[33] His concern is what he describes as a "massive expansion of Federal government control over healthcare in the United States,"[34] given that providing for wider access to health care need not require the state playing the dominant role, and concludes that views that express concern over violations of the subsidiarity principle tend to be dismissed by the Catholic "left" as "libertarian . . . as if only libertarians could possibly believe that limiting government power and encouraging private sector and civil society solutions to genuine social and economic problems are good things."[35]

The Dangers of Overpoliticization

Joseph Bottum, writing on the post-health care reform situation, bemoans the state of American politics, in which "commentator after commentator" has emphasized the high degree of polarization over the last half century, but especially over the last decade.[36] This state of affairs generates a climate in which debates take on a belligerent quality at the expense of the more subtle aspects of an argument, and the need to take a holistic approach to public policy questions that accounts for all important principles—such as the need to consider both solidarity and subsidiarity when invoking CST. Bottum astutely points out that James Madison in the *Federalist Papers* cites representation as the ostensible safeguard against the "factions" found in pure democracies—yet the representative legislative bodies find themselves behaving in the same passionate fashion as would "factions"—indeed they have become factions themselves. No Republican, in either the House or the Senate, voted for what no one would argue is not major legislation—with profound and sweeping impact, and now enacted law. To emphatically punctuate this scenario, even representation itself comes into question when one CNN poll suggested that, immediately after passage of the bill, 59 percent of the public was opposed to it—verifying Madison's very fear regarding legislative majority "factions." The relatively high levels of opposition that continued even into the November 2010 election that saw a rout of Democrats who supported the bill underscores this. The consequences for subsidiarity (and perhaps solidarity, particularly if some other "faction" finds itself in power) are considerable in the polarized policy arena. Indeed, Bottum observes that ". . . representative democracy has taken a beating, perhaps even pushed down toward a system in which we are free only to elect the tyrants who will rule us until the next election."[37]

Doing What Is Right: A Natural Law Perspective

The pressing concern in this case does seem to be the violation of subsidiarity, because of what appears to be a rising tide of what has been termed as "statism": a presumption that the best solution to public problems proceed forth from the highest levels of the state.[38] It is that presumption, not the involvement of the state per se, which presents the problem of a public administration which does not respect subsidiarity, and the accompanying danger that in acting, the state will not respect nonnegotiable principles such as the sanctity of human life. Bishops Finn and Naumann warn:

> Recent cautionary notes have been sounded by Cardinal Justin Rigali, Chair of the U.S. Bishops Secretariat for Pro-Life Activities, and Bishop William Murphy of the U.S. Bishops Committee on Domestic Justice and Social Development against the inclusion of abortion in a revised health care plan. At the same time, they have warned against the endangerment or loss of conscience rights protection for individual health care workers or private health care institutions. A huge resource of professionals and institutions dedicated to care of the sick could find themselves excluded, by legislation, after health care reform, if they failed to provide services which are destructive of human life, and which are radically counter to their conscience and institutional mission.[39]

The problem is, as Bishop Nickless warns, that openness to social progress in the form of greater access to health care for the poor also opens the door, in a manner similar to "pseudo-aggiornamento," to morally unacceptable side effects:

> Within these limits, the Church has been advocating for decades that health care be made more accessible to all, especially to the poor. Will the current health care reform proposals achieve these goals? . . . As Cardinal Justin Rigali has written for the USCCB Secretariat of Pro-life Activities, [HR 3200] circumvents the Hyde amendment (which prohibits federal funds from being used to pay for abortions) by drawing funding from new sources not covered by the Hyde amendment, and by creatively manipulating how federal funds covered by the Hyde amendment are accounted. . . . This will saddle the working classes with additional taxes for inefficient and immoral entitlements. The Senate bill . . . is better than the House bill, as I understand it. It subsidizes care for the poor, rather than tending to monopolize care . . . [the Senate Bill] also does not meet the . . . standard of explicitly excluding mandatory abortion coverage.[40]

Robert George sees statism as having no place in natural law theory.[41] Natural law theory, generally speaking, asserts that the fundamentals of morality and right-ordered action may be deduced from nature as a normative framework, without necessary recourse to any purely artificial system. It is in this manner that the highest values of a democratic society are both identified and safeguarded. George suggests that natural law theory, rather than promoting statism, recognizes the risks as well as the benefits of government and the consequent need to mitigate those risks through checks and balances.[42] There is no doubt that the U.S. founders envisioned a form of government safeguarded by virtue.[43] Accordingly, even without imposing a specific religious framework, if we take the "spirit of administration," as Frederickson puts it, as that virtuous spirit insisted upon by the founding fathers, then the guiding compass of secular administration must be no less than the natural law to defend against the "dictatorship of relativism" so aptly described by Pope Benedict XVI, then Cardinal Ratzinger.[44] And it is the natural law that suggests that man's dignity is served, his rights are vouchsafed, by a public administration that respects subsidiarity and promotes community virtue, rather than imposing a moral relativism upon lower levels of association, and ultimately the family. According to George, a morally valid authority derives the positive law (means of ordering society) from the natural law, which is in turn derived from *recta ratio* or "right reason" unfettered by emotional or other impediments.[45]

Jeff Mirus, in writing on the "natural logic" of the principle of subsidiarity, states that it is part of the dignity of the human person to be able to exercise control over his own destiny, that human needs should be met at the lowest possible level in the social order, and that a higher level of governing control should intervene only when necessary to compensate for deficiencies at lower levels.[46] He further suggests that health care reform may be something of a "wake-up call" in the American episcopate, as evidenced by the surge of recent statements from bishops defending the subsidiarity principle in the wake of the current legislative proposals.[47] For Mirus, this is the necessary vanguard in the face of the "growing dominance of a secular state."

Granted, health care is a complex topic that perhaps, in prudence, calls for a robust role for government and its attendant bureaucracies. In defense of the principle of subsidiarity, former Senator Rick Santorum acknowledges as much when he writes that "there are times when the federal government has to take the lead…in the early 1960s, the smallest social unit that could make racial justice happen *was* the federal government."[48] The key is to avoid a presumption that the issue of the government's role is anything *other* than a prudential matter, that government has any place in providing or administering health care as a foregone conclusion. Most importantly, social justice must be promoted and protected by a wholesome subsidiarity in a public administration which informs itself in both what is fundamentally valued by and maintains the dignity of the human person. The statement released by the U.S. Conference of Catholic Bishops upon the signing into law of the Patient Protection and Affordable Care Act of 2010 underscores this well when it states:

> For nearly a century, the Catholic bishops of the United States have called for reform of our health care system so that all may have access to the care that recognizes and affirms their human dignity. Christian discipleship means, "working to ensure that all people have access to what makes them fully human and fosters their human dignity" (United States Catechism for Adults, page 454). Included among those elements is the provision of necessary and appropriate health care. For too long, this question has gone unaddressed in our country. Often, while many had access to excellent medical treatment, millions

of others including expectant mothers, struggling families or those with serious medical or physical problems were left unable to afford the care they needed. As Catholic bishops, we have expressed our support for efforts to address this national and societal shortcoming. We have spoken for the poorest and most defenseless among us. Many elements of the health care reform measure signed into law by the President address these concerns and so help to fulfill the duty that we have to each other for the common good. . . . Nevertheless, for whatever good this law achieves or intends, we as Catholic bishops have opposed its passage because there is compelling evidence that it would expand the role of the federal government in funding and facilitating abortion and plans that cover abortion. The statute appropriates billions of dollars in new funding without explicitly prohibiting the use of these funds for abortion, and it provides federal subsidies for health plans covering elective abortions. Its failure to preserve the legal status quo that has regulated the government's relation to abortion, as did the original bill adopted by the House of Representatives last November, could undermine what has been the law of our land for decades and threatens the consensus of the majority of Americans: that federal funds not be used for abortions or plans that cover abortions. Stranger still, the statute forces all those who choose federally subsidized plans that cover abortion to pay for other peoples' abortions with their own funds. If this new law is intended to prevent people from being complicit in the abortions of others, it is at war with itself.[49]

Interestingly, the bishops proceeded to specifically address an explicitly administrative issue in their statement—i.e., an action by the President in the form of an Executive Order devised to win pro-life hold-outs in his party—framing not only the importance of the discipline of public administration but also its natural entanglement in political questions:

We share fully the admirable intention of President Obama expressed in his pending Executive Order, where he states, "it is necessary to establish an adequate enforcement mechanism to ensure that Federal funds are not used for abortion services." However, the fact that an Executive Order is necessary to clarify the legislation points to deficiencies in the statute itself. We do not understand how an Executive Order, no matter how well intentioned, can substitute for statutory provisions.[50]

George also addresses the issue of health care by acknowledging that health is a basic human good and that the preservation of health is a commensurately important goal.[51] For example, arguably traffic laws exist primarily to protect health and safety. Similarly, health care laws exist to promote the same essential goal. Yet, what shall that scheme of laws and regulations be? For George, any given traffic safety system is not deduceable directly from natural law, but this is rather the role positive law plays as legislators debate and alternately choose from among competing schemes. It therefore follows that a statist approach to health care as a common good is not any sort of a given, but that the appropriate role of all parties at all levels of association in society is a matter for public discourse, especially in a representative democracy.

Public Administration and the "Anti-Legal Temper"

A recent issue of the field's premier journal, *Public Administration Review*, contains an article which decries the "anti-legal temper" which has pervaded Public Administration since the waxing of managerialism in the early twentieth century, and consequently calls for the return of the rule of law as a guiding principle for administration.[52] I would make a slight adjustment to that call by placing the word "natural" in front of the word "law" to bring the field into line with a Catholic perspective. Avoiding the two administrative errors: callous managerialism which, per Frederickson, brings the danger of ignoring social equity, and, conversely, the introduction of an "ill spirit" in the interest of promoting agendas of societal progress at the expense of bedrock social values derived from the natural law would be well advised. The current state of affairs in the study and practice of public administration—the solving of public problems—with the rising tide of statism and apparent low regard of those in power for some of these values,[53] much less principles upheld as foundational by Catholic social teaching, suggests that, even with the arrival of the "New Public Administration," as well as goals for transparency and efficiency, a less than desirable direction for the field has been set.

Notes

1. Marc Holzer, Vache Gabrielian, and Kaifeng Yang. "Five Great Ideas in American Public Administration," in *Handbook of Public Administration: Second Edition,* eds. Jack Rabin, W. Bartley Hildreth, and Gerald Miller (New York: Marcel Dekker, 1998).

2. Rabin, Hildreth, and Miller, *Handbook of Public Administration.*

3. This paper is written from the perspective of the field of Public Administration as it is taught and practiced in the United States, which generally recognizes Wilson as the "founder" of the academic discipline as an offshoot of Political Science and draws heavily upon U.S. history and context to inform its literature and practice. It should be noted that the discipline also has significant classical roots (e.g., Machiavelli's writings have administrative implications) and European perspectives to consider, which have more of a sociological grounding in contrast to political science (e.g., the works of Germans Max Weber, who wrote on bureaucracy, and Lorenz Von Stein, who analyzed governmental systems).

4. Woodrow Wilson, "The Study of Administration," *Political Science Quarterly* 2 (June 1887).

5. Frank Goodnow, *Politics and Administration: A Study in Government* (New Brunswick, N.J.: Transaction Publishers, 2000).

6. Herbert Kaufman, "Administrative Decentralization and Political Power," *Public Administration Review* (Jan-Feb 1969): 3-25.

7. H. George Frederickson, "Toward a New Public Administration," in *Toward a New Public Administration: The Minnowbrook Perspective,* ed. F. E. Marini (Scranton, Pa.: Chandler Publishing Co., 1971).

8. *Catechism of the Catholic Church,* 1883.

9. Pontifical Council for Justice and Peace, *The Compendium of the Social Doctrine of the Church* (Washington, D.C.: USCCB Publishing, 2005).

10. Pius XI, Encyclical Letter *Quadgragesimo Anno*: AAS 23 (1931).

11. *Compendium of the Social Doctrine of the Church* (186).

12. *Compendium* (252).

13. Alexis de Tocqueville, *Democracy in America,* trans. Harvey Mansfield and Delba Winthrop (Chicago: University of Chicago Press, 2000).

14. J. J. Kirlin, "The Big Questions of Public Administration," *Public Administration Review* 56, no. 5 (1996): 416-23.

15. P. C. Light, *The Tides of Reform* (New Haven, Conn.: Yale University Press, 1997).

16. Frederickson, "Toward a New Public Administration."

17. Frederickson devotes an entire chapter of his book *The Spirit of Public Administration* (San Francisco: Jossey Bass, 1997) to the topic of what he terms "administrative discretion." It is essentially a balancing principle to Wilson's idea of politically neutral efficiency or managerialism in administration, whereby the equitable interests of the public ("social equity") are considered in administrative decisions.

18. H. George Frederickson, *The Spirit of Public Administration.*

19. Kirlin, "The Big Questions."

20. Cardinal Franc Rode, "From Past to Present: Religious Life Before and After Vatican II," *L'Osservatore Romano*, 28 January 2009, 8.

21. OMBWatch, "Background on the Rulemaking Process: II. A Brief History of Administrative Government," 3 October 2008, at www.ombwatch.org/node/3461,

22. Barack Obama, "Memorandum for the Heads of Executive Departments and Agencies," 21 January 2009, at www.whitehouse.gov.

23. America's Affordable Health Choices Act of 2009, H.R. 3200, http://thomas. loc.gove/cgi-bin/bdquery/z?d111:H.R.3200, 21 January 2009.

24. R. W. Nickless, "Voice Your Concerns over Healthcare Reform," at www.catholicculture.org, 4 September 2009.

25. R. W. Finn, and J. F. Naumann, "Joint Pastoral Statement on Principles of Catholic Social Teaching and Health Care Reform," at www.catholicculture.org, 4 September 2009.

26. Samuel J. Aquila, "Bishop Aquila on Health Care," at www.catholicculture.org, 4 September 2009.

27. Thomas C. Kohler, "In Praise of Little Platoons," in *Building the Free Society: Democracy, Capitalism, and Catholic Social Teaching*, ed. George Weigel and Robert Royal (Grand Rapids, Mich.: William B. Eerdmans Publishing Company, 1993).

28. Benedict XVI, Encyclical letter *Caritas in Veritate* (Boston: Pauline Books and Media, 2009). Also available on-line at www.vatican.va.

29. *Caritas in Veritate.*

30. Finn and Naumann, Joint Pastoral Statement.

31. Ibid.

32. Frank Morriss, "Limits of the State: Catholic Social Doctrine Begins with Subsidiarity," 30 March 2010, available at www.catholicculture.org.

33. Samuel Gregg, "What Is the USCCB's Problem with Subsidiarity?" *Acton Institute PowerBlog*, 26 May 2010, at http://blog.acton.org/archives.

34. Gregg, "USCCB's Problem."

35. Gregg, "USCCB's Problem."

36. Joseph Bottum, "Bad Medicine," *First Things* 203 (May 2010).

37. Bottum, "Bad Medicine."

38. George Will, "Will Obama's Statism Ever Retreat?" 23 August 2009. At http://www.realclearpolitics.com/articles.

39. Finn and Naumann, Joint Pastoral Statement.

40. Nickless, "Voice Your Concerns."

41. Robert George, *In Defense of Natural Law* (Oxford: Oxford University Press, 1999), 239.

42. George, *In Defense of Natural Law*.

43. For example, John Adams stated in a letter to his relative Zabdiel Adams: "The only foundation of a free Constitution, is pure Virtue, and if this cannot be inspired into our People, in a great Measure, than they have it now. They may change their Rulers, and the forms of Government, but they will not obtain a lasting Liberty." http://www.revolutionary-war-and-beyond.com/john-adams-quotes-3.

44. "Cardinal Ratzinger's Homily," 14 April 2005. At http://www.radiovaticana.org/en1/Articolo.asp?c=33987.

45. George, *In Defense of Natural Law*, 104-8.

46. Jeff Mirus, "Prospecting for Subsidarity," at www.catholicculture.org (3 September 2009).

47. Mirus, "Prospecting for Subsidarity."

48. Rick Santorum, *It Takes a Family*. (Wilmington, Del.: ISI Books, 2005), 65-72. See especially Chapter VIII, "Subsidiarity and Central Control."

49. USCCB News Release 10-054, "Bishops Encourage Vigilance That Health Care Legislation Protects Conscience, Does not Fund Abortion," 23 March 2010.

50. USCCB News Release 10-054.

51. George, *In Defense of Natural Law*, 237.

52. L. E. Lynn, Jr., "Restoring the Rule of Law to Public Administration," *Public Administration Review* 69, no. 5 (September/October 2009).

53. For example, a recent Gallup poll indicates a majority Americans self-identify as "pro-life." See Lydia Saad, "More Americans 'Pro-Life' Than 'Pro-Choice' for First Time." 15 May 2009, at http://www.gallup.com/poll/118399.

Chapter 6

COMPARATIVE POLITICS: MEANING, PURPOSE, AND THE COMMON GOOD

Anthony R. Brunello
Professor of Political Science
Eckerd College

How Much Does It Matter?

Comparative politics is presented with a particular set of challenges. The art of comparative politics demands that we compare people, politics, and systems without bias. We must operate in other cultures, encounter foreign languages, and understand diverse historical patterns, economies, and legal traditions, all with a certain goal. The goal must be to probe for the ideal government, while studying the real and practicable. Comparativists analyze the cause and effect of political change in diverse settings while employing comparison to come to critical judgments. A major distinguishing characteristic of comparative politics is that it is both a subfield of the discipline of political science, and it is also a method. This feature is not only unusual, but significant.[1] Comparative politics confronts the age old question of the *ends* of government, while applying social scientific methods to look inside the internal organs of political, social, economic, and cultural institutions in their interactions with each other.[2]

The last century has been one of dramatic change. Two significant aspects of these changes have been that our world has become increasingly secularized while experiencing what has been called the three waves of democratization. What does that mean? Clearly, secularization has not imposed itself so well that religious conflicts and movements no longer shape world politics. In fact, terms like secularization can be misleading in political study. What we mean by secularization is a process leading toward less religion and religious influence. Even so, such a process stated as a generalization can be an obstacle to good comparative political study. How much does the influence of religious tradition and history matter in understanding our current world?

Imagine for a moment if Spain in the 1500s had been a Muslim nation. Perhaps then we would find all of Latin and Central America today operating as Muslim countries with Islamic cultures and political systems. The mode of governing and legal systems would be completely different. Party systems, legislatures, and constitutional governments would reflect Sharia Law and the *Qu'ran*. Social relations, the family structure, roles of men and women, all of these would have evolved in modes expressing the many variations of an Islamic experience. Of course, these Muslim South American countries might still have had similar historical experiences as Latin America: for example, the strong influence and manipulation from North America and the United States, disequilibrium and dependency in economic development, and more. At the same time, consider the differences in cultural and social infrastructure. Democratization would have unfolded under wholly different auspices. We can only imagine the possible alternatives in global relationships and understandings. Our political world would not be the same.

The comparative approach has typically sought to identify differences and similarities among nations and cultures, as well as institutions, policies, and modes of operation. Fundamentally, comparativists are convinced that we cannot make legitimate evaluations of political behavior and phenomena by looking at a single case. For example, when someone says that the United Kingdom is a democratic republic, comparativists immediately begin to ask questions such as: How democratic? Is it like other republics? What does a republic mean? Did its manner of evolution toward democracy make a difference? Are the British more free and equal than Americans? the French?[3] Modern comparative politics seeks to balance the data uncovered in specific cases with common or universal patterns in political behavior and development. This has led to an emphasis on what political scientists call middle-range theory. In comparative politics middle-range theory can explain things that happen in a smaller or limited set of cases or countries that share similar characteristics. For example, the subset of states in Eastern Europe that made the transition from authoritarianism and Soviet domination at the end of the twentieth century gives us an area to apply middle-range theory to phenomena like "progress toward democratic institutions."[4]

Comparative political study is fruitless without a search for meaning. The key question for this chapter is what contribution a Catholic worldview can and has brought to this field of study. Robert Dahl was asked if he believed he was a scientist in connection to his turn toward comparative political study in the midst of his career.[5] He responded in the affirmative, saying that he was among those comfortable in linking normative theory with empirical social science. Dahl further observed that it was unfortunate that many political scientists did not share the same comfort level with this linkage. When asked to explain he said:

Because it is very hard to ask important research questions unless you define them in terms of their human value, in terms of what difference it will make if you answer them. Normative political theory, including the history of political ideas, is very useful for identifying relevant and important questions that are worth asking. Identifying a question that is important is a moral and normative issue, not a scientific issue.[6]

It is precisely here that the tradition of the Catholic Church and of Catholic scholars has offered significant alternative perspectives. Defining important questions is a moral issue. For centuries, the Church has taught that the purpose of government and social relationships must serve the happiness and elevation of the human soul in a very elemental way. As a touchstone, we can go to St. Augustine and the *Enchiridion on Faith, Hope and Love*, where he explains:

And now as to *love*, which the apostle declares to be greater than the other two graces, that is, than faith and hope, the greater the measure in which it dwells in man, the better is the man in whom it dwells. For when there is a question as to whether a man is good, one does not ask what he believes, or what he hopes, but what he loves. For the man who loves aright no doubt believes and hopes aright; whereas the man who has not love believes in vain, even though his beliefs are true; and hopes in vain, even though the objects of his hope are a real part of true happiness; unless indeed, he believes and hopes for this, that he may obtain by prayer the blessing of love.[7]

Robert Dahl and St. Augustine understand what makes questions that matter. The Catholic tradition in this regard is a guide to comparative study that answers questions that lie at the heart of the human experience. For example: Why *is* democracy undergoing its greatest expansion in the last century of human history? There are many reasons, but by stepping back from economic and structural hypotheses, or theoretical biases, we can see into the heart of the matter. Democracy in all its possible guises may expand because it offers a hope for greater happiness and justice for people. This is a human process that is universal, and it is good.[8] For centuries in comparative politics this process can be defined in terms of the interplay between the *telos* and *eidos* of the discipline.

Telos and *Eidos* in the Discipline

The discipline of comparative politics in Political Science has a long history and storied legacy. The legacy is bound by a relationship between *telos* and *eidos*. In short form, *telos* refers to the end, the purpose, or goals of study. For the philosopher Aristotle, the teleology was the effort to know the purposes and the ultimate reason for the existence of any creature, object, or human institution. Aristotle not only assumed that everything had its specific *telos* and evolved toward that end, his assumption rested on the idea that all things have meaning and purpose. *Telos* is about "meaning." *Eidos* can be seen as more of a Platonic concept referring to the ideal forms. Plato emphasized a philosophic object that is *the good*, existing beyond physical and material existence. The material world is one of change, and our understandings of this material world, especially in politics, are corruptible, oft distorted, and impermanent. Politically speaking, Plato would set our eyes on perfection and the ideal forms which operate beyond our physical senses.

In comparative politics the *telos* places value on establishing the purpose of things and seeing how differing forms operate together and produce certain ends in the material world. In contrast, the *eidos* refers to a comparative political scientist's pursuit of the best form of government, and the notion that beyond our human experience there exists an ideal and permanence that we must aspire to ultimately, or the dreams of humanity perish. There is a spiritual dimension in the quest for the best form of government. Part of the long legacy of comparative politics has been the effort to reconcile *telos* and *eidos*. The effort at a marriage of the two would change, evolve, and endure torment and even separation over the centuries. Comparative political science goes on today carrying this legacy.

From the beginning the goals of comparative politics have been divided in two fundamental categories. The first category is a normative or philosophical goal. The philosophical goal is to know "the good," and to gain self-knowledge. From the standpoint of comparative politics, we learn best how to be good citizens, or how to construct a better world, society, and forms of government through the study of others, and in the comparison of models and ideas. Philosophy, lest the pursuit of knowledge for its own sake because we are lovers of wisdom, asks not just *what is*, but forces us to consider *what ought to be*. The journey to define the most perfect or best form of society and government may never cease, but it is the *primary end* and philosophical goal.[9]

The second category is scientific. In modern comparative politics the scientific goal seeks empirical and theoretical knowledge of the political world. Like the philosophical goal, this pursuit justifies itself. For the sake of knowledge alone, we uncover objective and measurable data about political systems, political behavior and social organizations to broaden our understandings. The mode of analysis then requires that we compare these data. Comparativists seek to understand how things work and also why they fail. They search for the causes of change, the life cycles of social movements, the foundations of stability and the rise and functions of various institutions and structures. In the comparative field, this pursuit is undertaken through what has evolved as the diverse employments of the comparative method.

Above I used the phrase *from the beginning*. This is meaningful in the case of comparative politics for the roots of the discipline and method can be traced to a time over 2,300 years ago. When Aristotle determined that the science of politics was the chief science of all, he had already by that time established the rationale and method of comparative politics.[10] Contained in Aristotle's inquiries are both the philosophical and the scientific goals of modern comparativists. Aristotle clearly distinguished himself from his former teacher Plato by his determination to study the empirical world around him. Simply put, Aristotle was convinced that the best way to approach the question of *what ought to be* is to study the practical human world around us, and to compare, contrast, and otherwise analyze *what is*, and hence find the most practicable models in an imperfect world.[11] This process is sometimes referred to as the *art of the possible*. One could argue that, despite the ancient character of political inquiry and philosophy, comparative politics may lay claim to being the oldest discipline within political science. Aristotle grounded political science on comparative study, and as a by-product we inherited a methodology that remains compelling.

It is instructive to look at one of Aristotle's original questions to reveal the basic comparative method. Looking about his world, Aristotle was struck by the prospect of violent change and the rise and fall of governments. Modern political scientists today maintain a fascination for this subject, just as it has consumed and confounded human ingenuity for centuries. To understand the reasons for political collapse and rebellion, Aristotle sent his students out to gather together the case histories and constitutions of as many Greek city-states as possible. It is reported that the students returned with 158 case histories, of which the world only retains in written form the analysis of the city of Athens.[12] Even so, we do have the results of Aristotle's inquiry. Aristotle asked a question that could be answered in a comparative study: what causes some political systems to fail while others thrive? He then collected the descriptive data and classified each case history in categories according to the modes of organization of each state. Aristotle's three main categories were: 1) the number of rulers in government (e.g., single monarch, oligarchy, democracy); 2) the mode of decision making (e.g., group oligarchic, single despot, or democratic); and 3) the distribution of wealth or class structure (e.g., were wealth and power in the hands of one or a few elites or diffused and balanced by several classes).

Upon classifying the descriptive information, Aristotle began what we would today call correlations. Aristotle correlated the incidence of revolution and collapse of regimes with his three categories. Once correlated, he analyzed the results and drew his conclusions. According to Aristotle, the least stable regimes were either pure democracy or pure oligarchy and despotism. Why? Because Aristotle found through the comparative method that the least stable societies suffered from inequality of the distribution of wealth and power. This comes as no surprise to modern observers, especially when Aristotle seems right in line with the theories of so many since his time, including Cicero, Machiavelli, James Madison (in *Federalist*, no. 10), and of course Karl Marx, who declared that all of history was the "history of class struggle."[13] Aristotle established a standard and in some ways was not surpassed until the twentieth century.

The ancient inheritance from Aristotle offered a neat five-step method: 1) conceive of a problem answerable through comparative study; 2) collect empirical data; 3) classify and categorize the data; 4) correlate the data with relevant conditions and the original question; 5) analyze and draw conclusions from the correlations. Aristotle discovered that societies where wealth and power are balanced and evenly distributed across classes tended to be most stable. Yet, there is much more to the Aristotelian heritage than a method. We learn nothing without the *telos* of Aristotle and his effort to engage the Platonic *eidos* with his teleology. Everything Aristotle might have discovered was good to know, in itself, for the pure sake of knowledge, but the meaning lay in the importance of political life. Apart from the philosopher's contemplation, public life and the polis were the sources of the highest meaning in human existence.[14] To be a citizen engaged in the good of the whole community was the highest common calling. Aristotle's comparative method was employed in the search for meaning and the essence of earthly "immortality," rooted in politics, and ultimately realized in contemplative life.[15]

Thus, the purpose of comparative politics has always been to empirically comprehend our political worlds, compare them across space and time, and then perhaps discover something about the best form of government. Essentially the meaning and purpose of government is relevant to the meaning of life. Comparative political science can be difficult and makes steep demands on us to be cross disciplinary, employing anthropology, history, philosophy, psychology, economics, sociology, foreign languages, linguistics, and religious and cultural studies to do something that is among the most difficult of scientific tasks: to compare political systems, peoples, and cultures on an objective basis. How do you compare different political systems and cultures with fairness, and do so without seeing through the lens of your own cultural and ideological preconceptions of the world? How do you really learn from comparison? This challenge has kept comparative politics struggling with the *eidos* and the *telos* throughout its long history.

One model of the marriage of the *telos* and *eidos* has very Western roots that can be traced to Christianity and the Catholic Church. Especially as it was expressed in the work of Thomas Aquinas in the thirteenth century, a great synthesis was managed which attempted to bridge Platonism and Aristotelianism.[16] *Faith* and *Reason* were viewed as complementary and Thomas managed a universal system of harmony between God, nature, and human knowledge. In Thomism, faith was the fulfillment of human reason. Thomas's universe was a hierarchy we have since called the "Great Chain of Being" where the creator God looked down with great love from the summit of existence as the one uncontingent being upon his lowest creatures and objects below. Within the chain of being each part had its purpose, serving one another in natural harmony. Nature and contingent being had its material and physical constraints, but as the creation of God, they operated according to rules divine in their origin. These rules could be comprehended by human reason, and thus there was a place for natural science or philosophy as forms of contingent knowledge corresponding to contingent existences in the "Great Chain."

Like nature, society in Thomism also had purpose, and this is to order happiness in human affairs. Government had moral purpose, and the end of all government is to ensure justice and the common good within society.[17] Of course, the primary goal of human happiness for Thomas Aquinas was the ultimate heavenly life, but he conceived a system which recognized connections between the natural order, human endeavor, and divine perfection. Law, government, and peoples were part of an ordered hierarchy that manifested itself in a true harmony of *telos* and *eidos*, Faith and Reason, and the empirical and ideal realms. The synthesis did not endure, as the rise of science and the rift between Faith and Reason was enlarged to the point of near dissolution in later centuries. Even so, as unlikely as it may seem, the example of Thomas Aquinas demonstrated the value immanent to political discourse in the synthesis of the *telos* and *eidos*. Political inquiry is of little value without moral reasoning. Meaning, purpose, and the good are the real stuff of human relationships. Comparative political science attempts to maintain that quest in a modern world of diversity, complexity, and a demand for empirical measurement.

The Many Modern Evolutions of Comparative Politics

The study of comparative politics has been in constant evolution since the 1950s. Within these evolutions certain historical phases and foci can be identified. The following list of foci is illustrative:

1. the definition of politics and the scope of study
2. the nature and role of theory
3. the normative empirical dichotomy
4. the value and role of measurement and quantification
5. techniques employed in cross-cultural settings
6. configurative versus comparative study
7. the interdisciplinary nature of the field
8. the need for policy-oriented studies
9. the constant debate over theoretical approaches
10. the new conceptual complexity
11. the global and comparative intersection

The traditional study of the field coming into the twentieth century began with historical and philosophical inquiries but suffered from a configurative and descriptive method. Comparative politics was primarily about names, dates, and histories and was concerned with a kind of formal-legalism that relied on comparing different constitutions and legal systems. Institutions also dominated as executives, cabinets, courts, and bureaucracies in a European context prevailed. The parochialism expressed a conservative framework that tended to value enduring institutions and systems. Hence, modern comparative politics began the twentieth century methodologically insensitive to systematic analyses or standards of data collection. Preference for the moral and ethical systems of the West contributed to later criticisms of ethnocentrism in political evaluation.

The behavioral revolution, which arose full-blown in the 1960s, served as a kind of shock treatment to the discipline.[18] Rolling through the next three decades, the behavioralists emphasized empirical technique and quantitative data. The effort to escape bias and historicism, as well as the failure to move beyond the descriptive and judgmental, possessed a true revolutionary aspect. The effort to erect a new science of politics was initiated by a desire to shake off the shackles and blinders that led the world into two destructive world wars. Comparativists confronted a new world of rising nations, the end of colonialism, and diversity within a Cold War environment. This pushed the discipline to be more "pure" and objective in its selection of data. It encouraged the development of systems analysis, study of social movements and change,[19] political-economic development,[20] modernization studies,[21] political culture and socialization,[22] and a vast expansion of the boundaries of things necessary to study across multiple system types, cultures, continents, and levels of development. Collection of statistical data was used to support analyses of systems, structures, and their functions across national and cultural contexts. The ultimate goal was to make the entire field increasingly "scientific." Behavioral study demanded empirical rigor, and it asked questions that could only be resolved with quantitative measurement. Even so, criticisms of bias and parochialism remained.

The behavioral emphasis on sterile technique could not answer many questions concerning cultural variations, revolution and change, psychological development, war, poverty, nation building, power, freedom, leadership, and more. As early as 1960, August Heckscher warned: "Research which disavows any responsibility except that of being objective and non-utilitarian may well qualify as 'pure.' But it is the kind of purity which a society—particularly a society in an age of change—can overvalue."[23]

The new demand for a kind of scientific objectivity often masked buried prejudices favoring liberal democratic Western values and neo-classical economic systems. The new behavioral science showed indifference, if not hostility toward alternative means of development that did not fit the dominant and measurable social and economic paradigm. For decades, *development* meant the rise of secularization and market systems, and *political development* meant an evolution toward liberal democratic forms of governance.[24] In this milieu, rational choice theory established a preeminent position among methodologists in the comparative field, possessing a power to produce more elegant and discrete analyses of political phenomena. At the same time, rational choice tended to drown out studies aimed at any normative or ethical inquiry. At its worst, raw behavioralism refused to confront normative questions about human relationships and the common good, while concentrating on individual choices and preferences in an economic paradigm. In an ironic twist, behavioral methodological objectivity did not impede emerging views of cultural relativism. Nearing the end of the twentieth century, as Westerners became more sensitive to prejudicially judging other peoples, cultures, and nations against a "First World" value system, behavioral objectivity combined to make judgment and evaluation more difficult as well as unpopular. Questions that operated within the *telos* and *eidos* of political inquiry were pressed to the outskirts by a potentially false form of objectivity. Eventually, empiricism and relativism could have led to an inability to make evaluative judgments on any dimension. This was fortunately not the result.

Modern comparative political inquiry today has recognized these difficulties in a world where global interconnection and change are facts of life. The emergence of middle-range theory as a major portion of comparative research has been in part a response to these realities. The importance of *values* questions has not only survived, but they are a vital element of comparative politics. While embracing the importance of traditional and configurative forms of study and case-study methodologies, new abilities and understandings emerged. The importance of good empirical and quantitative analyses has advanced in light of increased sensitivity to cross-cultural settings. Political change and transformation, as well as consensus, legitimacy, and stability are studied with an eye for alternative measures and standards of development. Failed attempts at nation-building have brought wisdom, and demanded greater interdisciplinary study.[25] Most important, while weathering an era where the world and political science waded through debates concerning the "end of history,"[26] a "Clash of Civilizations,"[27] "Jihad vs. McWorld,"[28] or "the End of Ideology," comparative politics has evolved within a context of the emergent dynamic called globalization. With a diverse array of interdisciplinary tools, comparative politics offers new views on terrorism, parties and elections, democratization, revolutions, syndromes of corruption,[29] social movements, sustainable development, political identity, and even genetics and the "neuropolitics" of the human brain.[30] Modern comparativists must ask with ever greater care and urgency questions of meaning, purpose, and value. Theda Skocpol said this in an interview concerning the field of comparative politics:

> Political scientists study and engage the real world of political conflict, public policy making, and the operation of democratic and non-democratic governments. As a result, we have real-world audience—journalists, politicians and the general public—who want to hear what we have to say. This provides a powerful anchor for the discipline that protects against political science flying off into esoterics. I see excellent scholarship being done in political science, often by people who are talking to each other across theoretical and methodological divides and who are combining approaches.[31]

The challenges of global change have liberated comparative politics in the twenty-first century. It is at this juncture where normative inquiry in comparative politics reasserts its significance. Can a Catholic critique contribute to this dynamic? The answer lies in the connection of *telos* and *eidos*. The evidence of the possibilities lies everywhere.

Catholic Teaching, Democratization, and Comparative Politics

If we learn anything from a comparative study of the lives of people such as V. I. Lenin in contrast to Mahatma Gandhi, it is that when we act as if the *ends justify any means*, then the political consequences are frequently devastating. Niccolo Machiavelli did suggest in *The Prince* that the *ends* of political stability, preservation of the state, and possession of political power must justify the use of all *means* necessary.[32] Machiavelli confronted the necessities of *virtu* and the unpredictability of *fortuna* in *The Prince*, and in a narrowly conceived treatise written for a corrupt political milieu, presented the world a set of tactics he would not embrace in *The Discourses*. It was in *The Discourses* that Machiavelli allowed himself to engage in a form of unsystematic comparative and historical analysis, but it is clear that he saw republican forms of government as preferable over other forms. Republics link the people to the nation. They engender a desire to protect peoples' rights and the power to influence laws—powers that the citizens of republics naturally embrace. More to the point, Machiavelli argued in *The Discourses* that in a republic, where the people may govern, means and ends may not only complement one another, but that republics lead to the development of better human beings.[33] Lenin's hopes for a socialist democracy withered in the lies and violence employed by a Bolshevik party and regime that sacrificed the dream for political expediency.

The great social movements of the twentieth century led by Gandhi and Martin Luther King Jr. underscored just how significant the means employed are in the achievement of any good that has a moral purpose. Gandhi and King showed us that moral politics can lead to the ennoblement of humanity. Achieving the good does not mean "winning every day" especially if the goal is to change the hearts of men. Moral purposes are concepts that obviously lie in the field of contested ground, but if there is one universal moral purpose, it is the elevation of the human spirit, and the greater happiness of humankind.

The field of comparative politics has developed several defining areas of study, but the field of *democratization* is significant.[34] This makes sense if we employ Huntington's model of the three "waves" of democracy. The first wave began with the American and French revolutions at the beginning of the nineteenth century. The pace of democracy thereafter slowed and faltered through the periods of the two World Wars, and then a second wave emerged in the aftermath of World War II. After a brief reversal in the rise of communist states in the Cold War era, there was a third wave, beginning in the 1970s, throughout Southern Europe, Latin America, Asia, Africa, and finally Eastern Europe with the fall of the Soviet Union.[35] The numbers of states moving toward democratic systems in that time speaks for itself. As a result, the second and third waves led to the development of measurable indices, typified by the work of *Freedom House*. Meanwhile, the transitions from authoritarian to democratic governance were tirelessly researched by scores of scholars from the 1960s to this day.[36]

Scholarly research on democratization developed dramatically in the sixty years after World War II. Philosophical and ideological perspectives had to be balanced against Cold War politics of the times and a mire of contending theories. For example, there was a long held assumption that democratic institutions required a certain level of economic development. Most essentially, the emergence of free-markets and capitalism were linked to stable liberal democracy. Robert Dahl established in his seminal work *Polyarchy: Participation and Opposition* basic criteria for evaluating democracy and the success of democratic institutions.[37] It was a helpful beginning, but Dahl's criteria also generated much research and debate. Twenty years later Philippe Schmitter and Terry Lynn Karl argued that democracy is more fragile, does not always produce good policy, and has more requirements of its institutions than Dahl had earlier surmised. In "What Democracy Is…and Is Not," Schmitter and Karl clarified that democracy is not simply the existence of a certain set of institutions, but there are many types with varied results dependent upon time and procedure, practices, and socioeconomic conditions. Furthermore, no set of conditions or institutions guarantee how well democracy will unfold in one place or another.[38] Schmitter and Karl concluded:

> Democratization will not necessarily bring in its wake economic growth, social peace, administrative efficiency, political harmony, free markets, or the 'end of ideology.' Least of all will it bring 'the end of history.' No doubt some of those qualities could make the consolidation of democracy easier, but they are neither prerequisites for it nor immediate products of it. Instead, what we should be hoping for is the emergence of political institutions that can peacefully compete to form governments and influence public policy, that can channel social and economic conflicts through regular procedures, and that have significant linkages to civil society to represent their constituencies and commit them to collective sources of action.[39]

Democratic institutions must develop processes and procedures that are embraced by their people over time, especially in the areas of rule of law and public discourse.

Ultimately, the public realm must be a place of discourse and dialogue about collective norms that become binding on all of society, and then enforced by the powers of the state. This aspect of the democratization process is difficult and unpredictable. Competition and elections, as standard features of modern democracy are ancillary to the evolution of the varied roles of citizens and the public realm of standard rules of procedure and order. By the end of the twentieth century this understanding of democratization had broadened to where it can be seen as a set of universal values that are not necessarily linked to a particular economic system. Expansion of political rights and civil liberties, even amongst the poorest nations and peoples, may in itself foster future economic growth and development. As Amartya Sen pointed out:

> (D)emocracy's claim to be valuable does not rest on just one particular merit. There is a plurality of virtues here, including, first the *intrinsic* importance of political participation and freedom in human life; second the *instrumental* importance of political incentives in keeping governments responsible and accountable; and third, the *constructive* role of democracy in the formation of values and in the understanding of needs, rights and duties.[40]

We have witnessed remarkable examples of the struggle for democracy in Central and Eastern Europe, South Africa, South Asia, and even today in troubled Rwanda. Indeed, democracy is a universal value, but not linked to any particular economic prescription. Sen goes on to point out that there is absolutely no empirical evidence that the poor are inclined to reject civil and political rights; in fact, all the evidence is to the contrary. Democratization should be understood for its fragility, complexity, and desirability.

Modern comparative scholars today agree that democratic transitions from authoritarian rule have been the hallmark of our times, and yet consolidation of democracy is a complicated and not wholly predictable wager. The twentieth century was also an age of authoritarianism, and the study of their rise and fall preoccupied many comparativists. It is not enough to topple authoritarian regimes and dictators. The transition of overthrow of autocracy is simply the first step, but the follow through toward consolidation involves the evolution of viable political institutions, customs, and cultures. As Charles Tilly argued, a political and democratic *society* must establish itself wherein political conflict and dissent may be managed. Institutions must also be autonomous and relatively free of foreign influence and control to be legitimate.[41] The establishment of civil society where self-organized groups and movements can articulate values and interests was a key element emphasized in the work of Juan J. Linz and Alfred Stepan.[42] Political violence and war may overthrow autocracy, but deposing an autocrat and having elections is not enough. Guillermo O'Donnell and Philippe Schmitter offered a powerful metaphor to explain the process of the transition to democracy:

> To capture this situation, we propose the metaphor of a multilayered chess game. In such a game, to the already great complexity of normal chess are added the almost infinite combinations and permutations resulting from each player's ability on any move to shift one level of the board to another. Anyone who has played such a game will have experienced the frustration of not knowing until near the end who is going to win, for what reasons, and with what piece. Victories and defeats frequently happen in ways unexpected by either player.
>
> The analogy breaks down somewhat because transitional, multilayered political chess is played by several, even by an unknown number of players, not just two. Moreover, the number of players is indeterminate rather than fixed at three. Nor are there necessarily such clear winners and losers, since in the transitional game players cannot form alliances to protect each other's positions; they may also elaborate rules which have the effect of isolating certain parts of the board and of neutralizing the players' behavior with respect to these positions in such a way that their moves may have little or no effect upon the eventual outcome. In short, the risk of our exploiting the chess analogy is that the reader will imagine that we believe the transition process to be an orderly and cerebral game played by decorous and mild-mannered gentlemen. We ask the reader to conjure up a more tumultuous and impulsive version of the contest, with people challenging the rules on every move, pushing and shoving to get on the board, shouting advice and threats from the sidelines, trying to cheat whenever they can—but nevertheless, becoming progressively mesmerized by the drama they are participating in or watching, and gradually becoming committed to playing more decorously and loyally to the rules they themselves elaborated.... During the transition it is always possible for some contestants to kick over the board, or where authoritarian players still monopolize control over the pieces of organized violence, to remove their opponents by force.[43]

Schmitter and O'Donnell employed the chess analogy to explain years of empirical study of the second and third waves of democracy and to seek understandings of the possibilities of transitions from authoritarian rule in Latin America, Europe, Africa, and Asia. Through this kind of research, comparative politics evolved a subtle understanding of the nature of democratization. As a worldwide phenomenon it was indisputable, but it was varied, dynamic, and prone to setbacks. As Richard Rose demonstrated most recently, "democratization backwards" has been an area of serious concern, especially in Central and Eastern Europe, including Russia.[44] Our focus must include not only transition but also *persistence* in the process.

Regime change and removal of dictatorship, civil war, and violence do not beget democracy by themselves. Democratization is a game of multilayered chess with unclear rules, and with players who may determine to kick over the board. Foreign intervention does not guarantee the difficult birth of autonomous and legitimate institutions that must reflect local, cultural, and even regional diversity. Finally, social and economic development, though necessary, is difficult to impose in a short-term situation. Conditions for democratic consolidation have a way of defying nation-building efforts as an enterprise. In the end, aiding a nation to build schools, roads, hospitals, and viable agriculture and industry is critically important, but more likely successful over time and with few political strings attached.[45] Somewhere along the way civil society must develop to create the ties that bind; the social capital that leads to the eventual stabilization of institutions and democratic norms with indigenous roots. Hence, democratization is "on the march" but is an unpredictable wager that may ignore short-range political calculations.

The universal value of democracy could not avoid becoming ensnared in the great power politics in our time, but comparative scholars did their best to stay above the fray. At the same time, as Larry Diamond pointed out in *Squandered Victory,* it is also a scholar's responsibility to offer help and seek decent and productive outcomes when advising their governments.[46] Understanding the politics and problems of intervention and nation building as it evolved through the Cold War, after Vietnam, and into the post-September 11, 2001, worldview will be an area of research and debate for years to come. The result in the twenty-first century is a realization that democratic institutions are no guarantee when fostered by imposition or the force of war, notwithstanding the Japanese and German models after World War II.[47] Spreading freedom and democracy has been utilized as a justification for intervention and overthrow, but the value of democracy lies much deeper in the souls of people and their political culture.

As democratic institutions increased in the last sixty years on a global scale, so too have the problems associated with the uneven competition and market influences of globalization. Into this mix, concerns over the natural environment, global climate change, and the need for a sustainable future have combined with our understandings of the democratization process in innovative and useful ways.[48] Small-scale, microdevelopment is encouraged along with education and economic integration of women around the world to stabilize population growth rates, bring about sustainable economies, and nourish civil society. New definitions of governmental regulation of global financial markets are proposed with an eye to enhancing security, local agriculture, and markets and reigning in the corrupt and dangerous manipulations of financial institutions. There is an emerging understanding that a balance between markets, people, and the environment must be established to promote growth that is sustainable and encourages human development above profit. Greg Mortenson shows in *Stones into Schools* that over time more will be accomplished by books and schools than by bombs and violence in bringing civil society to Pakistan and Afghanistan.[49] Most importantly, authentic empowerment best develops where people are engaged in the building process with their own hands, in keeping with the Catholic principle of subsidiarity and the dignity of the human person. In story after story, Mortenson chronicles what he finally saw as an inconvenient reality in a Kirghiz school project:

> Only a few days later did I begin to comprehend that what the Kirghiz needed was something infinitely more precious and indispensable than whatever assistance might have been rendered by me, the American military, or anyone else who was not a part of their community. In place of our help what they needed most was the sense of empowerment that comes from knowing they had done it on their own. And by God's grace, they had achieved that in spades.[50]

Mortenson uncovered what has long been the vision of the Catholic Church for true liberation of the human spirit and *integral development*.

Modern Catholic social teaching has deep historical roots and can be clearly traced to Pope Leo XIII (1878-1903) and enunciated in his encyclical *Rerum Novarum* (1891) addressing the needs of working people.[51] Since that time, and by the 1960s, the Church was calling for all the things that we today identify as necessary for bringing about a more free and sustainable future. The social teachings encountered in *Populorum Progressio*, enunciated by Pope Paul VI in 1967, outlined what had historically been the Church's position on sustainable development models and their linkages to democratization.[52] In fact, Pope Paul defined the concept of *integral development*. As opposed to simple economic development and the encouragement of private markets, capital investment, and competition, Pope Paul VI saw development as inextricably linked (*integral*) to educational development, nutritional development, cultural development, and more. Of course, the guiding impetus for this was faith and salvation, and as Pope John Paul II said in 1979, this is expressed by the "voice of the Church, echoing the voice of human conscience . . . to make itself heard down through the centuries, amid the most varied socio-cultural systems and circumstances."[53] To follow in the path of Christ did not mean that one should not be pragmatic, or avoid the use of the total arsenal of scientific reason to achieve ends. Faith and reason are in harmony herein, as the Church argued that *integral development* must include development of the whole human being and hence the entire community. In the twenty-first century we are now in pursuit of the very goals that incited Pope Paul's vision in 1967.

Long ago, in *The City of God*, St. Augustine described the concept of a Christian commonwealth.[54] Human history was for Augustine defined by a contest between the earthly city of humanity and the City of God. The earthly city was filled with desire, possessions, and all the parts of material existence that support and also corrupt the human experience. The City of God is a place of a heavenly peace, salvation, and permanence. In line with this, of course, St. Augustine argued that the history of the church was the story of God in this world. One of the main tenets within Augustine's conception was the idea that humanity belongs to a single family. As John M. Headley points out in *The Europeanization of the World*, this had a significant impact on the idea of universal human rights and the evolution of democracy. The Augustinian notion of a Christian political sphere laid the foundations for the right to demand universal social justice, human rights, and individual freedom.[55]

In comparative politics, as much as we must focus on that which distinguishes people, it is the quest for the commonality and common goods that inspires the best research. Recently, new research connecting the moral self to biological underpinnings was highlighted by the American Political Science Association.[56] A series of pieces highlighted new research which begins with the idea that all human beings share a network of common biological functions and systems—for example, a sympathetic nervous system. The discovery of neurological and genetic markers for empathy and human fairness illustrates a modern quest for that which can be seen as universal in the human condition. At the same time, these can account for a wide array of cultural, political, and social differences.

In the *APSA-CP Symposium*, Peter Hatemi observes that "political scientists have been freed from traditional disciplinary constraints and the false choices of 'nature vs. nurture.'"[57] Environment is powerfully influential, but only in its interaction with the nature of the organism itself. In his research on "Genetic and Neurocognitive Approaches for Comparative Politics," Hatemi has been seeking to uncover the interaction between genetic and social variation. Upbringing and early childhood nutrition may have decided influence on cognitive development, behavior, and physical growth. These processes may account for differences in social organization, behavior, and cultural features. The interactions between biological and social systems are complex, but what is fascinating is to see how the moral universe might be shaped by, and also helps to shape, the material worlds we inhabit. Human biology and human nature are in constant interaction with our environments: social, political, cultural, historical, and natural. The universal and common conditions of the human experience lie below the surface of a world of apparent diversity and complexity. These discoveries are in line with St. Thomas Aquinas's philosophy of universal synthesis. In Thomas's all-encompassing system, God and nature welcome all the infinite diversity that accounts for existence. Human knowledge eventually forms a single piece and natural bond with eternity, and hence is the foundation for natural law. In this system there is no need to disembody nature from nurture.[58] Remarkably, modern science and genetics may offer support for the unity of God and nature found in Catholic teaching.

There has long been a place for Catholic social teaching for these understandings. Pope John XXIII in May 1961 released his encyclical *Mater et Magistra* (1984).[59] In many ways, this encyclical—along with *Pacem in Terris* (April 1963), *Gaudium et Spes* (1966), and Pope Paul VI's, *Populorum Progressio*

(1967)—began a period in which the Church stepped forward to enunciate the conditions in modern times for good society and good government.[60] *Mater et Magistra* established the Church's basic conditions for achieving the common good. Just wages and the protection of private property are juxtaposed alongside the problems of global underdevelopment, especially in the rural and agricultural regions of the world. In a time period when modernization theory was talking about one form of political and economic development in comparative politics, Pope John XXIII was discussing the bases for aid to underdeveloped countries. John XXIII addressed the role of government, and he suggested that the state must play a more progressive role in the life of the people. For Pope John these were both moral and practical imperatives. The common needs of humanity led directly to common sense visions of the moral universe and the primal spiritual calling of the Church. In the Cold War context of the times, this was remarkable. At the same time, it is important to note the Church's respect for the idea of balance. Markets and the rights of property are not only natural but contain rights to be respected among people. The nourishment of human life and of community requires the empowerment of all, and the church was not endorsing a political ideology or economic system. Even so, Pope John was offering a definition of the common good, well within modern comparative politics today:

> But the justification of all government action is the common good. Public authority, therefore, must bear in mind the interests of the state as a whole; which means that it must promote all three areas of production—agriculture, industry and services—simultaneously and evenly. Everything must be done to ensure that citizens of the less developed areas are treated as responsible human beings, and are allowed to play the major role in achieving their own economic, social and cultural advancement.[61]

In 1961 the world was organized around a conflict between the ideas behind state socialism versus liberal democracies characterized by the Cold War context. John XXIII was not choosing political sides in that time, but he was putting the Church on the side of people. The Church was ahead of its time as we consider the effects of globalization. Today there are some economists, such as Joseph Stiglitz, among others, who point toward the need for greater government regulation in a globalizing context.[62] Some of the negative effects of unregulated globalization are viewed as instigating regional poverty traps, catastrophic resource depletion, unsustainable economies, environmental destruction, and warfare.[63] The problems are complex, but toward the end of his work, *Pathologies of Power*, Dr. Paul Farmer made the following observation:

> Regardless of where one stands on the process of globalization and its multiple engines, these processes have important implications for efforts to promote health and human rights. As states weaken, it's easy to discern an increasing role for nongovernmental institutions, including universities and medical centers. But it's also easy to discern a trap: *the withdrawal of states from the basic business of providing housing, education, medical services usually means fur-*

ther erosion of the social and economic rights of the poor. Our independent involvement must be quite different from current trends, which have nongovernmental organizations relieving the state of its duty to provide basic services. We must avoid becoming witting or unwitting abettors of neoliberal politics that declare every service and every thing to be for sale.[64]

Paul Farmer is among those modern social entrepreneurs inspired by Catholic
social teaching and liberation theology that led directly to his global mission in
Partners in Health. Farmer argues that we are all responsible, and that the poor,
sick, and destitute cannot wait on government. Political empowerment, autonomy, and economic development require a delicate balance between the needs of
people and the resources of states. Government cannot and should not be asked
to manage and regulate all of our lives; but government must be responsible for
supporting the public good of citizens, especially the poor and weak, recognizing that subsidiary organizations, such as the local church and charitable bodies
of mutual aid be given proper scope as well.

In *Mater et Magistra*, Pope John also called for greater worker participation in the management of industry. This kind of "workplace democracy" expanded on acceptable conceptions of democratization. Our fixation late in the
twentieth century with the tribalistic conflicts inspired by "McWorld's" competition with "Jihad," may have distracted some political scientists from what was
becoming clearer every day. Healthy human societies require common standards
of nutrition. The world cannot be free where there is poverty and hopelessness
anywhere on the planet. Human development emerges best where people may
govern their own lives. Resource-based conflicts will continue, and as they arise,
forms of genocide may occur in places like the Congo, Darfur, Rwanda, Burundi, and elsewhere. Pope John's visionary expression of the moral imperative
to develop social and economic conditions that put people first was prescient.
Mater et Magistra placed an emphasis on improving local agriculture and also
changing the power and roles of workers and women.[65] At the end of the twentieth century, instead of believing that liberalism as an ideology and economic
system had defeated communism and hence, all other modern ideologies, world
leaders might have anticipated problems we are only now beginning to confront
in a comprehensive fashion. Comparative politics was equipped to address these
issues. Fields of study in development, democratization, social movements, and
revolution had laid the groundwork. Catholic social teaching had something
important to add to our understandings.

As Robert Dahl suggested, questions that matter are moral and normative in
nature. Catholic social teaching offered perspectives that the world of social
science too easily forgets. Salvation and the salvific design encompassed in social justice offers an opportunity for the oppressed and their oppressors to be
"saved" in this world in expectation of full salvation in the next.[66] In other
words, modern Catholic social teaching in its way brought together *telos* and
eidos and gave humanity a common footing not only in the earthly city, but perhaps too in the City of God. As Frank L. Wilson has argued, we inhabit today
a world of constant change.[67] At the same time, the conditions of the human

experience do not change so much that the lessons of Christianity will no longer apply.

The rise of liberation theology in the twentieth century emphasized the congruence of means and ends like few other spiritual and political movements. Following the lead of the church fathers, liberation theology sprang up around the Christian Base Community Movement in Latin America, but eventually found similar movements all around the world. Within the movement, social justice on behalf of the poor was interwoven with a critique of inequality and markets dominated by multinational corporations. The base communities sought political empowerment through education and literacy, especially among women.[68] The philosophy connected politics with education and spiritual salvation. The *preferential option for the poor,* which inspired people like Doctor Paul Farmer in Haiti as a young man, as well as Bishop Desmond Tutu in apartheid South Africa, was well in line with doctrines espoused by Pope John XXIII, Pope Paul VI, Pope John Paul II, and the church throughout history.[69] That certain Catholic theologians pressed a political formulation along Marxist lines too far is also apparent from the writings of John Paul II and Benedict XVI, who constantly reaffirmed the Church's pastoral role rather than its political activity.

Liberation theologians accepted the challenge to resist some of the most odious forms of oppression in human history. They operated in worlds inhabited by global corporations allied with dictators, death squads, organized crime, horrible poverty, and in some cases, the most powerful nations on earth. Liberation theology was nourished in Latin and Central America, but also found homes in South Africa, Haiti, and the United States. Like Mahatma Gandhi, the followers of liberation theology offered a movement that liberated the poor while also promising to save the rich, unscrupulous, exploitative, and the tyrannical for their sins against the poor.[70] The key factor in liberation theology, supported by the Church and John Paul II, was the focus on the workers, the poor, women, children, and the disenfranchised masses in rural poverty around the world. At its best this is what liberation theology was about. However, Pope John Paul II, in his opening address at the Puebla Conference, January 1979, admonished those who would forget that the calling of the Church was not new nor should it become mired in any particular political-economic ideology: "If the Church gets involved in defending or promoting human dignity, it does so in accordance with its mission. For even though that mission is religious in character, and not social or political, it cannot help but consider human persons in terms of their whole being."[71] Rome offered sharp criticism of some liberation theologians, and it was a necessary reminder to those like Jose Miranda that it is wrong to associate the teaching of Jesus Christ with any modern political *ism,* especially Marxism.[72]

Nicholas Kristof and his wife, Sheryl WuDunn, present an inspirational series of firsthand stories in their work *Half the Sky.*[73] In fact, Kristof has suggested that the bravest people he has ever seen working in the most terrible and dangerous circumstances on the planet are Catholic nuns and laypeople. One clear fact emergent in *Half the Sky* is the importance of people, especially women, working for themselves, taking responsibility for their own businesses, health, education, families, and communities. As Kristof reveals, the ultimate liberation of people comes in escaping oppression by expanding individual autonomy and opportunity.

Liberation theology defined class conflict in terms of spiritual awakening. It also pointed to an escape from unsustainable development and poverty traps that currently bedevil the world. Liberation theology linked political economic development to empowerment through education and social justice.[74] Where it failed was in the mistaken desire to transform Catholic social teaching into a narrow political movement. In liberation theology, the *telos* and the *eidos* of society were given spiritual depth by linking the political empowerment of those most vulnerable to the prospect of eternal salvation for all.

Knowing How Things Work

Comparative politics has historically sought to know how things work in political systems of all types. The methodology utilizes comparison to shed light on better practices in one place, and to highlight innovations or failures in another. Political success is evaluated along a continuum that includes the potential for political collapse and failure. For example, revolution is understood as a dynamic process separable from civil war and other forms of internal warfare that may even include ethnic cleansing or genocide. Today we possess indices which clarify and can even predict the potential for successful democratization.[75] Comparative political study cannot afford to be divorced from its normative, philosophical, and ultimately moral inquiries in dealing with these modern political pathologies.

In a world of rapid change comparative political inquiry has sought understandings of the structural transformations such change induces. Complexity and diversity defines the global landscape, but the compelling aspect of study remains those things that are constant, universal, and immanent to the human condition. All human beings may love and feel joy. Human beings all suffer, and feel pain, too. Humanity shares common needs for food, shelter, safety, but more we share a hope for the future, desires for meaningful lives, and the basic ability to utilize political empowerment to liberate and free ourselves to share in what are the common rights of all people. These things happen in thousands of different ways, in diverse cultural settings, and in all manner of societies. The youngster growing up in Palestine will take different paths from the child born today in Manhattan, New York; Bujumbura, Burundi; or Santiago, Chile. All the same, these universal needs and hopes are in each child's heart. The universals in us form the foundations for the "common paths" all people will walk. They make up our common goods.

Democratization as a process was a signal area in comparative politics where these factors in human relationships were analyzed, and in time, accounted for in the elements that lead to democratic institutions.[76] The Catholic Church presented the world with alternative models of democratization that were often ahead of the scholarship. How did this happen? Ultimately, it happened because the Church applied a moral and spiritual worldview to the universal condition of people. It could do nothing else as it followed in the footsteps of Jesus Christ. In so doing, it simply made common sense to stand for the poor. To offer enlightenment and empowerment, while seeking a better world, simply led to the right conclusions. Supporting the family, children, and the roles of women is the most natural and spiritual source of social capital in good societies. The social teaching found in the pronouncements and documents of John XXIII, Paul VI, and John Paul II demanded worker self-management, education of the poor, empowerment of women, redistribution of property and wealth, local land development, investment in home economies, investment in local community infrastructure, investment in children, and finally, prayed for a world order wherein "peace has found a home in the heart of each and every man, till every man preserves in himself the order ordained by God to be preserved."[77]

Catholic teaching anticipated the problems of our current world order, and this can be seen today in the research of scholars who link scarcity, poverty, and economic exploitation to violence, corruption, and the unsustainable destruction of the global environment.[78] In these problems all humanity commonly shares responsibility and the burdens of our actions, which must of course be taken in due prudence. At the global level of activity, the United Nations (UN) Millennium Goals offer one platform for action. However, as noted elsewhere in this book, the UN is not always the best locus for answering all human ills. Indeed, it has performed poorly in meeting many Millennial Goals, and several of the goals have admitted of progress simply through the general improvement of economies throughout the world in the recent decade owing to globalization effects. Often, there has been more success accomplished in the teeming cities, slums, and tribal villages where individuals, social entrepreneurs, doctors, and the ministries of the Church work face-to-face with women, children, and communities. The Church points to a path of sustainability and democracy based on understandings of universal truths. The Church balances the *telos* and *eidos*, and most important, offers a true harmony of faith *with* reason.

In the end, knowing how to compare societies and knowing the science of comparative politics should never be divorced from its normative and philosophical goals. The prospects for a spiritual political science can best operate on a normative plane, and the primary normative obligation is to study politics that can sustain life and engender peace. The ultimate goal of politics must be to sustain life with justice and freedom. Comparative politics has helped political scientists understand how things work, but it must keep its eyes fixed firmly on the ultimate journey. Can we imagine the difference it would make to study politics with love as both the ultimate destination and the method we employ? One of the most powerful elements of comparative study is the effort made to see the world through the eyes of others not like oneself. We know that culture is not static, and nothing could be more destructive than to engage in a pointless form of relativism. At the same time, we must see the world as others see it as much as possible. Then, as we see ourselves through the eyes of others, perhaps comparativists have the ability to also see with love.

Notes

1. Daniele Caramani, *Comparative Politics* (Oxford: Oxford University Press, 2008).

2. Frank L. Wilson, *Concepts and Issues in Comparative Politics* (Upper Saddle River, N.J.: Prentice-Hall Publishing, 1996).

3. William R. Clark, Matt Golder, and Sona N. Golder, *Principles of Comparative Politics* (Washington, D.C.: CQ Press, 2009), and Ruth Lane, *The Art of Comparative Politics* (Boston, Mass.: Allyn & Bacon, 1997).

4. Lane, *Art of Comparative Politics*.

5. Robert Dahl, "Normative Theory, Empirical Research and Democracy," in *Passion, Craft and Method in Comparative Politics*, ed. G. Munck and R. Snyder (Baltimore, Md.: Johns Hopkins, 2007), 113-49.

6. Dahl, "Normative Theory."

7. Augustine, *The Enchiridion on Faith, Hope and Love* (New York: Regnery Gateway, 1961), 135.

8. Amartya Sen, "The Importance of Democracy," in *Development as Freedom*, ed. Amartya Sen (New York: Anchor Books, 1999), 146-59.

9. See Lane, *Art of Comparative Politics*, and Clark et al., *Comparative Politics*.

10. See Aristotle, *The Politics*, trans. Ernest Barker (London: Oxford University Press, 1958).

11. Aristotle, *The Politics*.

12. Aristotle, *The Politics*.

13. See for instance, Marcus Tullius Cicero, *On the Commonwealth* (Indianapolis: Bobbs Merrill, 1976); Niccolo Machiavelli, *The Prince* (New York: W.W. Norton, 1992); James Madison, *Federalist,* no. 10, ed. Jacob E. Cooke (Middletown, Conn.: Wesleyan University Press, 1961); and Karl Marx, *The Communist Manifesto* (New York: W.W. Norton, 1988), 55.

14. Aristotle, *Nicomachean Ethics*, trans. Terence Irwin, (Indianapolis, Ind.: Hackett Publishing, 1985).

15. Hannah Arendt, *The Human Condition* (Chicago: University of Chicago Press, 1958).

16. Ralph McInerny, *St. Thomas Aquinas* (Notre Dame, Ind.: University of Notre Dame Press, 1977).

17. Thomas Aquinas, *The Political Ideas of St. Thomas Aquinas*, ed. Dino Bigongiari (New York: Hafner Publications, 1969).

18. Frank L.Wilson, *Concepts and Issues in Comparative Politics* (Upper Saddle River, N.J.: Prentice-Hall Publishing, 1996).

19. Samuel Huntington, *Political Order in Changing Societies* (New Haven, Conn.: Yale University Press, 1968).

20. Lucian W. Pye, *Aspects of Political Development* (Boston, Mass.: Little-Brown Publishing, 1966).

21. S. N. Eisenstadt, *Modernization: Protest and Change* (Englewood Cliffs, N.J.: Prentice Hall, 1966).

22. Gabriel Almond and Sidney Verba, *The Civic Culture: Political Attitudes and Democracy in Five Nations* (London: Sage Publications, 1989).

23. August Heckscher. "Research for Action," *Current Magazine* (July 1960).

24. See Jason Finkel and R. W. Gable, *Political Development and Social Change* (New York: John Wiley and Sons, 1966).

25. Francis Fukuyama, ed., *Nation-Building: Beyond Afghanistan and Iraq* (Baltimore, Md.: Johns Hopkins Press, 2006).

26. Francis Fukuyama, "The End of History?" *Foreign Affairs* (Summer 1989): 1-25.

27. Samuel Huntington, "The Clash of Civilizations?" *Foreign Affairs* 72, no. 3 (1993).

28. Benjamin R. Barber, *Jihad vs. McWorld* (New York: Times Books, 1995).

29. Michael Johnston, *Syndromes of Corruption: Wealth, Power and Democracy* (Cambridge: Cambridge University Press, 2005).

30. Adam Martin and K. R. Monroe, "Politics and the (Pro) Social Brain: Towards a Neuropolitics of Identity and Connections," *APSA-CP Symposium* 21, no. 1 (2010): 12-17.

31. Theda Skocpol, "States, Revolutions, and the Comparative Historical Imagination," In *Passion, Craft and Method in Comparative Politics*, ed. Gerardo Munck and R. Snyder (Baltimore, Md.: Johns Hopkins Press, 2007).

32. Niccolo Machiavelli, *The Prince*.

33. Niccolo Machiavelli, *The Prince and the Discourses* (New York: The Modern Library, 1950).

34. William R. Clark et al., *Principles of Comparative Politics*.

35. See, for example; Valerie Bunce, "Rethinking Democratization: Lessons from Postcommunist Experience," *World Politics* 55, no. 2 (January 2003): 170-189; Ronald H. Chilcote, ed., *Transitions from Dictatorship to Democracy: Comparative Studies of Spain, Portugal and Greece* (New York: Taylor Francis, 1990); and Juan J. Linz and Alfred Stepan, "Toward Consolidated Democracies," in *Consolidating the Third Wave Democracies: Theories and Perspective*, ed. Larry Diamond, Mark F. Plattner, Yun-han Chu, and Hung-Mao Tien (Baltimore, Md.: Johns Hopkins Press, 1997): 14-33.

36. Larry Diamond, *Squandered Victory: American Occupation and the Bungled Effort to Bring Democracy to Iraq* (New York: Henry Holt, 2005); Gerardo L. Munck, *Measuring Democracy* (Baltimore, Md.: Johns Hopkins Press, 2009); and Charles Tilly, *Democracy* (Cambridge: Cambridge University Press, 2007).

37. Robert Dahl, *Polyarchy: Participation and Opposition* (New Haven, Conn.: Yale University Press, 1971).

38. Philippe C. Schmitter and T. L. Karl, "What Democracy Is . . . and Is Not," *Journal of Democracy* 2 (Summer 1991): 75-87.

39. Schmitter and Karl, "What Democracy Is."

40. Amartya Sen, "Democracy as a Universal Value," *Journal of Democracy* 10, no. 3 (Summer 1999): 3-17.

41. Tilly, *Democracy*.

42. Linz and Stepan, "Toward Consolidated Democracies."

43. Guillermo O'Donnell and Philippe C. Schmitter, *Transitions from Authoritarian Rule: Tentative Conclusions* (Baltimore, Md.: Johns Hopkins, 1986).

44. Richard Rose, "Democratic and Undemocratic States," in *Democratization*, eds. Christian W. Haerpfer, Patrick Bernhagen, Ronald Inglehart, and Christian Welzel (New York: Oxford University Press 2009), 10-24.

45. Greg Mortenson, *Stones into Schools: Promoting Peace with Books, not Bombs, in Afghanistan and Pakistan* (New York: Viking Press, 2009).

46. Diamond, *Squandered Victory*.

47. Schmitter and Karl, "What Democracy Is."

48. David Bornstein, *How to Change the World: Social Entrepreneurs and the Power of New Ideas* (New York: Oxford University Press, 2007).

49. Mortenson, *Stones into Schools*.

50. Mortenson, *Stones into Schools*, 377.

51. Leo XIII, *Rerum Novarum* (1891).

52. Paul VI, *Populorum Progressio* (1967). In *Proclaiming Justice and Peace: Documents from John XXIII to John Paul II*, ed. Michael Walsh and Brian Davies (Mystic, Conn.: Twenty-Third Publications, 1984), 77-140.

53. In M. Walsh and B. Davies, *Proclaiming Justice and Peace*, 67.

54. Augustine, *The Political Writings of St. Augustine*, ed. Henry Paolucci (Chicago: Gateway Publication, 1962). This book contains extensive citations to the *City of God*.

55. John M. Headley, *The Europeanization of the World: On the Origins of Human Rights and Democracy* (Princeton, N.J.: Princeton University Press, 2008).

56. See the *APSA Comparative Politics Newsletter: Symposium* 21, no. 1 (2010).

57. Peter K. Hatemi, "A Partnership Between Science and Culture: Genetic and Neurocognitive Approaches for Comparative Politics," *APSA Comparative Politics Newsletter*, 11.

58. Aquinas, *Political Ideas*.

59. John XXIII, *Mater et Magistra* (1961). In *Proclaiming Justice and Peace*, ed. Walsh and B. Davies, 1-44.

60. Most papal encyclicals can be accessed on-line at www.vatican.org.

61. John XXIII, in Walsh and Davies, 27.

62. Joseph E. Stiglitz, "Globalism's Discontents," *The American Prospect* 13, no. 1 (January 2002); Jeffrey D. Sachs, *Common Wealth: Economics for a Crowded Planet* (London: Penguin Books, 2008); and James G. Speth, *The Bridge at the Edge of the World: Capitalism, Environment and Crossing from Crisis to Sustainability* (New Haven, Conn.: Yale University Press, 2008). These should be read in light, however, of the second demographic transition that is leading to massive depopulation in nearly 60 developed countries and also in light of the rights of subsidiarity that the Church has always defended.

63. See Colin H. Kahl, *States, Scarcity and Civil Strife in the Developing World* (Princeton, N.J.: Princeton University Press, 2006) and Charles Derber, *People Before Profit* (New York: Picador, 2002). Readers should recognize that economic organization of societies is regarded as a prudential matter for governments and peoples, with the Church urging respect for private property and for the preferential option for the poor.

64. Paul Farmer, *Pathologies of Power* (Berkeley: University of California Press, 2005), 244.

65. William Bausch, *Pilgrim Church* (Mystic, Conn.: Twenty-Third Publications, 1983).

66. This is the formulation of controversial liberation theologian Leonardo Boff, *Jesus Christ Liberator* (New York: Orbis Books, 1984).

67. Wilson, *Concepts and Issues in Comparative Politics*.

68. See, for example, Paulo Freire, *Pedagogy of the Oppressed* (New York: Continuum Books, 1985).

69. See John Eagleson and P. Scharper, eds., *Puebla and Beyond: The Major Addresses of John Paul II in Mexico* (New York: Orbis Books, 1980).

70. See, for instance, Gustavo Gutierrez, *The Power of the Poor in History* (New York: Orbis Books, 1983).

71. As quoted in Eagleson and Scharper, *Puebla and Beyond*, 66.

72. Jose P. Miranda, *Marx and the Bible: A Critique of the Philosophy of Oppression* (New York: Orbis Books, 1974).

73. Nicholas D. Kristof and Sheryl WuDunn, *Half the Sky: Turning Oppression into Opportunity for Women Worldwide* (New York: Alfred A. Knopf, 2009).

74. Paulo Freire, *Pedagogy of the Oppressed*.

75. For example, see Freedom House, *Freedom in the World, 2007: Annual Survey of Political Rights and Civil Liberties* (New York: Rowman & Littlefield, 2007); Staffan

I. Lindberg, *Democratization by Elections* (Baltimore, Md.: Johns Hopkins Press, 2009); and Gerardo L. Munck, *Measuring Democracy*.

76. See Amartya Sen, *Identity and Violence* (New York: W.W. Norton, 2006) and Amartya Sen, "The Importance of Democracy."

77. John XXIII, *Pacem in Terris*, 165.

78. See among many others, Colin H. Kahl, *States, Scarcity and Civil Strife*.

Chapter 7

A CATHOLIC CRITIQUE OF INTERNATIONAL RELATIONS THEORY

Andrew Essig
Associate Professor
DeSales University

Introduction

The study of international relations examines the interactions of various actors at the international level. It attempts to identify and understand these actors and what guides their behavior in an environment that lacks a centralized political authority. The anarchical nature of the international system has several important consequences, which the field must explore. International relations examines the role that principles and morality play in the interactions among the actors. It investigates the effects that anarchy has on the actors. And it looks at ways to mitigate the negative effects of anarchy.[1] As a field of study international relations consists of several subdivisions, which focus on particular aspects of the field in order to properly cover its depth and breadth. This chapter focuses on one of these subdivisions, international relations theory.

Theory helps to make observations more intelligible. The most effective theories accurately describe, explain, and predict a particular object of study through either quantitative or nonquantitative analysis. Both of these traditional methods of theory building attempt to discover causal explanations and test them. There are general theories that attempt to provide a complete account of the causes, and partial theories that are narrower in scope. Furthermore, there are empirical theories that relate to facts, as compared to normative theories that deal with values and value preferences, which may not necessarily be measurable.[2] This mixture of method, scope, and abstraction provides numerous permutations resulting in a plethora of theories, which abound within this subdivision.

Theoretical approaches found in the field of international relations face their share of challenges with which theorists must contend. David Singer describes one such challenge as the "level of analysis problem," whereby political scientists must choose from various levels of analysis—individual, state, international—when investigating a particular phenomenon. To select one level versus another may result in the lack of proper analysis.[3] Related to this issue is the predicament of having too much information. Theorists need to make educated decisions on which information is relevant and which is negligible. There are also questions of perception. Theorists periodically struggle with high degrees of abstraction, which may not necessarily reflect a complicated reality.[4] And finally, there is even a case to be made for having too many theories. Once again this calls for proper discernment on the part of theorists. But given these difficulties, international relations theory still has the potential to help individuals understand the chaotic world. It possesses many powerful tools and a rich history upon which it can draw.

Over its 2,500-year history, the subdivision of international relations theory has witnessed the formulation of numerous core and partial theories to help explain the workings of the international system from multiple levels of analysis. Attempts to theorize the workings of interstate relations are an ancient undertaking. In reviews of this rich history, scholars frequently begin with the Greek historian Thucydides' classic treatise *History of the Peloponnesian War*, which describes the early notions of power transition theory and the causes of war and peace.[5] His "Melian Dialogue" between the Athenians and the Melians captures a wide range of aspects relating to international relations theory: balance of power and alliances, among others.[6] Niccolo Machiavelli's *The Prince* stresses the role of power during the rise of the modern state system. The Englishman Thomas Hobbes's *Leviathan* paints the picture of the state of nature that is "nasty, brutish, and short," which is an apt descriptor of the international system.[7] The sixteenth-century Dutchman Hugo Grotius introduced international law through his works, in particular *Law of War and Peace*. John Locke, Jeremy Bentham, and Immanuel Kant's liberalism contributed intellectual insights into the workings of the international system. The writings of Karl Marx, John Hobson, and Vladimir Lenin influenced world affairs in their calls for the rise of the proletariat and the end of capitalist imperialism. More recent international relations theorists of note include: Hedley Bull, Kenneth Waltz, Robert Gilpin, Robert Keohane and Joseph Nye, E. H. Carr, and Hans Morgenthau, among many others. All of these individuals have contributed powerful ideas to make some sense out of what appears to be an incoherent, random world.

These political theorists are not simply important because they provide intelligible patterns of the international system. They do reflect the circumstances of their day. But more remarkably, they have changed them with their ideas, thus resulting in an evolutionary process. Some of their ideas will survive, while others will die through trial and error. These writers often react to the conflicts and struggles that surround them. War is often the primary catalyst for their questioning of the nature of the system. New observations are made, new theories produced, and sometimes new institutions, policies, and norms are created, along with other outcomes. The Industrial Revolution, World War I, and World War II had a dramatic impact on modern international relations theory. From these world-changing events arose the core theories of Marxism, Idealism, and Realism. Vestiges of these theories previously existed. As noted above, there were many intellectual precursors, but it is not until after these watershed events, that they are systematically formulated and accepted as competitive perspectives of international relations theory. These theories attempt to explain, describe, and predict at a general level the various aspects of international relations. Each perspective has its own particular actors and assumptions, its core concerns, major approaches, outlook on global prospects, motives of actors, central concepts, and policy prescriptions.[8] Critiquing these three core theories from a Catholic perspective will be the focus of this chapter.

The Catholic Church bears witness to a powerful intellectual heritage. She too has contributed to the rich history concerning international relations. Over the millennia Church scholars have provided vital insights into the workings of the international system and how actors should relate to one another. These Catholic writers include: St. Augustine, St. Thomas Aquinas, Francisco de Vitoria, Francisco Suarez, Pius XII, Pope John XXIII, and Pope John Paul II, to name a few. They remind the actors in the international system that while politics has a rightful autonomy from the Church, it is not independent from morality. Their distinctive method of moral analysis produces a Catholic international relations theory, whose traditional foundation can be found in Moral Realism. This distinct Catholic way of looking at international relations possesses three main pillars. First, politics is an arena of rationality and moral responsibility. These are not contradictory terms. Humans possess reasoning capabilities that allow them to make moral judgments. Politics is a human activity and inherently invokes questions on how human beings ought to live together. Second, Catholics view power from a classical tradition. Power is a means to an end, and that end is the achievement of the common good. Finally, Catholics hold a particular view of peace. The Church prescribes law, order, and proper governing institutions that promote the common good, which subsequently produces an authentic peace.[9] In light of these pillars of Moral Realism and its associated attributes and assumptions, a Catholic critique of international relations theory is possible. It is from this Catholic perspective that the core theories of Marxism, Idealism, and Realism will be considered. In order to do this, each of the core theories will be introduced. After discussing the main components of each theory at length, the foundation will be laid for a proper critique from the Moral Realist perspective.

Core Theories of International Relations

Marxism

During the Industrial Revolution of the nineteenth century, the abject poverty experienced by the working class sparked a proverbial revolution through the writings of Karl Marx and Friedrich Engels. Expressed in their major works, *The Communist Manifesto, Das Kapital,* and *The Condition of the Working Class,* they viewed history as a product of economic forces, which determined the institutional and ideological structures of society. Politics and economics were inherently intertwined; whoever controlled the means of economic production also controlled the political system, and vice versa. Consequently all of human history has been marked by a struggle between those in power and those out of power, in other words between socioeconomic classes. Marx breaks down this extensive history into five stages beginning with tribal societies and ending in communism. During the capitalist era of the nineteenth century, Marx's fourth stage of society, this struggle takes place between the bourgeoisie and the proletariat. While the nation-state system dominates this period of time, the key actors in this theory are still the classes. The endpoint of Marxism's historical trajectory is the establishment of a communist order where the class system no longer exists and all means of production are owned by the workers, resulting in a new peaceful world order.[10]

In its impact on international relations Marxism recognizes that all actors are operating in a capitalist global economy. The struggle between the owners of production and the workers of the world exists even at this level of analysis, since Marxism is not restricted to domestic politics alone. It is this class structure that is the primary source of conflict in the world, what the noted peace-researcher Johan Galtung referred to as "structural violence."[11] Thus, capitalism is the source of war and imperialism. The English economist John Hobson is the chief contributor to the communist theory of imperialism. He held that capitalist countries overproduced and underconsumed, thus inducing them to reinvest their surplus capital abroad. His works would later influence Lenin.[12] This capitalist world economy, which highly favors the owners of capital, creates a widening gap between the wealthy core countries and the poor periphery. The core states, mostly Western European countries, exploit the cheap resources and labor of the periphery states in Asia, Africa, and Latin America, and as a result of overproduction the core sells its surplus production to the periphery, thus increasing the core's wealth.

This world capitalist system produces other detrimental effects. It results in a dependency relationship from which the periphery is unable to break free. The poor countries become subject to the decisions made by the wealthy countries in economic, as well as political matters. The peripheral states lose their autonomy.[13] Furthermore, the class structure of the capitalist countries is reproduced in the poor ones, thereby perpetuating the system.[14] The division of labor, the motivation of greed among the capitalist class, and the resulting exploitation and poverty lead to a pessimistic outlook of global affairs.

Given this pessimistic state of affairs, the primary policy prescription of Marxist theory is revolution. This revolution consists of replacing the capitalist state with the workers' state. There are some questions as to whether or not Marx himself advocated a violent approach or believed in allowing history to take its natural course.[15] Lenin, on the other hand, was very clear that only a violent revolution could push Russia and the world to the endpoint of the historical trajectory of Marxist theory, communism.

While the fall of the Soviet Union raises questions about the death of Marxist ideology, the core theory of Marxism is still very much alive. In the contemporary literature it is expressed in the Global-North versus Global-South debate, theories of development and underdevelopment, and dependency theory. Each of these theories recognizes the predominance of the economic dimension of international relations. The economic structure of the system continues to be the main explanatory variable on how the actors interrelate with one another. The nature of the structure is still marked by an exploitative relationship between the core and periphery states. Demonstrative of this is the concept "third world," which can be found throughout this literature, although it has recently been replaced with the term "Global South." In the minds of dependency theorists this term continues to focus on exploitation and oppression, the lack of technology and development, underdevelopment brought about by colonialism and imperialism, and dependency upon the dominant capitalist system.[16]

Idealism

The arrival of Idealism, also referred to as Liberalism, as a competitive perspective in international relations theory was a consequence of the brutalities of World War I. Approximately 10 million soldiers died in the trenches of France, as well as along other fronts in this global war. Tragically the war might not have occurred in the first place if not mainly for the failure of the balance of power system that had kept Western Europe free from large-scale warfare since the end of the Napoleonic Wars in 1815. Idealists evidently viewed the balance of power system as inherently flawed; it was unable to provide the stable peace in which it prided itself. They believed, however, that the system could be corrected through the creation of proper institutions; ones which promoted collective action in meeting human needs. The lead advocate for this approach to international relations was U.S. president Woodrow Wilson, as expressed in his "Fourteen Points." This document proposed a "program of the world's peace" through the promotion of free trade, freedom of the seas, disarmament, self-determination, and more importantly the creation of a League of Nations "for the purpose of affording mutual guarantees of political independence and territorial integrity to great and small states alike."[17]

President Woodrow Wilson was not alone, however, in this conception of Idealism. He drew upon the powerful ideas of intellectual precursors in constructing this theory's twentieth century version. Chief among these notables is Immanuel Kant. In his major work *Perpetual Peace* Kant argues that international anarchy can be overcome through collective action, perhaps in the form of a federation of states. He highlighted the importance of international law in regulating state behavior. And he emphasized the power of reason and human learning in attempting to avoid war.[18] Kant is joined by other liberal stalwarts such as Jean-Jacques Rousseau and Jeremy Bentham. None of these individuals viewed human nature as necessarily the problem. It was the defective society into which humans were born; a society that perpetuated war through faulty institutions, such as the balance of power system and autocratic government. For that reason, all of them wrote of ideas to correct these societal flaws, and designed structures to institutionalize peace. These structures included elements such as: international law, international organizations, and democratization. They believed that the promotion of these would contribute to the freedom of the world's peoples, who if given the option would not choose war.

President Wilson summarized these beliefs in his address to Congress asking for a declaration of war against Germany in 1917. The central theme of his remarks was peace. Peace involves freedom, a partnership of democratic nations, and the end of autocratic regimes. But even more importantly, he states that "the right is more precious than the peace." There are causes worth fighting for at the expense of peace. One of these is "for a universal dominion of right by such a concert of free peoples as shall bring peace and safety to all nations and make the world itself at least free."[19]

Idealism, as its name suggests and demonstrated in Wilson's speech, is a highly normative theory. It has a positive view of human nature based in the traditions of Kant and Rousseau. Likewise, it holds a progressive outlook on the world, that an authentic peace is achievable. In order to actualize this optimistic vision, Idealism prescribes institutional reform to properly channel humans' good nature. This theory promotes the creation of institutions that transcend the state. While not necessarily calling for the end of the nation-state system, Idealists view, it as being marked by the pursuit of selfish national interests. The newly-created international organizations will focus on meeting human needs and providing mutual aid through the mechanism of cooperation rather than competition. This spirit of cooperation would spill over into social, economic, and environmental issues.

Upon this positive foundation, several pillars can be erected to promote international peace. One of these is economic interdependence. This calls for a dense network of interlocking economic relationships among states, which would consequently increase the costs of pursuing a policy of war.[20] The second pillar is democratization. Idealists are strong advocates for the democratic peace thesis, which argues that democracies rarely, if ever, go to war with each other. This type of government possesses certain values and norms that inhibit the recourse to arms when dealing with other democracies. Finally there is a strong emphasis on international law. The development of a body of law helps in alleviating the worst aspects of international anarchy. It facilitates conflict prevention and resolution, and can in certain circumstances legitimate the use of force.[21] These three pillars, built upon the foundation that human nature is good and structural reform is possible, will result in a harmonious, peaceful world order.

A vast amount of the contemporary literature in international relations falls within the purview of this core theory. Political integration, functionalism, neo-functionalism, regime theory, and liberal theories of international cooperation capture the basic elements of Idealism. All of these theories present ideas for overcoming sources of conflict in the international system through the creation of new political structures. The literature on democracy and war-proneness, international ethics and human rights, arms control, diplomacy, negotiation and conflict resolution, among others can be also added to the list.

Likewise, similar to other theories, Idealism is subjected to its share of development and revision. Theorists continually attempt to provide better explanations for the workings of the international system as new information presents itself. In the case of Idealism, this updating comes in the form of Neo-liberalism. In their book *Power and Interdependence* Robert Keohane and Joseph Nye describe the new foundations of this theory; complex interdependence and international regimes. Complex interdependence refers to the dense network of interactions between transnational actors, which creates a sense of vulnerability and sensitivity to the needs of others.[22] International regimes are norms, rules, and procedures for interaction agreed to by actors. They provide a certain degree of order in the anarchical international system by establishing long-term rules that regularize relations among the actors.[23] Neo-liberalism continues in the Idealist tradition by focusing on the role of international organizations and other transnational actors in promoting international peace.

Realism

The events of the Second World War upset the basic assumptions of Idealism. The League of Nations, point fourteen of Wilson's "Fourteen Points," ended in failure. It lacked the appropriate enforcement mechanisms to halt the actions of aggressive nations and achieve collective security. Disarmament efforts, promotion of a free trade system, and the rise of newly independent countries produced few benefits. Revisionist powers, both Communist and Fascist, abused the weak new structures put into place by the Treaty of Versailles, thus leading to war. The number of casualties resulting from this war dwarfed those of the previous generation. And as a result of these failures in Idealist principles, the field of international relations theory witnessed the revival of a supposedly discredited theory, Realism.

The revival of this core theory, interestingly enough, begins with a noteworthy book published just prior to the war. Edward Hallett Carr's *The Twenty Years' Crisis, 1919-1939* draws upon the lessons of the prominent Classical Realists Thucydides, Machiavelli, and Hobbes to analyze the causes of war. In his book he critiques Idealism, its normative approach, and view of human nature. He examines the huge gap between Idealism and Classical Realism, and calls for a balancing among these two perspectives. This book was followed several years later by Hans J. Morgenthau's seminal work *Politics Among Nations*. This book, written during the initial stages of the Cold War, introduced the main principles of Modern Realism. Morgenthau, similar to Carr, drew upon the rich history of Realism beginning with writings of Thucydides from the fifth century B.C. From this point in history he moves forward making references to more recent authors, such as Sir Halford Mackinder, and focuses on their discussions of power, national interest, and geopolitics. He even dabbles in the liberal enlightenment period with such thinkers as Rousseau and John Stuart Mill, emphasizing their views on balance of power. It is from these theorists, both ancient and modern, that other Realists take their cue.

Similar to Idealism and Marxism, Realism has its own particular key unit. While the Idealists emphasize the importance of transnational actors, and Marxists point to socioeconomic classes, Realists view the nation-state as the primary actor in the international system. The Treaty of Westphalia established this state-centric perspective in 1648, when the concept of national sovereignty became part of international law. And it has persisted ever since, although not without its challengers. While Realists recognize the existence of other nonstate actors, such as international organizations, they are viewed as being less important.[24] Realists consider the state to be a unitary, rational actor. These two characteristics assume that the state speaks with one voice in the international system, and that it prioritizes its goals, evaluates alternatives and consequences, and makes optimal choices.[25]

Realists describe the nature of the international system as being anarchical. There is no higher political authority than the state. This has a powerful impact on the state's decision-making process. In such a self-help environment, where states must rely upon themselves in order to survive, national security ranks high as a core objective. In order to achieve this goal, states must focus on the attainment of power. Power is a central concept in this core theory. It is the ability to get someone to do what they would otherwise not do. Realists place a heavy emphasis on acquiring hard power capabilities—such as military might, population, and landmass—in order to increase power relative to others. Thus, the international system is marked by a zero-sum competition among states.

Given this state of affairs, Realism focuses on the serious questions of war and peace. The central concepts of this theory, in addition to power, include: polarity, national interest, stability, and security. The strong emphasis on these concepts indicates the importance that Realism places on maintaining peace in an extremely hostile environment, one where life is considered to be short, brutish, and nasty. Peace in this case means the absence of war.[26] One of the main approaches prescribed by Realists to maintain a degree of stability in the system is the balance of power model. While Idealists are highly critical of this approach, as noted above, Realists view it as the optimal choice given the circumstances. This model predicts that states will strive to balance each other by forming alliances or increasing their own national power, so that no one state will become powerful enough to dominate the international system. Trying to achieve this balance is a challenging endeavor. Power transitions and the security dilemma make it difficult to judge the proper amount of power necessary to maintain the system and avoid war. Power transitions reflect the shifting distribution of power within the system, which may increase the probability of war. And the security dilemma describes the phenomena whereby states, by increasing their power to achieve a higher degree of security, may actually end up less secure due to the reactions along similar lines by other competing states.

The self-help, zero-sum environment, along with questions of war and security lead those who subscribe to the Realist school to hold a pessimistic view of the world. War or preparation for war is a constant. While peace is achievable, it is not the norm; and those who seriously question this, such as the Idealists, are often labeled as utopians. It is not only for their views on the anarchical nature of international system that places the Realists in the category of pessimist, but also their view of human nature. Here they rely heavily on the British Enlightenment thinker Thomas Hobbes, who believed that by nature humans are selfishly individualistic animals at constant war with each other. The state helps to alleviate this brutal condition among individuals, but finds itself under the same conditions in the international system.

The explanatory power of the international system is what marks Realism's more recent update, Neo-realism. In his book *Theory of International Politics* Kenneth Waltz explains that it is the nature of the international system which influences state behavior the most. Individual and state levels of analysis are dismissed. States are still the primary actors, but their actions are constrained by the structure of the system. While sovereign states all have a similar function, what differentiates them from each other is their capabilities. And power still matters, although it is no longer an end in itself, as propagated by the Realists, but becomes a means to an end.[27]

While the core theories of Marxism, Idealism, and Realism dominate the literature of international relations theory, this does not preclude the presence of others. A relatively new core theory that has been receiving some attention is Constructivism. This theory holds that ideas count. Individual perceptions and shared understandings of the world, which are supported by the social groups within which a person belongs, have a strong impact on state behavior. Elite beliefs are the powerful explanatory variables in this theory. Persuasion and activism are the primary policy prescriptions that lead to new normative changes. Alexander Wendt summarizes the two basic tenets of this theory in his book *Social Theory of International Politics*: "that the structures of human association are determined primarily by shared ideas rather than material forces, and that the identities and interests of purposive actors are constructed by these shared ideas rather than given by nature."[28] International relations is a social construct, which is capable of change. Consequently, human beings are no longer destined to live in a war-prone, chaotic international environment as argued by the Realists.

Along the lines of a social constructivism, Feminist and Gender Theory argues that the way individuals have been taught to think about world politics has led to the exclusion of women and their experiences in the field of international relations. This core theory attempts to introduce gender as a category of analysis.[29] The inclusion of the feminine experience would change the perceptions of the international system, thus creating new norms and values.

These two theories add a new dimension to understanding international relations. They focus on perceptions and the importance of norms and values, which they believe are not accurately captured by the other core theories. This raises an important point, which introduces the core theory of Moral Realism into the discussion. Theories are judged by their power to explain, describe, and predict. Each core theory has witnessed it own demise and resuscitation in one form or another, while attempting to explain traumatic changes within the international system. They have come about in reaction to the shortcomings of the other theories to properly explain the complex nature of international relations. In light of this theoretical tradition, the core theory of Moral Realism also hopes to contribute a better understanding of the workings of the international system.

Moral Realism

Marxism, Idealism, and Realism each contain their own primary assumptions, key units, core concerns, and policy prescriptions. Policy makers turn to these theories for guidance to make sense out of a complex international system. In turn policies are created which have a direct impact on how the actors interrelate with each other in the anarchical international system. It is in the creation of these policies, whether they establish international organizations or pursue a policy of war, that involves questions on how human beings ought to live together. Answering these inquiries inherently invokes moral judgments. It is here that the Catholic Church has something to say. While politics has a rightful autonomy from the Church, it is not exempt from morality. The U.S. Catholic bishops have confirmed this by stating that, "[Politics] should be about fundamental moral choices."[30] Therefore, the Catholic Church has developed a rich intellectual history concerning world politics, which is referred to as Moral Realism.

On first appearance the concept of Moral Realism seems to be a contradiction in terms. According to the core theory of Realism, morality should be detached from the actions of states. There is no room for individual morality in the calculation of national interest, and for the state to act along these lines will only lead to disaster in an environment that lacks a proper enforcement mechanism. Morgenthau declares in *Politics Among Nations*: "Realism maintains that universal moral principles cannot be applied to the actors of states in their abstract universal formulation, but that they must be filtered though the concrete circumstances of time and place."[31] The primary purpose of political leaders is the survival of the state in an anarchical international system. States are therefore held to a different standard, and are not in the position to make moral decisions similar to those of individuals. Idealists have often been critical of Realists for this lack of moral standards. In light of this, the word "realism" must mean something different in the context of Moral Realism.

Pope Benedict XVI offers a clue to the nature of this "realism" in his *Introduction to Christianity*. He writes of a Christian realism that is "beyond the physical world, realism of the Holy Spirit, as opposed to a purely worldly, quasi-physical realism."[32] In other words the pope is referring to a type of realism that is "otherworldly" in character. The core theory of Moral Realism provides a different approach to understanding the workings of the international system than the temporally oriented core theories of Marxism, Idealism, and Realism, while not completely rejecting them. St. Thomas Aquinas reinforces this "otherworldly" character in his *Summa Theologiae*. In answering Question 103 as to whether the end of government is something outside this world, he argues that the end of a thing directly corresponds with its beginning, and all things find their beginning in God.[33] This idea is derived from the biblical quotation: "The Lord has made all things for Himself (Prov. 16:4)." This is the ultimate foundation upon which Moral Realism is based. It is a more powerful sense of realism than that which belongs to the other core theories. Realism is God Himself.

The other half of the concept of Moral Realism focuses on the term "moral." The Catholic Church has consistently recognized her responsibility to intervene in the sphere of morality, even as it applies to politics. In addressing this issue, Pope John Paul II offers a definition. In *Veritatis Splendor*, he states, "It [the Church's Magisterium] has the task of 'discerning, by means of judgments normative for the consciences of believers, those acts which in themselves conform to the demands of faith and foster their expression in life and those which, on the contrary, because intrinsically evil, are incompatible with such demands.'"[34] Thus, the combination of these two words, "realism" and "moral," with their solid foundations in the Truth, as expressed in Sacred Scripture, Magisterial Teaching, and Divine Revelation, produces a powerful theory.

To develop an understanding of Moral Realism, George Weigel outlines several assumptions associated with this theory. He notes that while politics has its rightful autonomy from the Church, it is not independent from morality. This has been noted above. What is crucial however, is the underlying rationale that links politics and morality. One of the foundational principles of Catholic international relations theory is that human beings are political by nature. This follows in the tradition of St. Thomas Aquinas, who wrote that man is a political animal. Human beings naturally associate with each other. They possess reasoning capabilities that are inherently cooperative, since humans can learn from the experiences of others. They are also naturally communicative; individuals communicate with each other through various mediums, such as the written word and speech.[35] More importantly, Weigel adds that making moral judgments is inherent in the human person. Humans possess moral faculties to make decisions about what is right and wrong. Given these aspects of human nature, human beings require government to function properly. Political theory deals with the nature and purpose of human association; it poses questions on how and why humans relate to one another. Given this understanding of human nature and the need for political institutions, to create a distinction between morality and politics is counterintuitive. It would compartmentalize the human person, thus denying the fullness of the human experience.[36]

This discussion leads to the key unit of the core theory of Moral Realism. Whereas Realism considers the state to be the main actor, Idealism looks to transnational organizations, and Marxism emphasizes the importance of the class system, Moral Realism recognizes the human person as its primary unit. Pope John Paul II declared that "the human person must be the center of every civil and social order, of every system of technological and economic development."[37] Human beings are made in the image and likeness of God; and this is the source of their inherent human dignity. Recognizing and protecting this dignity is the primary concern that should motivate all of the actors in the international system. In his encyclical *Centesimus Annus* Pope John Paul II affirms that the duty of the state is to promote the common good and protect the rights of the individual.[38] The same can be said for the duty of international organizations, multinational corporations, and all other international actors. They are to promote the dignity of the human person and not destroy it by using it as a means to an end.

This motivational factor of recognizing and protecting human dignity distinguishes Moral Realism from the other core theories. Their primary concerns are war and security, institutionalizing peace, and poverty and exploitation. Moral Realism does not reject the legitimacy of the main actors and the core concerns associated with Marxism, Idealism, and Realism. Each has its own place to one extent or another in the natural order of things. This is captured by the principle of subsidiarity, which is one of the main pillars of Catholic Social Thought. Subsidiarity holds that "a community of a higher order should not interfere in the internal life of a community of a lower order, depriving the latter of its functions, but rather should support it in case of need and help to coordinate its activity with the activities of the rest of society, always with a view to the common good."[39] This principle recognizes a hierarchically ordered society where higher-level social authority supports, promotes, and develops lower-order societies. This protects individuals from abuse by assuming limitations on the higher order, since lower-level authority like civil society, the family, and the person have something original to offer to the community. Thus the state, transnational organizations, and economic classes have their rightful place, but all these must be geared toward the human person, otherwise the common good will not be achieved.[40] For instance, the state has its origins in human nature, which is divinely established, and therefore is part of the order God created. Since humans are social beings and require order to achieve happiness, which ultimately lies in God, the state's primary function is to provide peace and order.[41] It exists to protect the rights of lower-level societies that are prior to the state, such as the individual and the family.

In addition to the protection of human dignity, Moral Realism places a heavy emphasis on the notion of peace. The other core theories do not ignore this; in fact, they too possess normative elements to achieve this end. The difference, however, is that Moral Realism hopes to produce an authentic peace, rather than create a false sense of it. For example, Realists advocate that the major approach for maintaining peace in the international system is through the creation of a balance of power system. In order to pursue this policy, states must accumulate weapons or create alliances to increase their relative power. While peace may be achieved, it is unstable and short-lived. The increase in a state's power may tempt it to revert to the use of force or cause others to do so, as argued by power transition theorists. This course of action may also perpetuate the security dilemma, resulting in a continuous arms race that diverts resources from meeting societal needs. The end result is the reinforcement of an atmosphere of distrust in the international community, rather than one that promotes mutual interest and cooperation.

Moral Realism attempts to establish a more stable peace among the family of nations. It views peace as a supreme good through which other goods can be attained.[42] Drawing from Pope John XXIII's encyclical *Pacem in Terris*, authentic peace is based upon "four precise requirements of the human spirit: truth, justice, love and freedom."[43] These should be actively promoted, along with an increased awareness of the dignity of the human person. Essential to the message proclaimed by Pope John XXIII is his emphasis on truth. He considers it the basis of international peace, because it helps to overcome the myths of force and nationalism that prevent the nourishment of a sentiment of brotherhood among all men. With the development of a more fruitful solidarity comes the elimination of the roots of war.[44] Pope John Paul II follows up this message in his first World Day of Peace address entitled "To reach peace, teach peace," where he declared that education for peace should take place at all levels of society: within a person, among neighbors, within a country and between nations.[45] Authentic peace is possible, and it is a duty.

The core theories each prescribe their own major approaches for achieving peace, stability, and order in the international system. As noted above, Realists attempt to establish a balance-of-power system; Idealists promote international law, set up transnational organizations, and focus on democratization; Marxism calls for class struggle to reach the historical endpoint of communism. Moral Realism follows closely in the footsteps of the Idealist tradition. It believes that peace can be practically achieved through negotiation, dialogue, diplomacy, disarmament, and the rule of law. International organizations and international law play critical roles in the promotion of a cooperative environment. International organizations are seen as the embodiment of the community of nations, and can lead to the consensual establishment of a world public authority, which a moral order requires. This new public authority would not be a super-state or world government, but would operate according to the principle of subsidiarity and recognize the proper authority of the state.[46] What is called for here is international integration, the unity of the human race. This assumes that common interests exist among all the inhabitants of the world, and they should therefore pursue those interests through the spirit of community. This is a safe assumption to make in the light of Catholic Social Thought, where all are created in the image and likeness of God and are called to be in union with Him. International integration implies a sense of community founded upon common interest and coordinative efforts.[47]

Moral Realism also emphasizes the importance of international law. International law "rests upon the principle of equal respect for States, for each people's right to self-determination and for their free cooperation in view of the higher common good of humanity."[48] It has formulated "universal principles that are prior to and superior to the internal law of states and that take into account the unity and the common vocation of the human family."[49] International law has the strong potential to become the guarantor of peaceful relations among states and peoples by providing an ordering force for the regulation of human affairs. As states cooperate in the proper formulation of international law and the creation of international organizations, they are directing their authoritative power to the promotion of the international common good.

These two mechanisms—international organizations and international law—are the by-products of Moral Realism's major approach to international relations, which include negotiation, dialogue, and diplomacy, but also help to promote them as well. Where Idealists and Moral Realists begin to diverge is their outlook on global prospects. Idealists are optimistic and progressive in their outlook. They believe that institutions can properly channel humans' good nature to achieve a stable peace. Realists have criticized this particular view as utopian. Moral Realists agree with this criticism to a certain degree. Their overall outlook is best described as semi-optimistic.

Moral Realists take into account that reality exhibits the consequences of imperfection. A variety of blocs and civilizations are present which do or do not share a common system of values, which may lead to either cooperation or conflict. The numerous actors within the international system exercise power in both positive and negative forms. War, environmental degradation, underdevelopment, and international terrorism are examples of negative forms. Positive forms include humanitarian aid, international law, and collective security. These are not exhaustive lists, but they do illustrate why the core theory of Moral Realism advocates a semi-optimistic outlook. It recognizes that since human beings are capable of both good and evil, but are called to be good, there exists a powerful tendency towards hope, which is rooted in a their spiritual nature. And this human condition is constant.

Thus, Moral Realism strives for peace by focusing on the tools of negotiation and diplomacy, while continuing to recognize the dignity of the human person and the achievement of the common good. Alternative policies make it difficult to achieve authentic peace among nations. Deterrence, arms race, proliferation, and balance of power may achieve peace in the short run; but the inherent opportunity costs, the increased temptation to revert to the use of force, and the creation of an environment that is still susceptible to erupt into war make these policies less advantageous. Genuine peace and security are achieved by disarmament, negotiation, and the rule of law within an international order based upon global cooperation, mutual confidence, effective multilateral institutions, and international law.

Moral Realism views authentic peace as a common good. This concept of the "common good" is one of the foundational pillars of this core theory. Each of the core theories gives emphasis to certain central concepts. Marxism's major concepts include the division of labor, class, and core versus periphery; Idealism looks at collective security, law, integration, and international organizations; and

Realism highlights structural anarchy, power, national interest, balance of power, and polarity. Moral Realism's central concepts include: subsidiarity, solidarity, and the common good. Subsidiarity was previously discussed. It captures the idea that a hierarchy exists within the human community, whereby each level possesses its own legitimate authority and should not interfere in the affairs of the other levels. If higher associations usurp the duties of subordinate ones, a grave evil is being committed. Subsidiarity recognizes that the many actors in the international system have a place in the natural order of things, but expresses serious concern when they overstep their authority. For instance, the state should recognize and protect subordinate institutions within its territory, such as civil society and the family, and the same can be argued for international organizations and economic classes in their relations to a community of a lower order.

Solidarity is another central concept. Similar to the others, it points to Moral Realism's "otherworldly" character. It reflects man's communion with Christ and with his brothers and sisters here on Earth. It is a communion based on the words of Jesus Christ: "Truly, I say to you, as you did it to one of the least of these my brethren, you did it to me." (Mt. 25:40). It bears witness to the virtues of love and charity, which seek the good of others in the promotion of the common good. Among the family of nations it will help in the general task of alleviating those conditions that drive individuals to pursue violence.[50]

Finally, the notion of the common good originates from the dignity, unity, and equality of all mankind. Expressed in the Vatican II document *Gaudium et Spes*, it is "the sum total of social conditions which allow people, as groups or as individuals, to reach their fulfillment more fully and more easily."[51] It refers to the goods that are common to all persons, such as peace and security. Furthermore, it operates according the idea that human fulfillment can be found only by living in society. And that society consists of numerous institutions: the family, the economy, the political community, and the international community. All of these are necessary for achieving man's fullest potential.

It is easy to conclude from this discussion, and rightfully so, that Moral Realism's central concepts are inherently interconnected. They are all joined together in a triangle with human dignity at its core and held together by the virtue of love: love thy neighbor as thyself, love thy enemy, and love one another as I have loved you. Nor are they mutually exclusive from the major concepts of the other core theories. For example, deterrence can help to achieve the common good of preventing war, as long as it takes place in the context of progressive disarmament. Marxism places a heavy emphasis on solidarity among the working class. This is a narrow understanding of the concept, however, as it excludes certain elements of society which do not belong to this particular class. So while each of the core theories shares to some extent in the central concepts of Moral Realism, they are also lacking in their full application and understanding of them, thus making it difficult to achieve authentic peace in the international order.

One final issue that needs to be addressed in a Catholic critique of international relations theory is the topic of power. This term provides the cornerstone for all of the core theories. It is commonly defined as getting others to do what they would not otherwise do. Marxism views power from an economic perspective, as bourgeois domination over the proletariat. Idealism attempts to contain the destructive nature of power among nations through the establishment of international organizations and international law. Finally, Realism views power as an end in itself. Power is exercised in many forms. In international relations theory a distinction is often made between hard power and soft power capabilities. Hard capabilities focus on military affairs, economy, land size, and population. Soft capabilities consist of social, cultural, and economic attributes, and quality of leadership, among other factors. Realism stresses the importance of hard power, whereas Idealism and Marxism refer more frequently to soft power capabilities.

Moral Realism generally focuses on soft power. In the area of conflict resolution this core theory consistently calls for disarmament, negotiation, and diplomacy. And yet hard power capabilities do exist, and Moral Realism recognizes that they have their proper place. This ties in closely with its semi-optimistic outlook on global prospects. Poverty, hunger, and other forms of human misery exist, as well as a variety of government regimes that do not respect human rights. Given this reality, military and police capabilities play a protective function. Moral Realism attempts to make the case that the utilization of soft power is more productive and rational than hard power. Nevertheless, occasions arise when actors may legitimately revert to hard power capabilities to achieve the common good. To disregard this possibility leads to utopianism.[52]

A Catholic international relations theory views power from a different perspective. George Weigel defines it as "the capacity to achieve a corporate purpose of the common good."[53] Power is depicted as a means to an end. The end in this case is the common good. Thus, power is viewed in a positive light. In the context of international relations theory state power should be organized, whether hard or soft, in such a way as to promote the common good for all peoples. But taking into consideration the primary actors of the other core theories, no one is exempt from cooperating in the attainment and development of the common good.[54]

Conclusion

Theory helps to describe, explain, and predict the workings of the international system. By utilizing different methods, scope, and levels of abstraction, theorists have created a rich tradition throughout the millennia. The core theories of Marxism, Idealism, and Realism are products of this history. Each possesses its own key actors, assumptions, and major concepts to make the international system more intelligible. All of them capture reality to one extent or another, but none of them to its fullness. By critiquing these theories from a Moral Realist perspective, one is able to gain a better understanding of reality. This theory is based on a higher order, God's will for mankind. It is not a competitive perspective as the other core theories are to each other. Moral Realism captures the truth in each of them and places it within the proper context of solidarity, subsidiarity, and the common good, which never forgets the inherent dignity of the human person. It reflects the ultimate reality of God's goodness and His love for mankind. And similar to the other theories it provides a template for creating a world order and governing systems to best achieve this reality.

Notes

1. Robert J. Art and Robert Jervis, *International Politics: Enduring Concepts and Contemporary Issues* (New York: Pearson/Longman, 2005), 1-6.

2. Paul R. Viotti and Mark V. Kauppi, *International Relations Theory: Realism, Pluralism, Globalism* (New York: MacMillan Publishing Company, 1987), 3-5.

3. J. David Singer, "The Level of Analysis Problem in International Relations," *World Politics* 14 (1961), 77-92.

4. Patrick M. Morgan, *Theories and Approaches to International Politics: What Are We to Think?* (New Brunswick, N.J.: Transaction Publishers, 1994), 10-21.

5. See Thucydides, *The Complete Writings of Thucydides: The Peloponnesian War* (New York: The Modern Library, 1951).

6. Thucydides, "The Melian Dialogue," in *Classics of International Relations*, ed. John A. Vasquez (Upper Saddle River, N.J.: Prentice-Hall, 1996), 9-14.

7. Thomas Hobbes, *Leviathan* (New York: Penguin Books, 1968), 186.

8. Andrew Essig, "Catholic International Relations Theory: The Development of a Core Theory," *Fellowship of Catholic Scholars Quarterly* 30, no. 2 (Summer 2007), 30.

9. George Weigel, "World Order: What Catholics Forgot," *First Things* 143 (May 2004), 31-32.

10. James E. Dougherty and Robert Pfaltzgraff, Jr., *Contending Theories of International Relations: A Comprehensive Survey* (New York: Harper & Row Publishers, 1990), 224-27.

11. Johan Galtung, "A Structural Theory of Imperialism," *Journal of Peace Research* 8, no. 2 (1971), 81.

12. James E. Dougherty and Robert Pfaltzgraff, Jr., *Contending Theories,* 227-29.

13. Raul Prebisch, "The Dynamics of Peripheral Capitalism," in *Democracy and Development in Latin America*, ed. Louis Lefeber and Liisa L. North (Toronto, Ont.: York University Centre for Research on Latin America and the Caribbean, 1980), 25.

14. Ole R. Holsti, "Models of International Relations and Foreign Policy," in *American Foreign Policy: Theoretical Essays* Fifth Edition, ed. G. John Ikenberry (New York: Pearson Longman, 2005), 22-23.

15. George Klosko, *History of Political Theory: An Introduction, Volume II Modern Political Theory* (Belmont, Calif.: Thomson/Wadsworth, 1995), 454-60.

16. Ronald Chilcote, *Theories of Development and Underdevelopment* (Boulder, Colo.: Westview Press, 1984), 1-2.

17. Woodrow Wilson, "President Woodrow Wilson's Fourteen Points" (8 January 1918), The Avalon Project, avalon.law.yale.edu, 3 December 2009.

18. Karen Mingst, *Essentials of International Relations* (New York: W.W. Norton & Company, 2008), 60-61.

19. Woodrow Wilson, "The World Must Be Made Safe for Democracy," in *Classics of International Relations*, ed. John A. Vasquez, (Upper Saddle River, N.J.: Prentice-Hall, 1995), 35-38.

20. Robert O. Keohane and Joseph S. Nye, *Power and Interdependence,* Second Edition (New York: Harper Collins Publishers, 1989), 8-11.

21. Andrew Essig, "Catholic International Relations Theory: The Development of a Core Theory," 31-32.

22. Keohane and Nye, *Power and Interdependence,* 23-37.

23. Stephen D. Krasner, ed., *International Regimes* (Ithaca, N.Y.: Cornell University Press, 1983), 1-5.

24. Viotti and Kauppi, *International Relations Theory,* 6-7.

25. Viotti and Kauppi, *International Relations Theory,* 6-7.

26. Andrew Essig, "Catholic International Relations Theory: The Development of a Core Theory," 31.

27. Kenneth M. Waltz, *Theory of International Politics* (Reading, Mass.: Addison-Wesley Publishing Company, 1979).

28. Alexander Wendt, *Social Theory of International Politics* (Cambridge: Cambridge University Press, 1999), 1.

29. J. Ann Tickner, *Gender in International Relations: Feminist Perspectives on Achieving Global Security* (Irvington, N.Y.: Columbia University Press, 1992), 1-5.

30. The United States Conference of Catholic Bishops, *Faithful Citizenship: A Catholic Call to Political Responsibility* (Washington, D.C.: United States Conference of Catholic Bishops, Inc., 2003), 1.

31. Hans J. Morgenthau, *Politics Among Nations: The Struggle for Power and Peace* (New York: Alfred A. Knopf, 1978), 10-11.

32. Joseph Cardinal Ratzinger, *Introduction to Christianity* (San Francisco, Calif.: Ignatius Press, 1990), 276.

33. St. Thomas Aquinas, *Summa Theologiae,* Question 103.

34. Pope John Paul II, *Veritatis Splendor,* 6 August 1993, no. 110.

35. George Klosko, *History of Political Theory: An Introduction, Ancient and Medieval Political Theory* (Belmont, Calif.: Wadsworth/Thomson Learning, 2002), 247-51.

36. George Weigel, "World Order: What Catholics Forgot," 31-32.

37. Fr. C. John McCloskey, "Universal Church, Global Village," *National Catholic Register,* 25 July 2004, 4.

38. John Paul II, *Centesimus Annus,* 1 May 1991, no. 11.

39. John Paul II, *Centesimus Annus,* no. 48.

40. Pontifical Council for Justice and Peace, *Compendium of the Social Doctrine of the Church* (Washington, D.C.: USCCB Publishing, 2005), 81-82.

41. Heinrich A. Rommen, *The State in Catholic Thought: A Treatise in Political Philosophy* (St. Louis, Mo.: B. Herder Book Co., 1955), 248-49.

42. John Paul II, "Address to the Diplomatic Corps Accredited to the Holy See," 10 January 2005, no. 6.

43. John Paul II, *Pacem in Terris: A Permanent Commitment,* 1 January 2003, no. 6.

44. John XXIII, "Pacem in Terris," Christmas Message, 23 December 1959.

45. John Paul II, "To reach peace, teach peace," 1 January 1979.

46. Andrew Essig, "Catholic International Relations Theory: The Development of a Core Theory," p. 35.

47. Jacques Leclercq, *The Christian and World Integration* (New York: Hawthorn Books, 1963), 11-13.

48. Pontifical Council for Justice and Peace, *Compendium of the Social Doctrine of the Church,* no. 157.

49. Pope John Paul II, "Message of His Holiness Pope John Paul II for the Celebration of the World Day of Peace," *ZENIT News,* 1 January 2004.

50. Andrew Essig, "Catholic International Relations Theory: The Development of a Core Theory," p. 35.

51. Second Vatican Council, *Gaudium et Spes*, 7 December 1965, no. 26.

52. Andrew Essig, "Catholic International Relations Theory: The Development of a Core Theory," p. 34.

53. George Weigel, "World Order: What Catholics Forgot," 32.

54. Pontifical Council for Justice and Peace, *Compendium of the Social Doctrine of the Church*, nos. 164-67.

Chapter 8

A CATHOLIC CRITIQUE OF GLOBAL INSTITUTIONAL STUDIES

Robert F. Gorman
Professor of Political Science and International Studies
Texas State University

Introduction

The quest for peace, prosperity, and the respect of the dignity of persons is rooted in our nature as human beings. It is the promise of the Gospel of Jesus Christ as revealed in the New Covenant of Love. It is also the modern quest of global institutional studies, which, viewed from the standpoint of history, is a secularist residue of a much more ancient and hoary philosophical and theological system conveyed to the modern world by the Catholic Church which was the institutional mechanism and the dynamo for the rise of Western Civilization. This will seem to many modern students of international law and organization a rather outlandish claim, and yet it is true. In this chapter I critique the modern study of international law, organization, and human rights from the optic of Catholic political and social thought.

Within the Political Science subfield of international relations the study of international law and organization and the related fields of human rights and humanitarian law continues to be a burgeoning area of scholarship. I am here referring to these subfields of the subfield of international relations as "Global Institutional Studies (GIS)." This chapter surveys the approaches, assumptions, and preoccupations of contemporary GIS literature in light of the basic principles of Catholic social and political thought and practice. Indeed, the Catholic

Church regards international efforts to promote international order, peace, prosperity, and respect for human dignity as praiseworthy. All such endeavors when aimed at the true good of the human person are welcomed by the Church. Indeed in *Guadiem et Spes* (Vatican II Pastoral Constitution of the Church in the Modern World), the Church specifically applauds international organizations set up to "foster cooperation among nations."[1] But, as Pope Benedict XVI has recently warned, the Church is aware of the potentially perverse effects of intergovernmental organizations (IGOs), their inefficiencies and expense, their tendency to exhibit a secularism hostile to the goods of religious liberty and expression, their tendency to disregard rights of subsidiary bodies including the family, and even their potential injustice when disengaged from the objective order of truth and from the essentially spiritual nature of man.[2]

GIS traditionally are regarded by the realist school as the study of soft power and of the cooperative instincts of states, but also an arena in which states vie for power and control over international agendum. Idealists regarded these elements of international relations as the primary mechanisms through which states could eventually eliminate war. Indeed the idealist impulse gave rise after World War I to the Kellogg-Briand Pact that proposed to outlaw war and to the League of Nations, which was to guarantee global collective security. The colossal failure of these initiatives in the wake of World War II and the ensuing Cold War gave impetus to the realist proposition that preparing for war and interest-driven uses of force were necessary for the preservation of justice and world order. Although realist pessimism about the prospects for peace through bilateral and multilateral diplomacy continued to be born out by the behavior of governments in the twentieth century—given the persistence of international and especially of civil war—the proliferation of international law (in terms of both the number and the ambitious scope of international treaties) and of IGOs that aspire to establish relatively permanent regimes, and the dramatic rise to prominence of nongovernmental organizations (NGOs) in the post-World War II era, gave rise to a widely held belief among contemporary students of international relations, especially those in the liberal tradition, that global governance and multilateralism are not only here to stay, but also that they are the logical and necessary next stage in the transformation of the Westphalian state system into some form of incipient global governance. Often the hope for this eventuality has been dashed by the intransigence of national state claims to sovereignty, and by the corruption, incompetence, and failure of IGOs and multilateral initiatives to effectively address global issues. Still, hope springs eternal in the liberal institutionalist breast, as evidenced, for instance, in the recent book by Thomas Weiss, *What's Wrong with the United Nations and How to Fix It*, which ultimately complains that the boogey-man is the sovereign state system, and that the UN system is too much the creature of sovereign states, and that the solution is just to pitch these meddlesome states into the dustbin of history and get on with global government.[3] Similar—if less extravagant and extreme—arguments are routinely presented in textbooks by prominent international relations scholars, most of whom lament the slow progress being made in transforming the state system into a more efficient system of global governance.[4] A few discordant voices proclaim the ongoing relevance of a more realist outlook on the prospects for global governance, but it is no exaggeration to observe that the general tendency of GIS studies is to regard state sovereignty as a pernicious influence in international relations.[5] Thus many are constantly surprised by the longevity and resilience of the state system itself.

The Role of the Church as a Model of Transnational Organization

While the jury is still deliberating the fate of the sovereign state system and the capacity of multilateralism and global government to serve as effective post-Westphalian system mechanisms for the promotion of international stability, peace, justice, and prosperity, a Catholic appreciation of the problem of international institutionalism and order is perhaps both timely and pertinent. The Catholic Church has long experience in promoting human dignity, advancing prosperity, and advocating peace and justice. It has dealt with a rogue's gallery of tyrants and terrorists, emperors and kings, and pillaging barbarians and pretentious potentates in the course of its two millennia of existence. During the Middle Ages it built and sustained a millennium-long system for transnational order in Western Europe, the collapse of which following the Protestant Revolt gave rise to the modern state system we now observe. In the centuries since its demise as the cultural glue that held together the disparate nations of Western Europe until modern times, the Catholic Church has emerged with global ecclesiastical infrastructure of its own that is superior in numbers and cohesion of its adherents, and more global in scope than any other international institution. There is something to be learned in this longevity and in this global reach enjoyed by the Church. Indeed the secret of the Church's success may subsist as it claims in its supernatural origins, but it is also tied to its observance of a number of key organizational principles. Students of GIS could better understand both the apparent weakness of modern IGOs as instruments of effective policy making and the pesky intransigence of sovereign states, if they would only take a moment to consult the history and the organization of the Church. Modern texts on international relations and international organization all spend some time on developing modern history, and some spend a few paragraphs speaking about the Middle Ages and the role of the Church as an international moral and political authority prior to the Thirty Years War, but rarely do these texts perceive the institution-building capacity of the Church and its pervasive irenic, social, economic, educational, and humanitarian activity. This is understandable, but it is also a weakness of modern GIS scholarship, which lacks a macro-sense of institutional trends in history and of the role of religion in history.[6]

The Catholic Church considers itself to be at the service of eternal truth. It admits that there is a wide subjective and experiential dimension to truth, but it also regards the objective order of truth as real and knowable, and that ultimately all truth is one, rooted in the oneness of truth itself, which is not foremost a thing to be studied or a factum to be known, but a person to be loved: Jesus Christ, the only begotten Son of God the Father. From this derives the anthropological truth that all human beings are children of God, and part of the family of God, brothers and sisters one and all. Thus, the Church holds dear the truth that every human being that ever has been or ever will be conceived into this world is precious in the sight of his or her Maker. The dignity of the human person is bedrock to Catholic anthropology. The human person is regarded by the Church as rational, and thus naturally inclined by the intellect to truth. The human person possesses a free will which is ordered toward the good, and a heart that is naturally inclined toward and in need of both love of God and of neighbor as self. The human person knows with the knowledge "written on the heart" that life is precious, and thus to be protected and preserved and generated. The dignity of the person and the life of virtue is transmitted in the natural bonds of kinship and family that constitute the bedrock of all human society (a fact recognized in the Universal Declaration of Human Rights, which was heavily influenced by Catholic philosophy and Catholic thinkers and drafters, and reiterated in the Covenant of Economic, Social and Cultural Rights, Article 10) and in which the young are gradually formed toward wider participation in social and civil society that is itself oriented toward the common good. Human happiness is achieved within human societies when they respect human persons and subsidiary institutions, including families, local communities, churches, and other voluntary associations by which human communities produce the goods of life and promote good order, justice, and peace.

The Church, itself, is organized at the most local level to foster communities of justice and peace and flourishing human freedom ordered toward the true goods of man. It supports these local parish communities through a diocesan structure for ecclesiastical government across wider regions. The whole system is further united by papal authority and ecclesiastical governance capable of fostering the Church's primary missions of teaching, evangelization, and sacramental service to the faithful. In modern times, the Church has developed the capacity to engage in diplomacy with nation-states and intergovernmental bodies in order to advance its mission. The Church is ultimately a voluntary body. No one is forced to be a member of it, even though all are called to it. Although it once possessed the attributes of temporal power and authority, in ways that fell to it owing to the vagaries of human history, it now possesses only the prestige of its teaching office in regard to faith and morals. It is decidedly an institution possessing soft power, rather than hard power, but it nonetheless enjoys a formidable transnational ecclesiastical structure with extensive financial resources and wide humanitarian appeal. It maintains observer status at the United Nations. It has diplomatic relations with nearly 180 countries. Its charitable work in parishes, dioceses, and at the curial level continues to dwarf the humanitarian work of all IGOs combined, making the Catholic Church in its diverse institutional and private expressions the largest nongovernmental source of charitable aid.

This is admittedly an oversimplified sketch of both the history and current state of the Church as a major transnational actor, but from it can be drawn several principles that for the most part either escape the notice of GIS scholars or attract little careful scrutiny by them. Although lip service may occasionally be given in GIS literature to these principles, they deserve more diligent investigation since they are most certainly relevant to the study of international law, organization, and human rights. I begin with a discussion of the unity of knowledge and truth and then proceed to the dignity of the human person and the principle of subsidiarity, which protects the rights not just of individuals but also of the primary social institutions such as the family and the church, which are essential in both the formation of the human person and as the primary vehicles by which the dignity of the person is protected and preserved.

Truth and the Unity of Knowledge

GIS scholarship is generally open to the proposition that many and various academic disciplines have contributions to make to the understanding of international relations and international politics. International relations textbooks routinely include references to the latest scholarship and received wisdom from economics, anthropology, sociology, psychology, history, philosophy (political and moral), and even the natural sciences, technology, and the cultural arts. This basic thrust of GIS inquiry is aware of and open to how interdisciplinary knowledge enhances and enriches the understanding of international behavior. However, deep skepticism exists in the GIS field toward all normative and objective truth claims. Indeed, the principle of the "unity of knowledge" as understood in the Catholic tradition isn't just a collection of disciplinary literature, empirical studies, or cultural viewpoints and analytical perspectives, although the Church has no objection to and even applauds such variable analyses. Rather the unity of knowledge and of truth implies the existence of a real and intelligible universe invested by divine intelligence and principles of natural law and order that make human science even possible.

Indeed the Church historically supported the advancement of logic, evidentiary discovery, and scientific observation and analysis, confident that the deeper understanding of all nature would lead to the free and clear light of reason to discovery of the elements of eternal law that give coherence to the universe. Thus truth cannot contradict truth, and although reason and empirical analysis are limited and can only make truth claims in light of its limits, in the light of faith that completes reason, more certain knowledge is possible.[7] Today, such a claim is regarded by a large majority of GIS scholars as outrageously absolute. Indeed, within GIS, the predominant assumption is that of skepticism and relativism. A recent IR text entitled, *Understanding the Global Experience*, for example, proudly and explicitly commits itself to the theory of "cultural relativism."[8] This is an implicit assumption of nearly all contemporary international relations, international organization, and international law texts, but the authors of this text make no attempt to hide or qualify the relativism that guides their ideological perspective. IR and GIS college students are bombarded by such assumptions in nearly all of the texts they read, and these texts are furnished by many of the leading scholars in the discipline.

Thus, while there is a very strong commitment within GIS studies to an interdisciplinary perspective, to situate study at appropriate levels of analysis, and a very laudable commitment to mining the findings of a host of departmental and disciplinary bodies of knowledge, these bodies of knowledge are themselves largely committed to utilitarian, historicist, relativist, and empiricist assumptions.[9] Likewise, within the field of international law, the dominant orthodoxy remains that of positivism, although natural law perspectives are occasionally given voice, especially in the arenas of human rights and humanitarian law, although even in those specialized arenas, positivist assumptions are still dominant. This positivism considers the fashioning of new rights a matter of the activity of sovereigns, without regard to how the new norms and laws may violate long-standing and foundational principles of ethics. Indeed, the foundational role of ethics and the natural law as the soil in which law must be rooted to advance a truly human political and legal order is too often rejected or ignored by those who see law as merely a function of the decisions of sovereign parliamentary bodies capable of ignoring or revising the "law written on the heart," as St. Paul referred to it (Rom. 2:15). Indeed, the modern and regnant philosophies I have just described, often lead to very shallow, unfair, and historically incomplete treatments of religion in international relations scholarship. The dominant secularism of the profession feeds such outcomes. While religious believers make truth claims with confidence, GIS scholars by contrast generally make skeptical claims with confidence, and they tend to regard religious believers as obscurantist, parochial, and retrograde. Religion—coupled with its commitment to ultimate and objective truth claims—is often presented by GIS scholars as a primary source of conflict and violence in modern international relations.[10] This, clearly, is only a half-truth, and a poor assessment of the role of religion in human society.[11] Lost in modern assessments is the critical role religion has played as the institutional vehicle through which reconciliation, peace, harmony, altruism, and charity have been advanced in human history.[12] The secular lens through which GIS scholars view the world simply isn't adjusted to see religion in its full reality, and the IR scholar's ear, being attuned to strife and emergent strife rather than to concord and calm, often does not notice the underlying rhythms of religious harmony.[13] Rather religion is rarely noticed except when it is implicated in notable occasions of conflict. Indeed, GIS scholarship seems utterly unaware, given its poor appreciation of history and especially the history of Christendom as the bearer of Western Civilization, that its own secular version of how peace and harmony can be achieved by modern international organizations and international governance is just the latest and modern version of a Christian and, more precisely, Catholic understanding of the ultimate vocation of humankind toward the common good of justice and peace. There are, then, both a failure to explore and to learn from history and a philosophical reductionism at work in much GIS scholarship and writing.

Solidarity and Subsidiarity and Their Relevance to Global Issues

Students of GIS are rightly preoccupied with the international, interstate level of analysis, and to some extent with the governmental level of analysis since governments are still such prominent actors in international relations, and because their foreign policies are the empirical stuff essential to any full analysis of GIS. To the extent that individual or societal levels of analysis are included in GIS analysis, they focus on the individual characteristics of national leaders and national level interest groups vying for influence in foreign policy making. James Rosenau's path-breaking work on comparative foreign policy making has had the positive effect in GIS of distinguishing between levels of analysis and noting interactions between and among them.[14] However, often lost in GIS perspectives is the fundamental fact that most of the issues IGOs presume to manage and address are first and foremost very local issues that people in particular and local communities have long first addressed in very local, intimate, and immediate ways.

Many contemporary GIS textbooks and critiques of IGOs, regimes, etc. divide their subject into three sets of human concerns, including 1) collective security, order, and peace; 2) human rights and humanitarian action; and 3) economic prosperity and sustainable (ecologically friendly) development. These global studies issues and "agenda items" are profoundly local matters of concern long before they are multilateral matters of concern. They are the concerns of families and individuals, of neighborhoods and local communities, of churches and voluntary associations, and of local governments and civic societies. Too often the rich and varied texture of local practice, custom, and preference evident in each of these three issue areas is overlooked in GIS scholarship. It is as though the first, primary, and most important and dominating level at which any such issue should be addressed is that of either the national government or the multilateral institution. But this neither corresponds to the actual way in which people have dealt with political and social concerns throughout human history, nor is it, one might boldly assert, the way it should be dealt with.

On empirical grounds there is substantial evidence to suggest that the most effective means of maintaining security, promoting prosperity, and respecting human dignity are the local means by which people have customarily preserved and achieved these goals. This raises the very fundamental and essential question of subsidiarity and its relationship to solidarity. Many GIS scholars are very supportive of international solidarity, but too often they completely misconstrue the importance of subsidiary rights in connection to solidarity. Solidarity comprises acts of charity, concern, and support by peoples and nations for those in special need. But when international solidarity becomes a codeword for international bodies to usurp subsidiary rights and autonomy, it can no longer be regarded as real solidarity. True solidarity comes to the assistance of dysfunctional local bodies to help restore their vitality, and then it quietly and humbly steps aside to allow the local institutions to resume their role in providing security, prosperity, and human dignity. One must comb international relations and international organization texts for references to families, churches, or religious bodies as subsidiary agents of security, humanitarian support, and prosperity (if one finds them in the index at all, references to them are usually quite minimal), and yet throughout human history and even now these local and subsidiary institutions account for the vast majority of human effort in all of these areas.

Three examples help to illustrate how solidarity and subsidiarity interact. First, the UN has responsibility to promote the collective security of its member states, but under Article 51 of the UN Charter the inherent right of member states to self-defense is recognized, and this right confers on states, not the UN in the first instance, the obligation to protect, safeguard, and secure their territories and populations. If member states fail to do this, then the UN might (although it more often manifestly does not) do something to protect a member state, punish aggression, or restore peace. Promoting the safety and security of its citizens is the primary obligation of governments today, especially in terms of protecting borders and territory. But security for most people at most times is something they undertake for themselves on a personal level by locking doors, avoiding violent neighborhoods, maintaining personal vigilance, and the like. Local neighborhood associations may undertake watch programs. Local police enforce municipal ordinances. Cities and counties incarcerate individuals who violate the peace and good order of a community. States and provinces maintain larger forces and militias to quell more widespread threats to security and safety. Governments might eventually be called upon to assist in a general state of civil unrest, but only rarely is the UN needed to keep the local peace. Subsidiary bodies do it as a matter of routine, and only when they are utterly incapable of doing so in the context of a wider emergency or failure of function are more comprehensive and less local institutions called upon to offer shows of solidarity and support.

A second example of subsidiarity concerns human rights and humanitarian action. Human rights activists often fail to appreciate how very local and subsidiary is the activity that promotes and advances human rights, human dignity, and humanitarian action. While there has been an impressive development of international human rights treaties and institutions and human rights advocacy organizations at the international level made possible by the electronic communications revolution, it is still the case that both the preservation and violation of human rights are very immediately local concerns. Governments at the local, state, and national level have the immediate and first responsibility to protect and defend human dignity when it is threatened, but long before governments are engaged in this, the societal building blocks of the family, religious bodies, private associations, and self-help organizations are engaged in the work of promoting human dignity. The moral and civic formation of people begins in the matrix of the family and its local setting. This truth is recognized in Article 16 of the Universal Declaration of Human Rights and reasserted in Articles 10 and 13 of the UN Covenant on Economic, Social and Cultural Rights. Where families fail to form their members in regard to their duty to respect others and regard their rights, governments may well need to intervene to prevent outrages, abuses, and criminal behavior. Systems of law and order and of education provide support for the proper development of human interaction, but except in the most authoritarian settings, these are not regarded as the sole purveyors of human values, but rather more as backstops to intervene when local institutional mechanisms for advancing human dignity and respect have collapsed or fallen into dysfunction. National states have an obligation to perform such facilitative and restorative action as necessary. Intergovernmental organizations, being furthest removed from local capacity or accountability, may play an even more distant facilitative role, where national systems of human rights preservation have collapsed. Otherwise, the IGO role remains one of mere coordination of national aspirations, and one of general oversight and promotion of humane values. But there is a growing sensibility among human rights advocates that governments are largely lacking in clean hands and that international human rights agreements somehow trump governmental duties in the human rights arena. In addition, rights are often asserted apart from the recognition of duty and responsibility, and indeed, rights are often severed from their origins in natural justice and regarded as the byproduct of democratic assemblies. Such a theory of human rights, now quite popular and pervasive, provides no certain grounding in obligation, as national and international assemblies might easily dispense with old rights and create new ones that might indeed directly violate natural justice. Positivist accounts of rights lacking a ground in objective truth and in natural justice provide a flimsy philosophical basis for protection against flagrant abuse of human persons.

A third set of issues surrounds prosperity and economic survival. Most economic activity is of very local concern to individuals, families, churches, towns, and cities, long before they are a matter of even national let alone international significance. Most economic productive activity, even in the age of globalization and transnational corporations, is carried out by family businesses, small and local businesses, rather than massive international conglomerates. The same is true of efforts to promote respect for the duty of the human person, a formation process that begins with families and churches and then extends into local social and civic institutions. Indeed, students are educated locally, the environment is sustained locally, and human respect and dignity are preserved locally. Sometimes local bodies fail in their subsidiary responsibility in these areas, and some policy issues are by their nature not limited to merely local concern, and so more comprehensive institutions do have important roles to perform in support of improving local manifestations of economic, social, and political problems, but it is always the obligation of these less local bodies and less locally accountable bodies to respect the autonomy and authority of the local institutions, who will ultimately determine the longevity of externally devised policies and programs. This is so in part because solidarity is most keenly and deeply felt at the local level and is least intensely felt at the international level. It is also so because responsibility and accountability are far more personal and direct at the local level and least personal and least direct at the international level. GIS scholarship often fails to acknowledge these facts. Indeed, it is not unusual for international bodies, IGOs, and international NGOs to violate these principles, and GIS

analyses are often silent in the presence of such abuse, because of their preoccupation with the interstate level of analysis, even where more sinister motives are
not present, as they often are in matters of population control and women's
rights issues.[15]

Collective Security and Human Security

GIS scholarship on the collective security record of the UN system honestly
appreciates that the system is unreliable, often to the point of inoperability. This
leaves national governments largely still the primary actors maintaining international peace and security. But most human security is far more local and concerns not just life-threatening acts of violence but also access to basic necessities
of life. Thus there has emerged the notion of "human security." The emergence
of this concept in the 1994 UN Development Program's *Human Development
Report* led to a frenzy of scholarly interest in the concept, which still remains
poorly defined and hard to "implement."[16] For the UNDP and for many developing countries it became a kind of mantra justifying diverse ideological purposes
and highlighting the need for more international assistance to meet economic,
environmental, and infrastructural needs. The term usefully reminded those sitting in governmental, intergovernmental, and nongovernmental offices that ultimately security is essentially a local issue that human beings deal with in their
rich and varied communities. Thus, if human security is to be truly achieved, it
must ultimately develop from the grass roots, as it surely cannot be dictated or
stage-managed from the rarefied heights of international organization. The role
of IGOs must essentially be one of solidarity when local human security collapses and national capacities are too limited to respond. This is the primary
vocation of international humanitarian assistance, to be discussed momentarily,
which must also respect subsidiary rights, at least as far as Catholic social and
political thought are concerned. The state, in turn, has as its primary vocation the
protection of territory and population. This responsibility was ingrained even in
the Peace of Westphalia as the Catholic Holy Roman Emperor concluded separate treaties with his Catholic and Protestant subjects at the conclusion of the
Thirty Years War in 1648. The dignity and religious liberty of these subjects
was of major concern to the framers of the Westphalian system.[17] Recent scholarship seems to regard the "responsibility of states to protect" as a modern revelation, but it is actually built into the philosophical principle of the common
good, which hearkens all the way back to Aristotle's political philosophy and to
the constant teaching of the Catholic Church.

The human security literature has at least raised the awareness of IGO
scholars in recent years to the complicated nature of local security realities, especially in the context of civil wars, where the UN track record of success is
mixed. The literature in IGO collective security studies widely confirms the dif-
ficulty of implementing international collective security principles given the
changing nature of the international security climate, which is increasingly
marked less by international wars than by local violence, internal turmoil, insur-

gency, civil war, transnational terrorist acts, failed states, and other very local pathologies that serve in a globalized system as possible international threats. The publication of first Human Security Report (by the University of British Colombia), and subsequent electronic volumes, showed a steady improvement in the security climate throughout the world, which correlated to the growth of economic globalization. The scholarship reported in these reports and other research indicates that a combination of international factors such as international peacemaking and peacekeeping activities coupled with growing commercial activity, job growth, democratization of governments, and the emergence of stable states are associated with more positive human security climates. Peace and prosperity and good local governance seem to go hand in hand. The resurgence of violence in many Middle East countries where these conditions do not exist proves the point. Thus, positive developments in international relations are no doubt contributing factors to a better climate of security, but even more important are the decisions taken by national governments and their peoples to seek and secure their economic and political life. This is too often ignored by GIS scholars, who see the problem as too much sovereignty and too little international governance, and who sometimes equate the role of transnational NGOs as "democratic" and "accountable" agents of security, even though transnational organizations are precisely not accountable to any electorate, and may well be unwelcome and intrusive to local human communities.[18]

Problems of course persist in many countries and localities, and precisely when local problems indicate a collapse of security capacity, governments and IGOs/NGOs may need to be deployed to restore it. A closer inspection of the improvements in human security demonstrates that local initiative among peoples, though clearly affected by global trends, is still critical to the attainment of effective security, and that IGOs and international NGOs cannot simply deliver it, without the prior engagement of local capacities, as case after case of civil conflicts and international interventions have demonstrated. There is also a tendency among some scholars, though certainly not all, to regard human security as an individual matter, thus missing the significant role of the family, local partnerships, and subsidiary efforts in achieving security, as evidenced in this assertion from well-established IGO scholars:

> Human security bridges the traditional divisions of international organizational agendas, where questions of "war and peace" have been separated from "economic and social" ones. According to this new conceptualization, peace as the lack of direct violence is only one attribute of a secure environment, and international organizational action is the means of establishing this peace. Further, the notion of human security focuses the attention of international organizations directly on individuals and their circumstances, thereby constituting a subtle challenge to state sovereignty. . . . Pressing international organizations into the service of individually focused human security could therefore constitute an incremental step toward circumventing or marginalizing states and legitimizing supranational governance.[19]

In this formulation real human security is the work of IGOs and individuals, with "bad" governments in between who need to be subverted. But also invisible in this formulation is the primary role of families, neighborhoods, religious groups, churches, private partnerships, and local civil society, all of which build local and indigenous capacity. In fairness the authors go on to admit that human security is a fuzzy term, and that ultimately development of peace and prosperity is the work not just of the World Bank and other IGOs but also of "peoples" and "groups," "previously excluded individuals and groups" to satisfy "local needs" and to participate in "project planning," but IGOs and international NGOs are seen as the main providers, planners, empowering agents, and purveyors of the new model of security and of development.[20] This constitutes a new form essentially of internationalist or transnationalist imperialism. The problem with this particular interpretation of the role of IGOs as formators of individuals is that it violates not just the rights and duties of sovereign states but also the subsidiary rights of local peoples. There are occasions when violations of sovereignty can be justified, but for globalist IGO/NGO intervention itself to be justified in contravening national sovereignty, such international agents must recognize their duty to respect the rights of subsidiary and intermediary institutions to shape their own local and civic societies. International agencies must remain mere facilitators of local capacity and autonomy, not obtrusive agents of change. Otherwise the international interventions in the name of human security themselves violate justice, human dignity, and the natural order of subsidiarity.

Humanitarian Assistance and Human Rights

Nowhere have the demands and complications of solidarity and subsidiarity been more apparent in international relations than in the arenas of humanitarian assistance and human rights, which are increasingly relevant in areas where local violence and civil war have produced complex emergencies, often requiring the deployment of peacekeeping forces as well as humanitarian aid and sometimes even the restoration of stable government and civil society. Conflict obviously exacerbates human rights and humanitarian abuses, and there is a growing and rich literature on how governments, IGOs, and NGOs have been and should be engaged in these situations.[21] Indeed, scholars in this area, as well as the organizations they study are more attuned to these principles than perhaps in other subdisciplines. Even so, major intrusive attitudes persist, among the organizations and the scholars.

A special issue relating to global governance is the proper role of nongovernmental organizations as agents of emergency assistance and human rights advocacy. NGOs with an international focus and widespread international activity are responsible for increasing shares of humanitarian assistance and are often the workhorses that serve governments and IGOs as the agents of program implementation to the remote ends of the earth. Many of the best and largest are religious or church-based agencies, but many others are quite secular. They represent the best traditions of charity in the Western world, and they are evidence of the positive effects of freedom of association. Some GIS scholars view NGOs as the emerging force for democratization of the global order.[22] But NGOs, though a sign of democratic freedoms in the Western world, are not manifestly democratic in themselves, neither in their own internal organization nor in their roles as agents of international advocacy or assistance. Common folk do not elect NGO directors and managers, nor are NGO leaders politically accountable to any government or national population as such. Should NGO programs prove corrupt or even misdirected and harmful, there is no system for accountability. There are exceptions to this, as when an international arm of a church works with its indigenous counterpart in another country. Then some degree of accountability might be expected. But the work of NGOs in foreign countries raises a host of difficult moral and political issues. Practitioners have long been aware of this, and scholars of NGOs have frequently documented the difficulties. Mary Anderson and Michael Barnett and Thomas Weiss offer thoughtful critiques of NGO action in behalf of beneficiary populations in humanitarian emergencies, regarding how to avoid perpetuating conflict, how to promote peace and justice, and how to do so without violating the dignity and capacity of local civil society. This area of the GIS literature begins to grapple with important moral and political dilemmas in humanitarian assistance activities.[23]

Although operational NGOs must struggle with how best and most appropriately to understand humanitarian assistance, another increasing area of NGO activity is in the arena of international advocacy on human rights, development, and justice. This arena is fraught with even greater difficulties because they eventually involve potentially serious violations of subsidiary rights, especially in such areas as the integrity of family life, rights of religious liberty and expression, and the integrity of marriage and procreation of children. Human rights agencies bent on promotion of abortion as a human right, artificial contraception as a means of population control, and even secular education to counter traditional family values may seem from a Western secular perspective to be doing nothing more than the most sensible things. But for traditional families in traditional societies, these represent gross and damaging intrusions into the heart of family life and marriage. After many years of interviewing NGO advocates and officials, I myself have been struck by the smugness in which these policy attitudes are often held by NGO activists. Thus, the rights of subsidiarity are routinely abused as agencies purport these policies. Examples of this arrogant intrusion into the sovereign affairs of nations has been witnessed recently in Catholic countries of Latin America and even in European Union condemnations of its member states' national laws in these arenas (Slovakia and Lithuania serving as recent examples). International conferences on human rights, women's rights, and population and environment routinely see effort by Western secular governments, NGOs, and IGO secretariats to purport such policies as consistent with the human good. The Holy See, thus, finds itself allied to countries seeking to protect their religious liberty and the rights of families and national civil law against these secularist trends. Efforts by human rights advocacy groups to advance "forced pregnancy" as a war crime in the International Criminal Court Statute represented just one of the many occasions in which advocacy groups have attempted to do 'end-runs' around national legislatures to secure treaty norms protecting abortion as a human right. These kinds of advocacy efforts so common in international forums represent clear violations of the spirit of subsidiarity, not to mention a violation of the democratic spirit.

Economic Development and the International Pursuit of Happiness

Catholic teaching on the organization of local, national, and international economic policy has consistently asserted that the ultimate purpose of economic activity is to promote the life and dignity of persons. The tendency to regard economic activity in solely instrumental, utilitarian, and materialist terms typically degrades the human person. GIS debates surrounding economic policy have often pitted capitalist, communist, and socialist systems of thought and practice. A rich body of Catholic teachings starting with Leo XIII's *Rerum Novarum* and extending across the twentieth century to John Paul II's *Centesimus Annus* have supported the notion that the dignity of the person, the dignity of labor, and the basic rights of property and liberty must all be incorporated in a truly affirming policy. For this reason, Communist teachings on economic policy were condemned, but this did not extend to an open endorsement by the Church of the capitalist system as such, although capitalist and free enterprise economic systems were more often correlated to other human rights and liberties. In his most recent encyclical, Benedict XVI has offered yet another very textured appreciation on the need for genuine charity and respect for the dignity of persons and in the service of truth, being the only real path toward genuine economic development. Repeatedly papal teachings in this area have emphasized the rights of subsidiarity. The role of governments as agents of genuine solidarity has also been praised, recognizing the limits of government authority. In this arena of international relations, then, Catholic thought reiterates principles constantly affirmed in other aspects of the global order. Prudence indicates that many paths can be fruitfully followed toward genuine human flourishing. The rapid and largely (though not completely) salutary effects of economic globalization have removed a billion souls from the ranks of desperate poverty in the last two decades. But there remains nearly another billion who are stubbornly stuck in the grasp of poverty and underdevelopment. These peoples have the primary responsibility for their own development, but solidarity demands that governments, IGOs and NGOs should come to their assistance to facilitate their subsidiary efforts. Pope Benedict's *Charity in Truth* offers a blueprint on how such a humane world might best be achieved. GIS scholars would do well to consult its wisdom.

All politics aims at the advancement of the common good and the ends of human flourishing, although some systems of political thought and partisan action may well stifle rather than foster such flourishing. The natural inclinations of human beings orient them to appreciate the value of life itself, the necessity to nurture, protect, and preserve life and to form families in which new life is generated. This natural inclination to love and be loved is learned in the heart of family where the arts of friendship and of self-giving relationship are first learned. But the circle of friendship widens into contact with human society and into other subsidiary social and religious bodies, as well as into civic communities where the common good can be advanced. Thus man, as Aristotle asserted, is a political animal. The human intellect naturally desires the truth, and the human will seeks the good as it is best—but not always properly—understood. The ability to shape one's life in freedom toward the truth and the good is another universal aspiration of human persons. All of this aims at the attainment of happiness, understood as a state of being rather than mere sentiment. These observations about human nature are as old as the science of politics itself, and they are also deeply imbedded in the Judeo-Christian anthropology that claims universal application to all nations.

But the claims are not just a matter of philosophical and theological speculation. It turns out that the empirical literature on happiness that has emerged in recent years strongly confirms the correlation of human happiness with marriage and family; religious belief and practice; satisfying work; sacrifice for the good of others; charitable giving of one's time, talent, and treasure; traditional moral values and moral autonomy and freedom understood not as license leading to selfishness but as well-chosen love leading to self-recollection.[24] This same literature confirms that economic success, class status, possession of material goods, and even level of education are uncorrelated with happiness. For governments of all sorts, this should be chastening evidence, suggesting that the human spirit is not ultimately fulfilled by materialist gain, which is the primary preoccupation of modern government. Cradle-to-grave social systems of governments and IGO programs to advance the prosperity and material comfort of mankind, though perhaps worthy goals in themselves, are not likely to result in an increase in human happiness. Indeed, many such systems in Europe appear to be collapsing before our very eyes. Rather, the flourishing of subsidiary communities is far more likely to address the deepest and lasting spiritual and human needs.

Face-to-face charity nourishes prosperity and peace more directly than any national or international assistance program. This is work that must be done in the trenches of local life. No secretary-general of the United Nations can even begin to hope to provide this by the wave of a magic wand, nor can any IGO and NGO executive. The empirical evidence suggests that GIS scholarship, and the objects of GIS scholarship, that is the governmental/IGO/NGO nexus of institutional activity should pay much more attention to the deepest yearnings of the human spirit for a genuine human peace and security as well as a more human quest for flourishing work and economic prosperity that historically has been embedded in stable local institutions, foremost the family, the church, and other immediate subsidiary bodies, where genuine human interaction flourishes. To the extent that national governments, transnational NGOs, and IGOs can facilitate this local flourishing, they have important but clearly secondary roles to play. They have important roles to play in their own right to advance international cooperation between and among governments. But they have no right to manipulate and advance a secular agenda that in important ways detracts from rather than advances the true good of human beings. There is a compelling need for all scholars, policy-makers, and practitioners in the global institutional system for an attitude check, or perhaps an examination of conscience, to determine whether their global aspirations are truly in solidarity with the human spirit, and truly capable of advancing the genuine good of nations and peoples, or whether the GIS/IGO agendum sought today might seriously violate the subsidiary rights of concrete local communities of human flourishing, thus offering a false form of solidarity and ultimately a dessicating form of charity. If the latter appears to be so, the Church waits patiently and in charity, humbly offering an authentic model of the common good, rooted in faith, hope, and love.

Notes

1. *Guadium et Spes* para. 90.

2. Benedict XVI, *Charity in Truth*, para. 47.

3. Thomas Weiss, *What's Wrong with the United Nations and How to Fix It.* (Hoboken, N.J.: Polity, 2008).

4. Among the many current international relations texts reviewed include: Thomas Arcaro and Rosemary Haskel, eds., *Understanding the Global Experience: Becoming a Responsible World Citizen* (Boston: Allyn & Bacon, 2010); Michael Barnett and Thomas G. Weiss, *Humanitarianism in Question* (Ithaca, N.Y.: Cornell University Press, 2008); Michael Barnett and Martha Finnemore, *Rules for the World: International Organizations in Global Politics* (Ithaca, N.Y.: Cornell University Press, 2004); Russell Bova, *How the World Works: A Brief Survey of International Relations* (New York: Longman, 2010); Paul D'Anieri, *International Politics: Power and Purpose in Global Affairs* (Belmont, Calif.: Wadsworth, 2010); Paul F. Diehl, ed., *The Politics of Global Governance: International Organizations in an Interdependent World* (Boulder, Colo.: Lynne Rienner, 2001); Jeffrey A. Frieden, David A. Lake, and Kenneth A. Schultz, *World Politics: Interests, Interactions, Institutions* (New York: W.W. Norton and Co., 2010); Joshua Goldstein and Jon C. Pevehouse, *International Relations* (New York: Pearson, 2009); Jeffrey Haynes, *An Introduction to International Relations and Religion* (New York: Longman, 2007); Charles W. Kegley with Eugene R. Wittkopf, *World Politics: Trends and Transformation* (Belmont, Calif.: Thomson Wadsworth, 2006); Karen Mingst, *Essentials of International Relations* (New York: W.W. Norton and Co., 2008); John Allphin Moore, Jr., and Jerry Pubantz, *The New United Nations: International Organization in the Twenty-first Century* (Upper Saddle River, N.J.: Pearson/Prentice-Hall, 2006); Henry R. Nau, *Perspectives on International Relations: Power, Institutions, Ideas* (Washington, D.C.: CQ Press, 2008); Kelly-Kate S. Pease, *International Organizations* (New York: Longman, 2010); Donald J. Puchala, Katie Verlin Laatikanainen, and Roger A. Coate, *United Nations Politics* (Upper Saddleback, N.J.: Pearson, 2007); Michael G. Roskin and Nicholas O. Berry, *IR: The New World of International Relations* (New York: Longman, 2010); John T. Rourke and Mark A. Boyer, *International Politics on the World Stage* (Boston: McGraw Hill, 2010); and Thomas G. Weiss, David Forsythe, Roger A. Coate, and Kelly-Kate Pease, *The United Nations and Changing World Politics* (Boulder, Colo.: Westview, 2007).

5. John J. Mearsheimer, "The False Promise of International Institutions," *International Security* 19, no. 3 (Winter 1994/1995): 5-49.

6. See Jonathan Fox and Shmuel Sandler, *Bringing Religion into International Relations* (London: Palgrave Macmillan, 2006), who recognize this general oversight. A text that consults history and religion frequently is John T. Rourke and Mark A. Boyer, *International Politics on the World Stage*.

7. See *Charity in Truth*, paras. 1-9.

8. See Arcaro and Haskell, eds., *Understanding the Global Experience*.

9. On the importance of levels of analysis see James N. Rosenau, *Linkage Politics* (New York: Free Press, 1969).

10. See, for example, Goldstein and Pevehouse, *International Relations*, and Samuel P. Huntington, *The Clash of Civilizations and the Remaking of World Order* (New York: Touchstone, 1996), who draw a correlation between Islamic culture boundaries and other civilizations where conflicts abound.

11. Jeffrey C. Pugh, "Navigating Religion in the Global Context," in Arcaro and Haskell, eds., *Understanding the Global Experience* (Boston: Allyn & Bacon, 2010), 252-72.

12. Elizabeth Shakman Hurd, *The Politics of Secularism in International Relations* (Princeton: Princeton University Press, 2008).

13. See Fox and Sandler, *Bringing Religion*, among a spate of books assessing the "resurgence" of religion or the new awareness of religion in international relations.

14. Rosenau, *Linkage Politics*.

15. D. Brian Scarnecchia and Terrence McKeegan, *The Millennium Development Goals: In Light of Catholic Social Teaching* (New York: Catholic Family and Human Rights Institute, 2009), 73-85.

16. UN Development Program, *Human Development Report*, 1994.

17. Stephen Krasner, *Sovereignty: Organized Hypocrisy* (Princeton, N.J.: Princeton University Press, 1999).

18. Puchala et al., *UN Politics*, 197-99.

19. Weiss et al., *The United Nations*, 299-300.

20. Weiss et al., *The United Nations*, 300.

21. Mary Anderson, *Do No Harm: How Aid Can Support Peace—or War* (Boulder, Colo.: Lynne Rienner, 1999); Michael Barnett and Thomas G. Weiss, *Humanitarianism in Question*; and Larry Minear and Ian Smillie, *The Charity of Nations: Humanitarian Action in a Calculating World* (Sterling, Va.: Kumarian, 2004).

22. Puchala et al., *UN Politics*.

23. Anderson, *Do No Harm*, and Barnett and Weiss, *Humanitarianism*, are two laudable treatments.

24. See, for instance, two fine empirical and policy-based studies by Arthur Brooks, *Gross National Happiness: Why Happiness Matters for America—and How We Can Get More of It* (New York: Basic Books, 2008) and *Who Really Cares: The Surprising Truth about Compassionate Conservatism* (New York: Basic Books, 2007).

Bibliography

Abell, Peter. "Sociological Theory and Rational Choice Theory." In *The Black-well Companion to Social Theory*, edited by Bryan Turner, pp. 223-44. Malden, Mass.: Blackwell, 2000.

Anderson, Mary. *Do No Harm: How Aid Can Support Peace—or War*. Boulder, Colo.: Lynne Rienner, 1999.

Almond, Gabriel, and Sidney Verba. *The Civic Culture: Political Attitudes and Democracy in Five Nations*. London: Sage Publication, 1989.

America's Affordable Health Choices Act of 2009. House Resolution 3200. http://thomas.loc.gov/cgi-bin/bdquery/z?d111:H.R.3200 (21 January 2009).

Aquila, Bishop Samuel J. "Bishop Aquila on Health Care." www.catholic culture.org/culture/library/view.cfm?recnum=9101 (4 September 2009).

Aquinas, Thomas. *The Political Ideas of St. Thomas Aquinas*. Edited by Dino Bigongiari. New York: Hafner Publications, 1969.

Arcaro, Thomas, and Rosemary Haskell, eds. *Understanding the Global Experience: Becoming a Responsible World Citizen*. Boston: Allyn & Bacon, 2010.

Arendt, Hannah. *The Human Condition*. Chicago: University of Chicago Press, 1958.

Aristotle. *Nicomachaen Ethics*. Translated by Terence Irwin. Indianapolis, Ind.: Hacket Publishing, 1985.

———. *Nicomachean Ethics*. Translated by Joe Sachs. Newburyport, Mass.: Focus Publishing, R. Pullins Company, 2002.

———. *The Politics*. Translated by Ernest Barker. London: Oxford University Press.

Art, Robert J., and Robert Jervis. *International Politics: Enduring Concepts and Contemporary Issues*. New York: Pearson/Longman, 2005.

Augustine. *The Confessions*. Translated by Henry Chadwick. Oxford: Oxford University Press, 2009.

————. *The Political Writings of St. Augustine*. Edited by Henry Paolucci. Chicago: Gateway Publications, 1962.

————. *The Enchiridion on Faith, Hope and Love*. New York: Regnery Gateway, 1961.

Axelrod, Robert. "Political Science and Beyond." *Perspectives on Politics* 6, no. 1 (March 2008).

Barber, Benjamin R. *Jihad vs. McWorld*. New York: Times Books, 1995.

Barnett, Michael, and Martha Finnemore. *Rules for the World: International Organizations in Global Politics*. Ithaca, N.Y.: Cornell University Press, 2004.

Barnett, Michael, and Thomas G. Weiss. *Humanitarianism in Question*. Ithaca, N.Y.: Cornell University Press, 2008.

Barilleaux, Ryan. "Presidential Conduct of Foreign Policy." *Congress and the Presidency* 15 (Spring 1988): 1-23.

————. *The President and Foreign Affairs: Evaluation, Performance, and Power*. New York: Praeger, 1985.

————. "Evaluating Presidential Performance in Foreign Affairs." In *The Presidency and Public Policy Making*, edited by George Edwards, Steven Shull, and Norman Thomas, pp. 114-29. Pittsburgh, Pa.: University of Pittsburgh Press, 1985.

Bausch, William. *Pilgrim Church*. Mystic, Conn.: Twenty-Third Publications, 1983.

Bendix, Reinhard. *State and Society*. Berkeley, Calif.: University of California Press, 1968.

Benedict VI. *Charity in Truth*. Boston: Pauline Books, 2009.

Benestad, J. Brian, ed. *Ernest L. Fortin: Collected Essays*. Lanham, Md.: Rowman & Littlefield, 1996.

Boff, Leonardo. *Jesus Christ Liberator*. New York: Orbis Books, 1984.

Bornstein, David. *How to Change the World: Social Entrepreneurs and the Power of New Ideas*. New York: Oxford University Press, 2007.

Bottum, Joseph. "Bad Medicine." *First Things* 203 (May 2010).

Bova, Russell. *How the World Works: A Brief Survey of International Relations*. New York: Longman, 2010.

Brooks, Arthur C. *Gross National Happiness: Why Happiness Matters for America—and How We Can Get More of It*. New York: Basic Books, 2008.

————. *Who Really Cares? The Surprising Truth about Compassionate Conservatism*. New York: Basic Books, 2007.

Brown, Courtney. "Politics and the Environment: Nonlinear Instabilities Predominate." *American Political Science Review* 88 (June 1994): 292-303.

Budziszewski, J. *The Line through the Heart*. Wilmington, Del.: Intercollegiate Studies Institute, 2009.

————. *What We Can't Not Know*. Dallas, Tex.: Spence Publishing Company, 2004.

————. *Written on the Heart: The Case for Natural Law*. Downers Grove, Ill.: InterVarsity Press, 1997.

————. *The Nearest Coast of Darkness*. Ithaca, N.Y.: Cornell University Press, 1988.

Bunce, Valerie. "Rethinking Democratization: Lessons from Postcommunist Experience." *World Politics* 55, no. 2 (January 2003): 170-89.

Campbell, Colin. "Management in a Sandbox." In *The Clinton Presidency: First Appraisals*, edited by Colin Campbell and Bert Rockman, pp. 51-87. Chatham, N.J.: Chatham House, 1995.

Campbell, Colin, and Bert Rockman, eds. *The Clinton Presidency: First Appraisals*. Chatham, N.J.: Chatham House, 1995.

Canavan, Francis, S.J. *The Pluralist Game: Pluralism, Liberalism, and the Moral Conscience*. Lanham, Md.: Rowman & Littlefield, 1995.

Caramani, Daniele. *Comparative Politics*. Oxford: Oxford University Press, 2008.

Catechism of the Catholic Church. Citta del Vaticano: Libreria Editrice Vaticana, 1997.

Ceaser, James W. *Liberal Democracy and Political Science*. Baltimore, Md.: Johns Hopkins University Press, 1990.

Chilcote, Ronald H., ed. *Transitions from Dictatorship to Democracy: Comparative Studies of Spain, Portugal and Greece*. New York: Taylor Francis, 1990.

Chilcote, Ronald H. *Theories of Development and Underdevelopment*. Boulder, Colo.: Westview Press, 1984.

Cicero, Marcus Tullius. *On the Commonwealth*. Indianapolis, Ind.: Bobbs Merrill, 1976.

Clark, William R., Matt Golder, and Sona N. Golder. *Principles of Comparative Politics*. Washington, D.C.: CQ Press, 2009.

Code of Canon Law. 1983. www.vatican.va.

Compte-Sponville, Andre. *A Small Treatise on the Great Virtues*. New York, Henry Holt, 2002.

Congregation for the Doctrine of the Faith. *Doctrinal Note on Some Questions Regarding the Participation of Catholics in Political Life*. 2002.

————. *Donum Veritatis*. 1990.

Cohen, Patricia. "Field Study: Just How Relevant Is Political Science?" *New York Times on-line*. 19 October 2009 at www.nytimes.com/2009/10/20books/20poli.html (22 February 2010).

Coulter, Michael L., Stephen M. Krason, Richard S. Myers, and Joseph A. Varacalli, eds. *Encyclopedia of Catholic Social Thought, Social Science, and Social Policy*. Lanham, Md.: Scarecrow Press, 2007.

Dahl, Robert. "Normative Theory, Empirical Research and Democracy." In *Passion, Craft and Method in Comparative Politics*, edited by G. Munck and R. Snyder, pp. 113-49. Baltimore, Md.: Johns Hopkins Press, 2007.

————. *Polyarchy: Participation and Opposition*. New Haven, Conn.: Yale University Press, 1971.

D'Anieri, Paul. *International Politics: Power and Purpose in Global Affairs*. Belmont, Calif.: Wadsworth, 2010.

Dawson, Christopher. *Dynamics of World History*. Edited by John J. Mulloy. Wilmington, Del.: Intercollegiate Studies Institute Books, 2002.

———. *Religion and the Rise of Western Culture*. New York: Doubleday, 1957.

Derber, Charles. *People Before Profit*. New York: Picador, 2002.

Diamond, Larry. *Squandered Victory: American Occupation and the Bungled Effort to Bring Democracy to Iraq*. New York: Henry Holt, 2005.

Diehl, Paul F., ed. *The Politics of Global Governance: International Organizations in an Interdependent World*. Boulder, Colo.: Lynne Rienner, 2001.

Dougherty, James E., and Robert Pfaltzgraff, Jr. *Contending Theories of International Relations: A Comprehensive Survey*. New York: Harper & Row Publishers, 1990.

Douglass, R. Bruce. "Introduction." In *Catholicism and Liberalism: Contributions to American Public Philosophy*, edited by R. Bruce Douglass and David Hollenbach, pp. 1-18. New York: Cambridge University Press, 1994.

Drury, Shadia. *The Political Ideas of Leo Strauss*. New York: St. Martin's Press, 1988.

Dulles, Avery Cardinal. *Magisterium: Guardian and Teacher of the Faith*. Naples, Fla.: Sapientia Press, 2007.

Eagleson, John, and P. Scharper, eds. *Puebla and Beyond: The Major Address of John Paul II in Mexico*. New York: Orbis Books, 1980.

Easton, David. *The Political System*. New York: Knopf, 1953.

Eisenstadt, S. N. *Modernization: Protest and Change*. Englewood Cliffs, N.J.: Prentice Hall, 1966.

Essig, Andrew. "Catholic International Relations Theory: The Development of a Core Theory." *Fellowship of Catholic Scholars Quarterly* 30, no. 2 (2007): 30-36.

Fairlie, John A. "Political Developments and Tendencies." *American Political Science Review* 24, no. 1 (February 1930).

Farmer, Dr. Paul. *Pathologies of Power*. Berkeley: University of California Press, 2003.

Finkel, Jason, and R. W. Gable. *Political Development and Social Change*. New York: John Wiley and Sons, 1966.

Finn, Bishop Robert W., and Archbishop Joseph F. Naumann. "Joint Pastoral Statement on Principles of Catholic Social Teaching and Health Care Reform." wwwcatholicculture.org/culture/library (4 September 2009).

Fishman, Ethan. *The Prudential Presidency*. Westport, Conn.: Praeger, 2001.

Fortin, Ernest, L. "The Trouble with Catholic Social Thought." *Boston College Magazine* (Summer 1988): 37-42.

Fox, Jonathan, and Shmeul Sandler. *Bringing Religion into International Relations*. London: Palgrave Macmillan, 2006.

Frederickson, H. George. *The Spirit of Public Administration*. San Francisco, Calif.: Jossey Bass, 1997.

———. "Toward a New Public Administration." In *Toward a New Public Administration: The Minnowbrook Perspective*, edited by Frank E. Marini. Scranton, Pa.: Chandler Publishing Co. 1971.

Freedom House. *Freedom in the World, 2007: Annual Survey of Political Rights and Civil Liberties.* New York: Rowman & Littlefield, 2007.

Freire, Paulo. *Pedagogy of the Oppressed.* New York: Continuum Books, 1985.

Frieden, Jeffrey A., David A. Lake, and Kenneth A. Schultz. *World Politics: Interests, Interactions, Institutions.* New York: W.W. Norton and Co., 2010.

Fukuyama, Francis, ed. *Nation-Building: Beyond Afghanistan and Iraq.* Baltimore, Md.: Johns Hopkins Press, 2006.

Fukuyama, Francis. "The End of History?" *Foreign Affairs* (Summer 1989): 1-25.

Fustel de Coulanges, Numa. *The Ancient City: A Study on the Religion, Laws, and Institutions of Greece and Rome.* Garden City, N.Y.: Doubleday & Company, 1956.

Gaddis, John Lewis. *The Cold War: A New History.* New York: Penguin, 2005.

Gale Reference Team. *Human Security Report 2005: War and Peace in the 21st Century.* Electronic Document. 2006.

Galtung, Johan. "A Structural Theory of Imperialism." *Journal of Peace Research* 8, no. 2 (1971): 81-117.

George, Robert P. *The Clash of Orthodoxies: Law, Religion, and Morality in Crisis.* Wilmington, Del.: Intercollegiate Studies Institute Books, 2001.

———. *In Defense of Natural Law.* Oxford: Oxford University Press, 1999.

Gilson, Etienne. *The Christian Philosophy of St. Thomas Aquinas.* Notre Dame, Ind.: University of Notre Dame Press, 1956.

Glenn, Gary. "Defending Strauss Against the Criticism That His Ancients/ Moderns Reading of the History of Political Philosophy Unjustly Depreciates Christianity's Contribution to That History." Presented at the Society of Catholic Social Scientists Annual Convention. Queens, N.Y.: St. John's University School of Law, October 2007.

Goerner, Edward A. "On Thomistic Natural Law: The Bad Man's View of Thomistic Natural Right." *Political Theory* 7, no. 1 (1979): 101-22.

Goldstein, Joshua, and Jon C. Pevehouse. *International Relations.* New York: Pearson, 2009.

Goodnow, Frank. *Politics and Administration: A Study in Government.* New Brunswick, N.J.: Transaction Publishers, 2000.

———. "The Growth of Executive Discretion." *Proceedings of the American Political Science Association*, 40.

Grasso, Kenneth L. "Neither Ancient nor Modern: The Distinctiveness of Catholic Social Thought." *Catholic Social Science Review* 14 (2009): 49.

———. "The Subsidiary State: Society, the State and the Principle of Subsidiarity in Catholic Social Thought." In *Christianity and Civil Society: Catholic and Neo-Calvinist Perspectives*, edited by Jeanne Hefferan Schindler, pp. 31-65. Lanham, Md.: Lexington Books, 2008.

Gregg, Samuel. "What Is the USCCB's Problem with Subsidiarity?" *Acton Institute PowerBlog*, 26 May 2010, at http://blog.acton.org/archives.

Gutierrez, Gustavo. *A Theology of Liberation.* New York: Orbis Books, 1984.

———. *The Power of the Poor in History.* New York: Orbis Books, 1983.

Hallowell, John H. *The Moral Foundation of Democracy*. Chicago: University of Chicago Press, 1954.

Hatemi, Peter K. "A Partnership Between Science and Culture: Genetic and Neurocognitive Approaches for Comparative Politics." *APSA-CP Symposium* 21, no. 1 (2010): 6-11.

Haynes, Jeffrey. *An Introduction to International Relations and Religion*. New York: Longman, 2007.

Headley, John M. *The Europeanization of the World: On the Origins of Human Rights and Democracy*. Princeton, N.J.: Princeton University Press, 2008.

Heckscher, August. "Research for Action." *Current Magazine* (July 1960).

Hobbes, Thomas. *Leviathan*. New York: Penguin Books, 1968.

Holden, Matthew. "The Competence of Political Science." *American Political Science Review* 94, no. 1 (March 2000): 1-19.

Holsti, Ole R. "Models of International Relations and Foreign Policy." In *American Foreign Policy: Theoretical Essays*, edited by G. John Ikenberry, pp. 14-39. New York: Pearson/Longman, 2005.

Holy Bible. New American Bible. Catholic Study Edition.

Holy Bible. Revised Standard Version. Catholic Edition.

Holzer, Marc, Vache Gabrielian, and Kaifeng Yang. "Five Great Ideas in American Public Administration." In *Handbook of Public Administration*, edited by Jack Rabin, W. Bartley Hildreth, and Gerald Miller, pp. 49-102. New York: Marcel Dekker, 1998.

Hooper, J. Leon. *The Ethics of Discourse: The Social Philosophy of John Courtney Murray*. Washington, D.C.: Georgetown University Press, 1986.

Hunt, Robert P. "Political Philosophy." In *Encyclopedia of Catholic Social Thought, Social Science, and Social Policy*, edited by Michael L. Coulter, Stephen M. Krason, Richard S. Myers, and Joseph A. Varacalli, pp. 827-29. Lanham, Md.: Scarecrow Press, 2007.

———. "Christianity, Leo Strauss, and the Ancient/Modern Distinction." *Catholic Social Science Review* 14 (2009): 53-63.

———. "Kraynak: Christianity v. Modernity?" *Catholic Social Science Review* 9 (2004): 47-52.

Huntington, Samuel P. *The Clash of Civilizations and the Remaking of World Order*. New York: Touchstone, 1996.

———. "The Clash of Civilizations?" *Foreign Affairs* 72, no. 3 (1993).

———. *Political Order in Changing Societies*. New Haven, Conn.: Yale University Press, 1968.

Hurd, Elizabeth Shakman. *The Politics of Secularism in International Relations*. Princeton, N.J.: Princeton University Press, 2008.

John XXIII. *Mater et Magistra* (1961).

———. *Pacem in Terris* (1963).

———. "Pacem in Terris": A Christmas Message. 23 December 1959.

John Paul II. Address to the Diplomatic Corps Accredited to the Holy See. www.vatican.va (10 January 2005).

———. "Message of His Holiness Pope John Paul II for the Celebration of World Day of Peace." *ZENIT News*, 1 January 2004.

————. *Pacem in Terris: A Permanent Commitment.* 1 January 2003.

————. *Fides et Ratio.* 1998.

————. *Veritatis Splendor.* 1993.

————. *Centesimus Annus.* 1991.

Johnston, Michael. *Syndromes of Corruption: Wealth, Power and Democracy.* Cambridge, Mass.: Cambridge University Press, 2005.

Kahl, Colin H. *States, Scarcity and Civil Strife in the Developing World.* Princeton, N.J.: Princeton University Press, 2006.

Kaspar, Walter. *The Christian Understanding of Freedom and the History of Freedom in the Modern Era: The Meeting and Confrontation between Christianity and the Modern Era in a Postmodern Situation.* Milwaukee, Wis.: Marquette University Press, 1988.

Kathlene, Lyn. "Power and Influence in State Legislative Policymaking: The Interaction of Gender and Position in Committee Hearing Debates." *American Political Science Review* 88 (September 1994): 560-76.

Katznelson, Ira. "At the Court of Chaos: Political Science in an Age of Perpetual Fear." *Perspectives in Politics* 5, no. 1 (March 2007): 3-15.

Kaufman, Herbert. "Administrative Decentralization and Political Power." *Public Administration Review* (January-February 1969).

Kegley, Charles W., with Eugene R. Wittkopf. *World Politics: Trends and Transformation.* Belmont, Calif.: Thomson Wadsworth, 2006.

Keohane, Robert O., and Joseph S. Nye. *Power and Interdependence.* New York: HarperCollins Publishers, 1989.

Kirlin, John J. "The Big Questions of Public Administration." *Public Administration Review* 56, no. 5 (1966): 416-23.

Klosko, George. *History of Politcial Theory: An Introduction, Ancient and Medieval Political Theory.* 2 vols. Belmont, Calif.: Thomson/Wadsworth, 1995.

Kohler, Thomas C. "In Praise of Little Platoons." In *Building the Free Society: Democracy, Capitalism, and Catholic Social Teaching,* edited by George Weigel and Robert Royal, pp. 31-50. Grand Rapids, Mich.: William B. Eerdmans Publishing Company, 1993.

Koyzis, David T. *Political Visions and Illusions: A Survey and Christian Critique of Contemporary Ideologies.* Downers Grove, Ill.: InterVarsity Press, 2003.

Krasner, Stephen D. *Sovereignty: Organized Hypocrisy.* Princeton, N.J.: Princeton University Press, 1999.

Krasner, Stephen D., ed. *International Regimes.* Ithaca, N.Y.: Cornell University Press, 1983.

Krason, Stephen. "The Importance of the Society of Catholic Social Science Apostolate." *Catholic Social Science Review* 11 (2006): 371-73.

————. *Liberalism, Conservatism and Catholicism: An Evaluation of Contemporary American Political Ideologies in Light of Catholic Social Teaching.* Catholics United for the Faith, 1991.

Kraynak, Robert P. *Christian Faith and Modern Democracy: God and Politics in the Fallen World.* Notre Dame, Ind.: University of Notre Dame Press, 2001.

Kristof, Nicholas D., and Sheryl WuDunn. *Half the Sky: Turning Oppression into Opportunity for Women Worldwide.* New York: Alfred A. Knopf, 2009.

Lane, Ruth. *The Art of Comparative Politics.* Boston, Mass.: Allyn & Bacon, 1997.

Leclercq, Jacques. *The Christian and World Integration.* New York: Hawthorne Books, 1963.

Levi, Margaret. "Why We Need a New Theory of Government." *Perspectives on Politics* 4, no. 1 (March 2006): 5-19.

Light, Paul C. *The Tides of Reform.* New Haven, Conn.: Yale University Press, 1997.

Lindberg, Staffan I. *Democratization by Elections.* Baltimore, Md.: Johns Hopkins Press, 2009.

Linz, Juan J., and Alfred Stepan. "Toward Consolidatede Democracies." In *Consolidating the Third Wave Democracies: Theories and Perspective*, edited by Larry Diamond, Mark F. Plattner, Yun-han Chu, and Hung-Mao Tien, pp. 14-33. Baltimore, Md.: Johns Hopkins Press, 1997.

Lowell, A. Lawrence. "The Physiology of Politics." *American Political Science Review* 4, no. 1 (February 1910).

Lynn, Laurence E., Jr. "Restoring the Rule of Law to Public Administration." *Public Administration Review* 69, no. 5 (September/October 2009): 803-13.

Machiavelli, Niccolo. *The Prince and the Discourses.* New York: The Modern Library, 1950.

———. *The Prince.* New York: W.W. Norton, 1992.

Madison, James. "Federalist no. 10." In *The Federalist*, edited by Jacob E. Cooke, pp. 56-65. Middletown, Conn.: Wesleyan University Press, 1961.

Martin, Adam, and K. R. Monroe. "Politics and the (Pro)Social Brain: Towards a Neuropolitics of Identity and Connections." *APSA-CP Symposium* 21, no. 1 (2010): 12-17.

Marx, Karl. *The Communist Manifesto.* New York: W.W. Norton, 1988.

McAllister, Ted V. *Revolt Against Modernity: Leo Strauss, Eric Voegelin, and the Search for a Postliberal Order.* Lawrence, Kans.: University Press of Kansas, 1995.

McCloskey, C. John. "Universal Church, Global Village." *National Catholic Register*, 25 July 2004, 4.

McInerny, Ralph. *St. Thomas Aquinas.* Notre Dame, Ind.: University of Notre Dame Press, 1977.

Mearsheimer, John J. "The False Promise of International Institutions." *International Security* 19, no. 3 (Winter 1994/1995): 5-49.

Merriam, Charles. "Progress in Political Research." *American Political Science Review* 20, no 1 (February 1926).

Minear, Larry, and Ian Smillie. *The Charity of Nations: Humanitarian Action in a Calculating World.* Sterling, Va.: Kumarian, 2004.

Mingst, Karen. *Essentials of International Relations*. New York: W.W. Norton and Co., 2008.

Miranda, Jose P. *Marx and the Bible: A Critique of the Philosophy of Oppression*. New York: Orbis Books, 1974.

Mirus, Jeff. "Prospecting for Subsidiarity." 4 September 2009. At www.catholic culture.org/commentary/blog.

Moore, John Allphin, Jr., and Jerry Pubantz. *The New United Nations: International Organization in the Twenty-First Century*. Upper Saddle River, N.J.: Pearson/Prentice-Hall, 2006.

Moore, Matthew J. "Political Theory Today: Results of a National Survey." *Political Science and Politics* 43, no. 2 (April 2010): 265-72.

Morgan, Patrick M. *Theories and Approaches to International Politics: What Are We to Think?* New Brunswick, N.J.: Transaction Publishers, 1994.

Morgenthau, Hans J. *Politics Among Nations: The Struggle for Power and Peace*. New York: Alfred A. Knopf, 1978.

Morriss, Frank. "Limits of the State: Catholic Doctrine Begins with Subsidiarity." www.catholicculture.org (16 October 2010).

Mortenson, Greg. *Stones into Schools: Promoting Peace with Books, not Bombs in Afghanistan and Pakistan*. New York: Viking Press, 2009.

Munck, Gerardo L. *Measuring Democracy*. Baltimore, Md.: Johns Hopkins Press, 2009.

Munck, Gerardo L., and R. Snyder, eds. *Passion, Craft and Method in Comparative Politics*. Baltimore, Md.: Johns Hopkins Press, 2007.

Murray, John Courtney. *We Hold These Truths: Catholic Reflections of the American Proposition*. New York: Sheed & Ward, 1960.

————. "Governmental Repression of Heresy." *Proceedings of the Third Annual Meeting of the Catholic Theological Society of America*. Chicago: 1948.

Nau, Henry R. *Perspectives on International Relations: Power, Institutions, Ideas*. Washington, D.C.: CQ Press, 2008.

Newman, Cardinal John Henry. *The Idea of the University*. London: Baronius Press Ltd., 2006.

Nickless, Bishop R. Walter. "Voice Your Concerns over Healthcare Reform." www.catholicculture.org (4 September 2009).

Obama, Barack. "Memorandum for the Heads of Executive Departments and Agencies." www.whitehouse.gov (21 January 2009).

O'Donnell, Guillermo, and Philippe C. Schmitter. *Transitions from Authoritarian Rule: Tentative Conclusions*. Baltimore, Md.: Johns Hopkins Press, 1986.

OMBWatch. "Background on the Rulemaking Process: II. A Brief History of Administrative Government." www.ombwatch.org/node/3461 (3 October 2008).

Paul VI. *Populorum Progressio* (1967).

Pease, Kelly-Kate S. *International Organizations*. New York: Longman, 2010.

Pinckaers, Servais, O.P. *The Sources of Christian Ethics*. Translated by Sr. Mary Thomas Noble, O.P. Washington, D.C.: Catholic University of America Press, 1995.

Planned Parenthood v. Casey, 505 U.S. 833 (1992).

Plato. *The Apology*. In *The Trial and Death of Socrates*, translated by G. M. A. Grube. Indianapolis, Ind.: Hackett Publishing Company, 2000.

Pontifical Council for Justice and Peace. *Compendium of the Social Doctrine of the Church*. Washington, D.C.: USCCB Publishing, 2005.

———. *Compendium of the Social Doctrine of the Church*. Citta del Vaticano: Libreria Editrice Vaticana, 2004.

Prebisch, Raul. "The Dynamics of Peripheral Capitalism." In *Democracy and Development in Latin America*, edited by Louis Lefeber and Liisa L. North. Toronto, Ont.: York University, 1980.

Puchala, Donald J., Katie Verlin Laatikanainen, and Roger A. Coate. *United Nations Politics*. Upper Saddleback, N.J.: Pearson, 2007.

Pugh, Jeffrey C. "Navigating Religion in the Global Context." In *Understanding the Global Experience*, edited by Thomas Arcaro and Rosemary Haskell, pp. 252-72. Boston: Allyn & Bacon, 2010.

Putnam, Robert D. "The Public Role of Political Science." *www.apsanet.org* 1, no. 2 (June 2003): 249-55.

Pye, Lucian W. "Political Science and the Crisis of Authoritarianism." *American Political Science Review* 84, no. 1 (March 1990).

———. *Aspects of Political Development*. Boston, Mass.: Little-Brown Publishing, 1966.

Rabin, Jack, W. Bartley Hildreth, and Gerald Miller, eds. *Handbook of Public Administration*. New York: Marcel Dekker, 1998.

Rawls, John. *A Theory of Justice*. Oxford: Cambridge Press, 1971.

Ratzinger, Josef Cardinal. *The Church, Ecumenism, and Politics*. San Francisco, Calif.: Ignatius Press, 2008.

———. *Values in the Time of Upheaval*. San Francisco, Calif.: Ignatius Press, 2005.

———. "Truth and Freedom." *Communio: International Catholic Review* 23 (Spring 1996): 16-35.

———. *Introduction to Christianity*. San Francisco, Calif.: Ignatius Press, 1990.

Rehfeld, Andrew. "Offensive Political Theory." *Perspectives on Political Science* 8 (2008): 465-86.

Ricci, David M. *The Tragedy of Political Science: Politics, Scholarship, and Democracy*. New Haven, Conn.: Yale University Press, 1984.

Rochester, J. Martin. *Between Peril and Promise: The Politics of International Law*. Washington, D.C.: CQ Press, 2006.

Rode, Cardinal Franc. "From Past to Present: Religious Life Before and After Vatican II. *L'Osservatore Romano*, English ed., 28 January 2009, 8.

Rommen, Heinrich A. *The State in Catholic Thought: A Treatise in Political Philosophy*. St. Louis, Mo.: B. Herder Book Co., 1955.

Rose, Richard. "Democratic and Undemocratic States." In *Democratization*, edited by Christian W. Haerpfer, Patrick Bernhagen, Ronald Inglehart, and Christian Welsel, pp. 10-24. New York: Oxford University Press, 2009.

Rosenau, James N. *Linkage Politics*. New York: Free Press, 1969.

Roskin, Michael G., and Nicholas O. Berry. *IR: The New World of International Relations*. New York: Longman, 2010.

Rourke, John T., and Mark A. Boyer. *International Politics on the World Stage*. Boston, Mass.: McGraw-Hill, 2010.

Saad, Lydia. "More Americans 'Pro-Life' Than 'Pro-Choice' for First Time." www.gallup.com (15 May 2009).

Sachs, Jeffrey D. *Common Wealth: Economics for a Crowded Planet*. London: Penguin Books, 2008.

———. *The End of Poverty*. London: Penguin Books, 2005.

Santorum, Rick. *It Takes a Family*. Wilmington, Del.: Intercollegiate Studies Institute Books, 2005.

Scarnecchia, D. Brian, and Terrence McKeegan. *The Millennium Development Goals: In Light of Catholic Social Teaching*. New York: Catholic Family and Human Rights Institute, 2009.

Schall, James V. *The Mind That Is Catholic: Philosophical and Political Essays*. Washington, D.C.: Catholic University of America Press, 2008.

———. *Roman Catholic Political Philosophy*. Lanham, Md.: Lexington Books, 2004.

———. *At the Limits of Political Philosophy: From "Brilliant Errors" to Things of Uncommon Importance*. Washington, D.C.: Catholic University of America Press, 1996.

———. *Reason, Revelation, and the Foundations of Political Philosophy*. Baton Rouge, La.: Louisiana State University Press, 1987.

———. *The Politics of Heaven and Hell: Christian Themes from Classical, Medieval and Modern Political Philosophy*. Lanham, Md.: University Press of America, 1984.

Schindler, Jeanne Hefferan, ed. *Christianity and Civil Society: Catholic and Neo-Calvinist Perspectives*. Lanham, Md.: Lexington Books, 2008.

Schmandt, Henry F., and Paul G. Steinbicker. *Fundamentals of Government*. Milwaukee, Wis.: Bruce Publishing Company, 1954.

Schmitter, Philippe C., and T. L. Karl. "What Democracy Is . . . and Is Not." *Journal of Democracy* 2 (Summer 1991): 75-87.

Seeley, John R. *Introduction to Political Science*. London: Macmillan and Company, 1896.

Sen, Amartya. *Identity and Violence*. New York: W.W. Norton, 2006.

———. "Democracy as a Universal Value." *Journal of Democracy* 10 (Summer 1999): 3-17.

———. "The Importance of Democracy." In *Development as Freedom*, edited by Amartya Sen, pp. 146-59. New York: Anchor Books, 1999.

Singer, J. David. "The Level of Analysis Problem in International Relations." *World Politics* 14 (1961): 77-92

Skillen, James V. *Recharging the American Experiment: Principled Pluralism for Genuine Civic Community*. Grand Rapids, Mich.: Baker Books, 1994.

Skinner, Quentin. "Meaning and Understanding." In *Meaning and Context: Quentin Skinner and His Critics*, edited by James Tully. Princeton, N.J.: Princeton University Press, 1988.

Skocpol, Theda. "States, Revolutions, and the Comparative Historical Imagination." In *Passion, Craft and Method in Comparative Politics*, edited by Gerardo Munck and R. Snyder, pp. 649-708. Baltimore, Md.: Johns Hopkins Press, 2007.

Society of Catholic Social Scientists (SCSS). "Symposium: The Ancients/ Moderns Distinction: Catholic Perspectives." *The Catholic Social Science Review* 14 (2009): 9-84.

———. *Public Statements of the Public Policy and Church Affairs Committee 1993-1995*. Steubenville, Ohio: SCSS mimeograph, 1995.

Somit, Albert, and Joseph Tanenhaus. *The Development of American Political Science: From Burgess to Behavioralism*. Boston, Mass.: Allyn & Bacon, 1967.

Sorokin, Pitirim. *The Ways and Power of Love*. West Conshohocken, Pa.: 2002.

———. *The Crisis of Our Age*. Oxford: Oneworld Publications, 1992.

Speth, James G. *The Bridge at the Edge of the World: Capitalism, Environment and Crossing from Crisis to Sustainability*. New Haven, Conn.: Yale University Press, 2008.

Spitzer, Robert J. *New Proofs for the Existence of God: Contributions of Contemporary Physics and Philosophy*. Grand Rapids, Mich.: William B. Eerdmans Publishing Company, 2010.

Stiglitz, Joseph E. "Globalism's Discontents." *The American Prospect* 13, no. 1 (January 2002): 200-206.

Strauss, Leo. *The City and Man*. Chicago: University of Chicago Press, 1964.

———. *What Is Political Philosophy?* Westport, Conn.: Greenwood Press, 1959.

———. *Natural Right and History*. Chicago: University of Chicago Press, 1953.

Taylor, Charles. *Sources of the Self: The Making of the Modern Identity*. Cambridge, Mass.: Harvard University Press, 1989.

Thucydides. *The Complete Writings of Thucydides: The Peloponnesian War*. New York: The Modern Library, 1951.

———. "The Melian Dialogue." In *Classics of International Relations*, edited by John A Vasquez, pp. 9-14. Upper Saddle River, N.J.: Prentice-Hall, 1996.

Tickner, J. Ann. *Gender in International Relations: Feminist Perspectives on Achieving Global Security*. Irvington, N.Y.: Columbia University Press, 1992.

Tilly, Charles. *Democracy*. Cambridge: Cambridge University Press, 2007.

Tocqueville, Alexis de. *Democracy in America*. Translated by Harvey Mansfield and Delba Winthrop. Chicago: Chicago University Press, 2000.

Truman, David. "Disillusion and Regeneration: The Quest for a Discipline." *American Political Science Review* 59, no. 4 (December 1965): 865-73.

Tully, James, ed. *Meaning and Context: Quentin Skinner and His Critics.* Princeton, N.J.: Princeton University Press, 1988.

UN Development Program. *Human Development Report*, 1994.

United States Conference of Catholic Bishops. *Faithful Citizenship: A Catholic Call to Political Responsibility.* Washington, D.C.: USCCB Inc., 2003.

Viotti, Paul R., and Mark V. Kauppi. *International Relations Theory: Realism, Pluralism, Globalism.* New York: Macmillan Publishing Company, 1987.

Voegelin, Eric. "What Is Political Theory?" In *The Drama of Humanity and Other Miscellaneous Papers, 1939-1985: Collected Works*, vol. 33, edited by William Petropulous and Gilbert Weiss. Columbia: University of Missouri Press, 2004.

Walsh, Michael, and Brian Davies, eds. *Proclaiming Justice and Peace: Documents from John XXIII to John Paul II.* Mystic, Conn.: Twenty-Third Publications, 1984.

Waltz, Kenneth M. *Theory of International Politics.* Reading, Mass.: Addison-Wesley Publishing Company, 1979.

Weigel, George. "World Order: What Catholics Forgot." *First Things* 143 (2004): 31-38.

———. "A Better Concept of Freedom." *First Things* 121 (2002):

Weigel, George, and Robert Royal, eds. *Building the Free Society: Democracy, Capitalism, and Catholic Social Teaching.* Grand Rapids, Mich.: William B. Eerdmans Publishing Company, 1993.

Weiss, Thomas G. *What's Wrong with the United Nations and How to Fix It.* Hoboken, N.J.: Polity, 2008.

Weiss, Thomas G., David Forsythe, Roger A. Coate, and Kelly-Kate Pease. *The United Nations and Changing World Politics.* Boulder, Colo.: Westview Press, 2007.

Wendt, Alexander. *Social Theory of International Politics.* Cambridge: Cambridge University Press, 1999.

Wiker, Benjamin. *Moral Darwinism: How We Became Hedonists.* Downers Grove, Ill.: InterVarsity Press, 2002.

Will, George. "Will Obama's Statism Ever Retreat?" 23 August 2009, at http://www.realclearpolitics.com/articles/2008.

Wilson, Frank L. *Concepts and Issues in Comparative Politics.* Upper Saddle River, N.J.: Prentice-Hall Publishing, 1996.

Wilson, James Q. "Interests and Deliberations in the American Republic." *PS: Political Science & Politics* 23 (December 1990): 558-62.

Wilson, Woodrow. "President Woodrow Wilson's Fourteen Points." *The Avalon Project.* New Haven, Conn.: Lillian Goldman Law Library, 2008.

———. "The Law and the Facts." *American Political Science Review* 5, no. 1 (February 1911).

———. "The World Must Be Made Safe for Democracy." In *Classics of International Relations*, edited by John A. Vasquez. Upper Saddle River, N.J.: Prentice-Hall, 1996.

———. "The Study of Administration." *Political Science Quarterly* 2 (June 1887).

Index

abortion, 45, 78, 80, 90, 91, 155; health care and, 90, 93, 95
Afghanistan, 112
American Political Science Association (APSA), 6, 8, 66, 68, 79, 113; addresses by presidents of, 8-12; James Madison Award of, 66. *See also American Political Science Review*
American Political Science Review (APSR), 39n14, 72-73
American politics, 65-98; public management and, 86
American Sociological Association, 81
Anderson, Mary, 155
Aquila, Bishop Samuel, 90
Aquinas, Thomas, 4, 13, 17, 33, 49-50, 59, 60, 104-5, 113, 125, 133; natural law teaching of, 49-50; *Summa Theologiae* of, 133
Arendt, Hannah, 47
aristocracy, 6
Aristotle, 1-2, 6, 17, 32, 44, 49-50, 53, 59, 67, 75-76, 77, 79, 101-2, 103, 104, 152, 157; comparative politics and, 101-4; *Nicomachean Ethics* of, 2, 67; *Politics* of, 1, 75; regime types and, 6, 102-4; teleology of, 2, 101-2
arms race, 12, 135, 136
Arrow, Kenneth, 70
artificial contraception, 155; non-governmental organization

programs (NGOs) and, 155
Augustine, 4, 12, 33, 53, 55, 76, 101, 112, 113, 125; *City of God* of, 112-13; *Enchiridion* of, 101; "two cities" concept of, 51-52, 112-13
autocracy, 110; authoritarian governance and, 108, 110-11, 151
Axelrod, Robert, 10-11

balance of power, 124, 127, 128, 130, 134-35, 136-37; European system of, 127
Balkans crisis, 72
Barnett, Michael, 155
behavioralism, 4, 13, 16, 68-69, 71, 74-75, 77, 81, 106; Catholic attitudes toward, 13; "Creed" of, 16, 68-69, 74, 77, 80-81
Benedict XVI, 15, 79, 90, 94, 116, 133, 144, 156; *Caritas in Veritate* of, 15, 90, 156
Bentham, Jeremy, 124, 128
Bonaventure, 4
Bottum, Joseph, 92
bureaucracy, 46, 73, 89-90
Burundi, 115
Brooks, Arthur, 13
Brown, Courtney, 72
Brownson, Orestes, 33
Brunello, Anthony, 17
Brust, Steven, 16
Budziszewski, J., 76-77, 80; *The Line through the Heart* of, 80; *The*

About the Contributors

Robert F. Gorman is Professor of Political Science and International Studies at Texas State University. He has a B.A. in Political Science from Seattle University (1973) and an M.A. (1975) and Ph.D. (1979) in Political Science from the University of Oregon. Professor Gorman is the author or editor of more than a dozen books and series including *The Cold War* (Salem Press, 2010), *A to Z of Human Rights and Humanitarian Organizations* (Scarecrow, 2009), and *Great Debates at the United Nations* (2000) as well as numerous articles on topics of international relations, international law and organization, humanitarian and refugee policy, and the history of ethics and philosophy. He served as Council on Foreign Relations Fellow (1983-84), Ford Foundation Scholar at Africare in Washington, D.C. (1984-85), and as Distinguished Teaching Professor of Humanities at Texas State University (1999-2002). He was ordained a deacon in the Archdiocese of San Antonio in 2000, where he has since served his parish of Sts. Peter and Paul. He also teaches theology at John Paul II Catholic High School in Schertz, Texas. He and his wife Mary reside in New Braunfels, Texas, where they are members of the Amici Christi of the Mission of Divine Mercy. They have three children, Aaron, Teresa, and Ryan, and six grandchildren.

Ryan J. Barilleaux is Professor of Political Science at Miami University of Ohio, where he served as chairman from 2001 to 2009. He is the author or editor of nine books on the presidency and American politics, and has published dozens of scholarly articles as well. His latest edited book is *The Unitary Executive and the Modern Presidency* (Texas A&M University Press, 2010). He has been a member of the Miami faculty since 1987, and he was the Miami University Effective Educator for 2010-2011. He received a B.A. from the University of Louisiana at Lafayette (1979) and an M.A. (1980) and Ph.D. (1983) from the University of Texas at Austin. Earlier in his career, he served as a staff aide in the United States Senate. He and his wife Marilyn have six children.

Anthony R. Brunello is Professor of Political Science at Eckerd College in St. Petersburg, Florida, where he has taught for the past twenty-five years. He previously held teaching positions at the University of New Mexico and the University of Oregon, where he earned his Ph.D. He also has served as Associate Dean of General Education at Eckerd College. He co-edited *The Wider World of Core Texts* (Green Lion Press, 2004) and is the author of many articles and essays in comparative politics, political theory, and religion and politics. He is the winner of teaching awards at New Mexico and Eckerd. He, his wife Monica, and their three children are members of Blessed Trinity Catholic Church in St. Petersburg.

Steven J. Brust is Associate Director of the Tocqueville Forum on the Roots of American Democracy at Georgetown University, where he also serves as a Visiting Lecturer. He has a Bachelor of Science in Business Administration from the University of Southern California, Master of Arts degrees in Philosophy (Franciscan University of Steubenville, 1997) and in Politics (The Catholic University of America, 2001), and a Ph.D. in Politics (The Catholic University of America, 2006). His dissertation is entitled The Origin and Nature of Political and Spiritual Power: Natural Rights and Natural Law in the Thought of Francisco Suarez. His articles on political thought have appeared in the *Catholic Social Science Review* and in the *Catholic Social Thought, Social Science and Social Policy Encyclopedia*.

John Corso is program director and senior faculty member of the Strategy and Performance Management certificate program at Georgetown University's Center for Continuing Professional Education. He holds a bachelor's degree in Finance from the University of Maryland, a master's degree in Administration from Central Michigan Unviersity, and a doctorate in Public Administration from the University of Southern California. He is a regular contributor to *Nurse Leader*, a health care management journal. Dr. Corso has served as a consultant in the public management field for more than a decade. His special interest is in human, team, and organizational performance as it relates to strategy. He resides in Potomac, Maryland, with his wife Lourdes. They are members of the Mount St. Sepulchre Fraternity of the Secular Franciscan Order in Washington, D.C.

Andrew Essig is Associate Professor Political Science at DeSales University in Center Valley, Pennsylvania. He has earned a B.A. in Economics (1989) from St. Joseph's University in Philadelphia, and an M.A. (1993) and Ph.D. (2001) in Political Science from Penn State University. He studied at the Christian-Albrechts-Universitat in Kiel Germany from 1994 to 1996. He has published several articles on international relations topics, including "John Paul II and the New International Order" in *Catholic Social Science Review*, and "Catholic International Relations Theory" in *Fellowship of Catholic Scholars Quarterly*, among others. He teaches a variety of courses in international relations, American government, and political philosophy. Essig lives in Allentown, Pennsylvania, with his wife Anne and two boys, David and Daniel.

Robert P. Hunt is Professor of Political Science at Kean University, where he has taught since 1986, and where he currently serves as the Chair of Political Science. He received his B.A. (1978) and M.A. (1980) in Government and Politics from St. John's University and his Ph.D. in Political Philosophy from Fordham University (1984). He has co-edited several books, including, most recently, *Catholicism and Religious Freedom: Contemporary Reflections on Vatican II's Declaration on Religious Liberty* (2006). His articles and reviews have appeared in journals such as *First Things*, *The Review of Politics*, and the *Catholic Social Science Review*. He and his wife Diane have two children, Maura and Timothy.